# ROBERTSON DAVIES
## A Mingling of Contrarieties

REAPPRAISALS:
CANADIAN
WRITERS

# *ROBERTSON DAVIES*
## A Mingling of Contrarieties

Edited by
Camille R. La Bossière
and Linda M. Morra

**University of Ottawa Press**

**REAPPRAISALS**
Canadian Writers

Gerald Lynch
General Editor

**National Library of Canada Cataloguing in Publication Data**

Main entry under title :

Robertson Davies : a mingling of contrarieties

(Reappraisals, Canadian Writers)
Includes bibliographical references.
ISBN 0-7766-0531-3

1. Davies, Robertson, 1913-1995 — Criticism and interpretation.
I. La Bossière, Camille R.   II. Morra, Linda M.   III. Series.

PS8507.A67Z848 2001          C813'.54          C2001-901470-8
PR9199.3.D3Z793 2001

University of Ottawa Press gratefully acknowledges the support
extended to its publishing programme by the Canada Council
and the University of Ottawa.

We acknowledge the financial support of the Government
of Canada through the Book Publishing Industry Development
Program (BPIDP) for our publishing activities.

UNIVERSITY OF OTTAWA
UNIVERSITÉ D'OTTAWA

Cover design: Robert Dolbec

ISBN 0-7766-0531-3
ISSN 1189-6787

© University of Ottawa Press, 2001

Reprinted 2003

542 King Edward, Ottawa, Ont. Canada K1N 6N5
press@uottawa.ca   http://www.uopress.uottawa.ca

*Printed and bound in Canada*

# Contents

VI

# Introduction:
# Davies Tristram-gistus

CAMILLE R. LA BOSSIÈRE

The ANTITHESIS, or SEESAW, whereby Contraries and Oppositions are balanced in such a way, as to cause the reader to remain suspended between them, to his exceeding delight and recreation.

> – Alexander Pope, *Peri Bathous, or the Art of Sinking in Poetry*

The middle of the day is like the middle of the night. Life seems suspended when it is most intense. . . .

> – *Amiel's Journal*, translated by Mrs. Humphrey Ward

The meridian demon was upon him; he was possessed by that . . . post-prandial melancholy which the coenobites of old knew and feared. . . .

> – Aldous Huxley, *Crome Yellow*

[A] qualified Yes, conditioned by a prudential No . . . a fine credulity about everything, kept in check by a lively scepticism. . . . It [is a cast of thought] that keeps you constantly alert to every possibility. It is a little understood aspect of the Golden Mean.

> – Robertson Davies, *Murther and Walking Spirits*

Once upon a time, in 1949, Robertson Davies revisited the time of his youth to recall of his first reading in Aldous Huxley that it lifted him into "the sunshine world of high comedy" and cast over his life "a summer glory . . . which no conceivable winter could dispel" (*Enthusiasms* 230). The book was *Antic Hay* (1923), taken up at the suggestion of a lad of his own age who aspired to priesthood in the Church of England. "Enthralled" by the "wonderfully amusing people," "easy scholarship," and "witty pedantry" he met with in that novel, the teenaged Davies immediately "knew that this man Huxley stood in a very special relation" to him (229). Some twenty years later, in "The Conscience of the Writer" (1968), Davies extended his account of that very special relation, from his "surprise" at the appearance of *Eyeless in Gaza* (1936) to his considered understanding of Huxley's mid-life change from neo-Augustan satirist to religious mystic: "But what was significant about *Eyeless in Gaza* was that it was written when Huxley was forty-two, and ripe for change. If there had been no change, we should soon have tired of the old Huxley wearing the young Huxley's intellectual clothes" (*One Half* 127). The Davies of "The Conscience of the Writer" continues to prize the young Huxley's work for "the brilliance of its wit," its "strong satirical edge," and "stringent charm" (126), even as he more or less explicitly acknowledges the persistence of Huxley, "one of the most far-ranging, capacious and powerful intellects of our time" (*Enthusiasms* 141), as *éminence grise* in the continuing progress of his own "spiritual" life: "And from that time [of *Eyeless in Gaza*] to the end of his life . . . [Huxley's] exploration of mystical religion and his discussions of morality were at the root of everything he wrote" (*One Half* 127).

But signs of disenchantment, not long in coming after "The Conscience of the Writer," seem clear enough in the record of Davies' subsequent commentary on Huxley's intellectual clothes, whether new-Restorationly flashy or latter-day-monastic in cut. Certainly, both the young Huxley and the old come in for a somewhat circumspect ruffling in *World of Wonders* (1975), where an intermittent discussion of "intellectual fopperies" touches on unworldly "non-attachment" as much as on "the Ironic Spirit" of the early 1930s (175, 204). And when the theme of Huxley's shift in garb is revisited in a Davies lecture of November 1976, it is by a critic apparently much altered in his view since 1968: though Huxley "became fascinated with those things which he had formerly derided," according to Davies in "Thunder without Rain," he continued to suffer from "his earlier defect–he thought too much and felt too little" (*One Half* 253, 254). Like the "heartless[ly]" witty proceeding of *Crome Yellow* (1922), *Antic Hay*, and *Point Counter Point* (1928), the mystical Huxley's enterprise, as Davies now sees it, was impelled by a "negative and life-diminishing" spirit: his quest for "Absolutes" effectively occluded the "infinitely complex mingling of contrarieties" essential for the generating of "a new and stronger spirit in man" (253, 258, 263). Now altogether privileged over Huxley are Powys, Mann, and, of course, Jung, agents for a "Mystical Marriage of Opposites" that results not in a static, deadening "perfection," but in an inspiriting, dynamic "wholeness" (263, 268). The Davies of "Thunder without Rain" leaves little doubt as to the traditional theological import of his critique: Huxley young and old suffered from the cardinal vice of the modern age, "Wanhope" or "Accidie," the "very old sin" attributed in the Middle Ages to "monotony of life" (248, 258).

For all its surface transparency, though, the seasoned Davies' pronouncement of his break with Huxley on the grounds of persistent unfeeling or acedia remains substantially curious, perhaps even mystifying. And the curiosity is this: that Davies, in effect, takes a page from Huxley even as he turns from him. Readers familiar with Huxley's "Accidie" (in his first volume of essays, *On the Margin*, published in the same year as *Antic Hay*) will recall his early recognition of "the meridian demon's triumph" in "the most characteristic modern literature" (22)–and, with duly cogent obliqueness, in his own productions as ambivalent, ironic wit of "the Golden Mean" as well.[1] And the still-young Huxley, in his *Point Counter Point* and *Do What You Will* (1929), surely made explicit enough his adoption of a Blakean model for overcoming the melancholy and indolence in which he found himself more or less (un)happily mired: "in favour of life and wholeness," the "sane, harmonious Greek man" Blake "was civilized . . . *civilized*. Civilization is harmony and completeness. Reason, feeling, instinct, the life of the body. . . . Barbarism is being lopsided. [ . . . ] Blake strikes a balance [of] . . . the conscious soul and the unconscious, physical, instinctive part of the total being" (*Point* 141-42, 123); as exemplified by *The Marriage of Heaven and Hell*, the "life-worshipper's aim is to achieve a vital equilibrium, not by drawing in his diversities, not by moderating his exuberances . . . , but by giving them reign one against the other. His is the equilibrium of balanced excesses, the safest perhaps of all (is it not between the projecting extremities of a long pole that the tight-rope walker treads his spidery bridge?)" (*Do What* 279). Rabelais, Montaigne, Shakespeare, and Mozart figure prominently in the genealogy for the Blakean ideal of "moderation in terms of balanced excesses" that *Do What You Will* advances (223).

Nor do Davies readers familiar with *Eyeless in Gaza*–the crucial moral concern of which progressively issues from Huxley's meditating on a wisdom of balance-and-mean rehearsed from such Augustan notables as Dryden, Pope,

Johnson, Gibbon, and Hume, and developed from his *Limbo: Six Stories and a Play* (1920) to *Point Counter Point*–have all that much reason to be surprised by the coincidence in spiritual discernment that Huxley's pivotal testament and the text of "Thunder without Rain" inscribe. As the protagonist of *Eyeless in Gaza* comes to recognise with his entry into mid-life, the *daemon meridianus* is upon him: his is the "besetting sin" of that "indifference" or "inner sloth" to which practitioners of "the Higher Life," whether mystical coenobites or savants ironic in the best *dix-huitièmiste* mode, are naturally susceptible (*Eyeless* 13, 617, 171). The central perception of the book that stands at the pivotal point of Huxley's spiritual progress could hardly meet more closely with the moral theology that Davies comes to invoke against the whole of his oeuvre: "Indifference is a form of sloth, and sloth in its turn is one of the symptoms of lovelessness" (*Eyeless* 15). Such an instance of close agreement on what for Davies as for Huxley is the crucial, perennial problem in higher living–"Sloth," Davies accordingly emphasises in a Queen's University convocation address of 1962, is "the deadliest of the sins" (*One Half* 62)–provides some indication of the closeness of their special relation. In 1962, Huxley published his last novel, *Island*, in which the once "indifferent," "nay-saying" Will Farnaby, heir to Voltaire and Hume (like Theodore Gumbril Jr., bored schoolmaster and the main figure of lazy felicity in *Antic Hay*), comes to experience "a marriage between hell and heaven," of antithetical yet "complementary philosophies," "the paradox of opposites indissolubly wedded, of light shining out of darkness, of darkness at the very heart of light," in an uplifting transport accompanied by counterpoint from the composer of *The Well-Tempered Clavier* (27, 130, 129, 274, 288). What, in a sense, could be more substantially agreeing with Davies?

Now, this preliminary narrative is not at all meant pre-emptively to cast Davies in the role of Impercipient Reader or Absentminded Professor. Quite the contrary. It is intended, rather, to evoke, by way of historical analogy and liminal introduction, something of the complexity of Davies–his subtly evasive, seriously playful wit, the abiding pertinence of his substantial moral concerns, the artfulness of his theatrical maskings, and his marked disposition to a logic and rhetoric of doubleness, balance, paradox or irony–to which the essays of *A Mingling of Contrarieties* (developed from the first-ever conference on Davies, at the University of Ottawa, May 1998) variously and complementarily attest, with due sense of responsibility. As Elspeth Cameron had good reason to observe in her introduction to *Robertson Davies: An Appreciation* (1991), the writings of

Davies must seem "deeply intractable" to "critics" who would attempt to find a strictly logical "coherence in life . . . to locate a didactic programme" in his opus (4).[2] The tribute to Davies the artist of logical intractability and mystic profusion that ends Cameron's introduction figuratively resumes the still-abiding lot and condition of a criticism adjusted as veridically as it can to its subject as a master of sleight-of-hand: "To his critics, or admirers, or friends, Davies seems variously a Prospero, a Magus, a Wizard of Oz, a Wizard of the North, and an Emperor with imaginary clothes–always a magician whose crafty tricks may be benign or sinister. But whose ability to create and sustain illusion on a grand scale is formidable" (8). *Odi et amo*, a sentence formidable enough in itself in its power to conjure a Mystical Marriage of Opposites benign or sinister, might aptly serve as the *mot d'ordre* for *Robertson Davies: A Mingling of Contrarieties*.

The collection opens with Michael Peterman's "Perspectives on the Masks of Robertson Davies," a carefully measured account of critical biography that calls into question the wisdom of reading "the phenomenon" of "intriguing" Davies in unambiguously judgmental terms. As Peterman cautions, the "writerly ego" behind such a triumph of perceptive, richly comprehensive humanity as *Fifth Business* could also sometimes show a distinct tendency to "kick out ruthlessly in response to those things that mattered most to him." Peterman's recollection of his own grappling with "the problem" of locating the "complexity" that is Davies judiciously recommends a siting on "the middle ground," "somewhere between the extremes of response," either in favour or against. The Davies who emerges from this account, "an Ontario phenomenon born and bred," began "to perfect" his theatrical art of the "deliberately half-shadowed mask" early in life, from the time of his performing on the boards at age five in sombre, all-too-clear yet unsunny Thamesville. Allusion to the Melvillean "carpet bag of the ego . . . stuffed with masks and costume changes" discreetly aligns the subject of Peterman's discourse with the quick-change artist of *The Confidence-Man: His Masquerade*, whose Faustian, diabolico-angelical wisdom issues from an apperception of the conflict of convictions played out in the theatre of the world: "YEA AND NAY–EACH HATH HIS SAY: / BUT GOD HE KEEPS THE MIDDLE WAY" (Melville, *Poems* 10).

Faith Balisch's "'A Hint of the Basic Brimstone,'" on Davies' "humour," nicely follows on Peterman's contribution, locating as it does the source of that funniness in "the perception of shadows." "Ambiguity is the essence of humour," since what humour does is to explore "the great contra-dictions and incongruities that are an essential part of human experience." An attending to the concept of humour as a lively funning born of a Heraclitean-style "reconciliation of opposites" in mystery, so Balisch suggests, affords insight into the substantial attraction of "a Jungian spirituality" for a merry wit. Ample reference to Davies' affinity with the physician and Franciscan priest Rabelais supports the case for a Davies (in his own words) "'fully in sympathy with the medieval view that work is an ignoble way of passing the time,'" though Balisch is careful to align her subject with a "Renaissance" ethos of devilish fun difficult to reconcile with the praise of labour in the last of Chaucer's tales of pilgrimage to Canterbury and the Benedictine principle that to work is to pray. "Workaholic" Davies (the qualifier is Peterman's) loved to play in the shadows.

But, initially at least, the twilight world revisited in David Creelman's "Shadows of Determinism in the Salterton Novels" seems more grim than merry. By Creelman's reckoning, the Salterton novels image the travails of a mind at sixes and sevens, imbued with a "sense of scepticism" and practising an art of "antithesis" snugly fitted to a "middle-of-the-road" reading of the (in)efficacy of the human will. The resorting to Romance solutions to Realist problems reflects the depth of those travails. Rather than working to diminish the value of the Salterton tales, though, this essay proceeds to suggest that novelist Davies' early balancing in the "gaps" between contesting versions of determinism prepared his progress to a Jungian "internalizing" of external forces in The Deptford Trilogy. The "powerful ideological struggle" in Davies' early fiction represents a stage in his growth toward a less tension-filled ambiguity, and, as Creelman argues, a more dynamically constructive, since more cogent, apprehension of the human condition.

Relative to Creelman's contribution, which opens with a reference to the "perhaps surprisingly unified voice" of commentators on *Tempest-Tost*, *Leaven of Malice*, and *A Mixture of Frailties*, Todd Pettigrew's "Magic in the Web: Robertson Davies and *Shamanstvo*" proceeds *à rebours* by initially setting the question of why the diametrically opposed valuations of novelist Davies' achievement as a whole. Pettigrew's answer to that question involves a paradoxical *jeu d'esprit* whereby a "monologic domination" is understood to "liberate" the reader by "ensnarement" in the weave of a storyteller's text. A playful analogy of text and "web" works to invite a recognition of the artist as spider whose inherently reflexive constructions centred "on points in between" leave readers at liberty to travel up and down the non-sticky radial strings of the tales that he spins. "Ambiguous" again is the qualifier of great moment for "the magic" that, like the *shamanstvo* epitomised in Part Two of Goethe's *Faust*, Davies the wonder worker and crafty weaver of tales achieves in effect.

The insightful humour of K.P. Stich's "The Leaven of Wine and Spirits" is perhaps even more entertainingly dry in its contextual siting of Davies as a purveyor of high culture. Genealogical reference to Dionysus, Orpheus, and Hermes, "polymorphous" gods companioned in their power to represent "paradoxes and enigmatic initiations" in human affairs, figures prominently in this essay on "liquid 'Fifth Business.'" Though an "irreverent praise of half-drunk genius" on occasion "occurs intemperately" in the world of Davies' fiction, more often than not the novelist's "emphasis" is "on the sunny rather than the sinister side of drink." As in Rabelais, "it is the moderate . . . drinkers who abound." "Intemperate temperance," a paradox of vice/virtue cognate, so Stich suggests, with the figure of a high-flying wit ever sensitive to the folly of excess, emerges as a *bête noire* repeatedly revisited in the world of cultural or moral values that the eleven novels of the Davies opus collectively sign. The spirit of animated yet prudential humour epitomised in Leacock's "'wet' sunshine" remains very much alive, substantially informs the whole of that achievement.

If the lesson of moderation even in moderation that Stich finds configured in "the Great Theatre of Life" according to Davies might seem as old-fashioned as reflexively self-consistent, the moral sense so advanced hardly precludes the possibility of reading his art in a "postmodern" context. As Lois Sherlow's essay makes the telling point, the dramatic writings of Davies evince "a strong tendency to enjoy the self-referentiality of theatre and to manipulate the drama/culture complex as far as his invention allows–and not only in his plays–in the interest of estranging unexamined habits of perception common in Canada." The postmodern character of his plays is demonstrated by reference to the features of "ambivalence" and "doubleness," the "vertiginous degree of relativisation and scepticism," which they recognizably share with the Canadian theatre of the eighties and nineties, in French as in English. Ironically enough, though, and in a way consistent with its subject as a practitioner of a scepticism understandably doubtful of itself, Sherlow's essay concludes with a remarking of Davies the dogmatist and Davies the theatrical relativist near allied: if the plays are "uproarious" in their postmodernly nay-saying to such modern dramatic practises as indicate an "either nihilistic or propagandist" intention, they themselves are "overburdened with moralizing messages."

And the figure of Davies as dramatiser of dubiety and ambivalence, of *skepsis* as inquiry in unknowing, surely dominates in Mark Silverberg's "'Where There's a Will, There Are Always Two Ways.'" Rich in the language of "sneakiness," "duplicity," and "paradox"–"the uncanny"–this essay argues for *World of Wonders* as "a novel of constant debate." Opposites do not simply collide in the "extremely complicated" world of that narrative; they make each other possible. "Dialogical," virtually polyphonic, in its voicing, according to Silverberg, *World of Wonders* is a book of bafflement, marvel, and reflection that draws the reader into a universe where all action or being finds itself logically represented "between poles of opposition and affinity." The narrative's affective working registers a process of negative capability that makes any discriminating ethical reading impossible to sustain with any certainty. "The Double," Silverberg offers by way of conclusion, "is the Other finally recognised as the Self. Paul's encounters with Willard and Sir John are instances of self-meeting and figure as necessary stations on the road to self-actualisation." If *World of Wonders* has any lesson to convey, it is that extremes meet.

David Hallett's "Authentic Forgeries . . . in *What's Bred in the Bone*" also attends to the synthetic logic basic to novelist Davies, but to an end that is distinctly unambiguous in affirming the ethical sense of the matter that it interprets. Contemporary notions bearing on "horizon[s] of expectation," wed to an archival recollection of Hermes/Mercury as "reconciler of opposites," prepare the ground for Hallett's interpretation of *What's Bred in the Bone* as "a didactic work of art in a modernist manner in the midst of the postmodern era." *What's Bred in the Bone* is undeniably consistent with itself, since it narrates the possibility of "making" a picture, even in imitation, that is all one's own. The oxymoron of "authentic forgeries" designates the achievement of an artist whose fundamentally Platonic mode of valuation–the ideal is the real–subtends his sense of Romance as ethically pragmatic. Hallett's measured demurring from Stanley Fish's theory of Renaissance wisdom-writing as *pharmakon* by ostensibly healthful self-consumption helps advance the argument for *What's Bred in the Bone* as a "text" that "makes overt, conscious use of the idea of a contemporary artist working effectively" in the "didactic" mode of "an earlier era." "Authentic Forgeries" ends fittingly, in Renaissance style, with an aphorism and a pun, to the effect that "Being human is a chronic condition; the prescription of challenging art always needs renewal."

Tatjana Takseva Chorney's meditation on the "loving" agency of the storytelling practised in The Deptford Trilogy further advances the theme of renewal. Her contribution's "seriously fanciful" engaging of "the ways in which the characters [of that trilogy] reach out from the page toward the reader" works to draw its own readers into a sympathetic recognition of their "urge . . . to share in the magic of the text, not as its co-creator, but as [listeners] . . . who accept its gift appreciatively and with an undeniable freedom to interpret it." In concert with her co-contributors to *A Mingling of Contrarieties*, Chorney locates teller and receptor in a place "in between," on which shared ground both parties to the action of giving and receiving are naturally invited to apprehend "the truth" of "metaphor" or "myth" as modes of conjoining, communion. "A quality of fine ambivalence," of "buoyant earnestness," must needs be experienced and shared by any participant in the communion of writer and reader when each acts in mutual "good faith." Chorney's concluding reference to the "magic" of Davies, "his enchanter quality," bespeaks the potential efficacy of just such a faith.

No less aptly, though less peripatetic in its proceeding, the last essay of *A Mingling of Contrarieties* revisits the case for a "Janus-faced" Davies who "operates best" in the "'gap' between antithetical elements" in his narratives, especially as evinced in *The Lyre of Orpheus*. As Andrea C. Cole's "'Converting the Clerisy': Quest/ioning, Contradictions, and Ethics in the Cornish Triptych" represents it, the "Quest" for the liberation from "Limbo"–"a type of suspense"–which that ensemble of texts signs is "achieved" by "the reader" in the experience of "an epiphany" born of a "collision" of perspectives and elements in a world of invincible uncertainty. By narrative design, the weave of italicised *ETAH* commentary in *The Lyre of Orpheus* textualises as it enacts the proposition that process rather than fate is all: "The real story is how the story is told." "The reader"–so Cole emphasises on the last page of her contribution–"is not meant to accept any position unquestioningly; a true clerical, or ethical reading, must remain open." Thus understood, Davies the crafty spinner of tales and Davies *skeptikos*, moralist of inquiry, doubt, and wonder, appear to be all of a piece.

"'Medical Consultation' for *Murther and Walking Spirits* and *The Cunning Man*," a sprightly, instructive reading derived from Davies' correspondence with physician Rick Davis, is appended to *A Mingling of Contrarieties* as a potentially ironic envoy. As this narrative of "consultation" eloquently attests, Robertson Davies, purveyor of magic, illusion, and feeling, was also very much a careful student, a man of intellect and erudition who attended, in an eminently practical way, to the "facts" of the visible universe.

Like the "anatomists" Rabelais and Burton, university scholars and aficionados of the *recherché* whose endeavouring to overcome melancholy he consulted time and again, Davies was quite at home in the world of scholarly letters and learning. Professor Peter Brigg, facilitator of the reading that ends this book, affectionately recalls something of the value of his academic mentor as a man of "common sense" and "immense forbearance" who recommended "the Plain Style." *Voler bene*!

The Symposium Committee of the University of Ottawa's Department of English is delighted to thank Mrs. Davies for her gracious permission to print from her husband's letters, and to acknowledge such financial aid as the Social Sciences and Humanities Research Council of Canada and the University of Ottawa's Research Committee, in concert with its companion committee in the Faculty of Arts, generously saw fit to provide. This volume would not have appeared without their support. The efforts of Angela Robbeson, Marie Tremblay-Chénier, and Veronica Tremblay in helping to organise the Davies Symposium no less deserve recognition here.

CRL
Douglas/Renfrew 12.99

## NOTES

1. For an account of young Huxley's "delighting like Swift in self-torment," see Tindall (101). The "ambivalence of his early novels" is remarked by Woodcock (16), who recalls his experience of more than just surprise on first reading *Eyeless in Gaza*: "I remember, when *Eyeless in Gaza* was published thirty-four years ago, reading it with bewilderment and a sense of betrayal" (13). For an account of Huxley's sustained commitment to a morality of "tact and taste, of balanced contradictions," and his savvy evasiveness as debunker and celebrant of indolence in the whole of his oeuvre, see La Bossière (45-48).

2. More recently, Diamond-Nigh confirms such an intractability in a monograph that recalls Davies as a professor of higher learning and a figure of high intellectual culture whose novel *The Rebel Angels* evinces "his valorization of instinct over intellect" (33).

# WORKS CITED

Cameron, Elspeth. Introduction to *Robertson Davies: An Appreciation*. Peterborough, Ont.: Broadview Press, 1991.

Davies, Robertson. *The Enthusiasms of Robertson Davies*. Ed. Judith Skelton Grant. Toronto: McClelland & Stewart, 1979.

–. *Murther and Walking Spirits*. Toronto: McClelland & Stewart, 1991.

–. *One Half of Robertson Davies: Provocative Pronouncements on a Wide Range of Topics*. Toronto: Macmillan, 1977.

–. *World of Wonders*. 1975. Harmondsworth: Penguin, 1977.

Diamond-Nigh, Lynne. *Robertson Davies: Life, Work, and Criticism*. Toronto: York Press, 1997.

Huxley, Aldous. *Antic Hay*. London: Chatto & Windus, 1949.

–. *Crome Yellow*. London: Chatto & Windus, 1952.

–. *Do What You Will*. London: Chatto & Windus, 1956.

–. *Island*. New York: Harper & Row, 1962.

–. *On the Margin*. London: Chatto & Windus, 1971.

La Bossière, Camille R. *The Progress of Indolence: Readings in (Neo)Augustan Literary Culture*. Toronto: York Press, 1997.

Melville, Herman. *Poems*. New York: Russell & Russell, 1963.

Tindall, William York. *Forces in Modern British Literature, 1884-1956*. 2nd ed. New York: Vintage, 1956.

Woodcock, George. *Dawn and the Darkest Hour: A Study of Aldous Huxley*. New York: Viking, 1972.

# The Concert of His Life: Perspectives on the Masks of Robertson Davies

MICHAEL PETERMAN

It is the spring of 1985 and Robertson Davies is writing to his old friend Gordon Roper about an exhausting publicity trip he has just undergone to promote *What's Bred in the Bone*. He writes from Windover, his well-appointed rural retreat in the Caledon Hills north of Toronto, where above his desk hangs Yousuf Karsh's photographic portrait of Carl Jung. Having complained to Roper about how shabbily he had been treated while giving readings at New York University and the National Library of Canada, he launches into an amusing story about his experiences at the National Library prior to his reading:

> Before things got going I was invited into a room where there hangs portraits by Karsh of Canadian writers, blown up to huge proportions. And there was I, in a picture I hate deeply; it was Karsh's notion of a Funny Man. I so well recall when he took it; he bamboozled me for over an hour, assuring me that a humorist must appear to the world as exactly that, and what that meant was a clownish picture indeed. Mr. Karsh, I should explain, has no sense of humour of any kind. O God! I asked if it could not be exchanged for another, but the National Librarian of Canada–a fat woman who ha[d] come right out from behind the Checking Out desk somewhere in the north, would not believe that I was serious. If you are a Funny Man, you see, you are never serious. So I read a passage from the new book about a dwarf tailor who hanged himself because his life was one long humiliation, and I think ALMOST convinced the

National Public Librarian that it wasn't meant to be funny.[1]

I begin with this anecdote for several reasons. I have called this paper "The Concert of His Life: Perspectives on the Masks of Robertson Davies" because as I wrestled with the problem of how to begin this first-ever conference on Davies, I found myself returning time and time again, as I think many interested readers do, to the problem of coming to grips with the man behind the genial and courtly, but deliberately half-shadowed, mask. If we are to try to measure the resonances of Davies' writing, I would argue that we have to know him as well as we can; indeed, we need to know more of him than he was willing to project outward to the public. In knowing him better we can begin to separate the writer from his writing, and thus can attend more judiciously and informedly to the dynamic relation between the man and his works. By his "writing" I refer particularly to the eleven novels upon which, despite a wide range and volume of work in other genres and fields, his literary reputation must finally stand. The vast number of critical articles on Davies' fiction confirms this focus of attention.

What I have to say, at least initially, focuses on the "phenomenon" of Robertson Davies. It is more than two years since his rather sudden and surprising death. Most members of the literary community of Canada (a many-sectored club, one of which includes academic Canadianists, but a club nevertheless) had some contact–pro or con, positive or negative, welcoming or off-putting–with Davies, the man. In a way that is rare among Canadian authors of note, his was a presence that struck the eye, that left a lingering impression. The image he projected was among the most caricatured in the Canadian press over the last three decades. People who encountered him either liked him or disliked him–there was, it seems, little middle ground. For those who had some opportunity to observe him over time, that sense of presence left a lingering sensation, oddly reminiscent of the way in which, in the final two Salterton novels, Mrs. Louisa Bridgetower contrived, for reasons perfectly clear to herself, to extend her "Dead Hand" of control over those around her. Davies himself had a passion for control, especially over the way he projected himself and, by implication, over the way in which he wished to be perceived. One can feel that "hand" still at work in the recent posthumous collections of Davies' occasional writing, *The Merry Heart* and *Happy Alchemy*. The latter volume achieves a kind of dead-hand eeriness by prefacing each of the selected essays with candid excerpts from Davies' theatre diaries.

In using the term "phenomenon," I refer specifically to the man who as a little boy first appeared on stage at the age of five in Thamesville.[2] In effect, he never thereafter left the boards, at least so long as there was an audience poised to witness and remark upon his Concert. And as he progressed in the sophistications of self-presentation, he perfected a series of personae or self-images that audiences of the day readily recognised and even anticipated. I mix theatrical traditions (something Davies himself liked to do) in saying that he "g[a]ve 'em the old razzle-dazzle" Edwardian style: the beard, the cape, the jaunty hat, the hint of gaslight, the genial, gracious presence, the whiff of sulphur, and the promise of a man who, while he could and would be Funny, also had important truths and dark revelations to impart to those who were prepared to listen closely. He gave 'em G.K. Chesterton, Max Beerbohm, and G.B. Shaw with a grounding of Havelock Ellis, Sigmund Freud, and Carl Jung. I only wish that he had made room for something a little more vulgar, energetic and sassy, in the mode of Bob Fosse. And, in fairness, he did try, but to be "larky" is not to be "sassy," and what was sexy apparently held little attraction for him.[3] His models were precisely to his own taste; they were largely of a well-clothed, genteel English cut that hearkened back to the nineteenth century and they were not to be altered, especially by anything that was American, jazzy, and erotic. His abiding need was the desire to be profound, and that need took different shapes as he evolved in his life experience and reading. For Davies, initially there was the desire, rooted in his curiosity, to provide counsel and advice related to "depth psychology." Thus, he was known at Oxford as "the Havelock Ellis of Balliol."[4] In the 1940s and early 1950s he was a devotee of Freud, often writing from a clear Freudian perspective; over the final four decades, he consciously transformed himself into "the Carl Jung of Canadian letters."[5] I must confess, however, that I prefer the early, subtle sense of Jung in Davies' work, as when, in *Fifth Business*, he was the "fantastical duke of dark corners."

In the anecdote about his Karsh photograph at the National Library, Davies signals several things. A look at the picture may provide some surprise (as it surprised me), for it is not a picture I recalled having seen. We would only see it were we leafing through *Karsh Canadians* (1978) or *Karsh: The Art of the Portrait* (1989), or if we were visiting the Canadian Authors Room at the National Library.[6] Taken in Davies' own study in 1977, the picture shows a man of great good humour, geniality radiating comfortably from him. His finger is raised near his nose as if in tribute to a good joke or *bon mot*. We can almost hear the chortle that was so characteristic of Davies when, among companions or in an audience, he reacted with jolly boisterousness and pleasure, with full and uninhibited engagement, to something he found amusing. When I sought out the photograph in *Karsh Canadians*, I was further surprised to find that, on the opposite page, Karsh provided his own three-paragraph account of his subject and their sitting, an account that offers a very different view of the experience of photographing Davies:

> The exotic ambience of the Master's Lodge at Massey College, Toronto, where Canada's pre-eminent man of letters resides, suits him perfectly. In the classic statues, antiques, and richly bound rare books around his home is evidence of his love of literature, art, and music. He is a civilized man, a scintillating conversationalist with a gift of combining erudition and earthy humour.
>
> I find it interesting (and, I suspect, quite wrong) that Davies has interpreted his attachment to civilization as a special Canadian characteristic. "I'm not a great lover of the wilderness," he once remarked. "In this I think I'm a real Canadian. My forbears were genuine pioneers and their idea was to get inside and keep the wilderness outside. The struggle was always toward civilization rather than toward all that rubbish out there that you had to clear up."
>
> The impeccable English tea that I shared with Davies and his wife, Brenda, was proof that he carries on the family tradition of exorcising the wilderness from his urban refuge. I doubt that Davies, so profoundly right about many other things, has correctly judged the old instincts of his people. Nowadays, most of them live in cities, yet the wilderness constantly pulls them back to its solitude and mystery, forever colouring and haunting the subconsciousness of a nation conceived in lonely places.[7]

Evidently, Karsh had his reservations about certain of Davies' pronouncements. The commentary suggests a tension between the two that lingered on in both their memories. Karsh did not accept Davies' assertion of the "garrison mentality" view of Canada's historical and psychological roots. That he said so in print, juxtaposing Davies' civilised bearing and "earthy humour" with his frank dismissiveness of the land and the wilderness, encapsulates the iciness that underlay their interaction. Perhaps, then, it is not surprising that Davies should have used the occasion of his National Library reading to revisit his own disappointment with Karsh and to let loose his anger at the result of the sitting.

The Karsh portrait was not one he seems to have used for publicity purposes; he was, after all, a man who was very often photographed and who seems to have taken great pleasure in being projected and preserved in his various guises and moods.

In the anecdote, I note particularly Davies' insistence upon Karsh's failure to capture his true essence: hence, his "deep" hatred for the product and the whole experience. A bubble of residual anger underlies his recollection. Though there is nothing in the record to suggest that Karsh sought to render Davies "clownish," one can sense Davies' deep-seated preoccupation with and desire to control his personal image, a preoccupation especially apparent in his awareness of the kind of enlargement he has received among his equally enlarged peers–his image "blown up to huge proportions." From this letter, however, we know only of HIS portrait. It is all he sees. Much as he dislikes it, his eyes can't leave it. Moreover, although he actively eschews the label of Funny Man, a label he had once been quite willing to promote, he is very much the humorist at work in the anecdote.

Underlying this episode is Davies' firm sense of having become a figure of greater seriousness and consequence, of having moved well beyond the funny-fellow image that readers had learned to associate with Samuel Marchbanks and the amusing high jinks of the early Salterton novels. The publicity photos used for those early books (for obvious reasons there was no photo for either of the first two Marchbanks texts) and for newspaper profiles were, to be sure, not always marked by a laugh, but they suggested an amused and affable author. And certainly the comic photo of Marchbanks as Davies for *Liberty* magazine stressed the madcap impression.[8]

The personalised story he offers to Gordon Roper is a gift to amuse an ailing friend, but the bare bones of its construction tell us a good deal. Typically, Davies insists on stereotypes to ensure the greater complexity of his own individuality. Beyond his characterisation of Karsh as humourless and insensitive photographer, we catch Davies, in a characteristic manoeuvre, capitalising the stereotypes he uses–here the misunderstood Funny Man and the conventionalised Librarian are set at odds. The Librarian, Canadian style, is a vivid caricature in herself, "com[ing]," and I relish the phrasing, "right out from behind the Checking Out desk somewhere in the north." One blanches, however, for the real-life National Librarian who is clearly Davies' straw woman in the anecdote, imaged as an overweight bureaucrat who, like the culture she formally represents, doesn't get it when it comes to the complex essence of his writing; indeed, she does not seem quite able to get it even with so graphic a case of the death of Blairlogie's dwarf tailor before her.

There is, for me, something essential about Davies in this anecdote; we see him trying out a personal story, beginning to transform it so as to tap its comic and cultural potential, yet characteristically needing to exact a kind of revenge on those who, like Karsh or the insensitive National Librarian, have not, in his estimate, paid him appropriate attention or due homage. Had he lived longer and found a place for it, I suspect that the anecdote, further teased out and developed, might well have become a part of novel number twelve or thirteen.

It matters little to most readers and fans of Davies–and they are many–that some critics should dwell upon the complexities of temperament and ego that underlie his work as a novelist. Still, it is important to recognise Davies as public performer and to measure various aspects that follow from or are masked by his performances–to make note, for instance, of his appetite for attention and recognition, his craving for fame and success as a writer, and the sting in the manticore's tail when his expectations were in some particular way disappointed or violated. If his central theme was initially the problems faced by the artistic sensibility in the chilly (northern) cultural climate of Canada, his most intense and consistent focus of attention was upon the process he later came to call "individuation." He was, virtually from the beginning, drawn to the struggles of the individual to find and develop his own strengths. Only later did he begin to explore the complex, sometimes dark, forces underlying those strengths. As readers, we have seen the theme of individuation, the active pursuit of self-knowledge and healthful accord with oneself, voiced over and over, by Davies himself and by critics responding to his fictional representations of the process. But what has surprised me on revisiting Davies this time around is a glimpse of the raw hunger he had for attention and adulation, and the kind of desperation he expressed when he felt the control pass from his hands. There seems to have been a childlike craving in him to be valued as he wished to see himself, to be rewarded for a good and compelling and serious show. When he was disappointed or when he felt himself misjudged or undervalued, the gospel of growth and healthful maturation fell away like a mantle or a cape, leaving a not-quite-naked but often mean-spirited ego alone on stage.

Here I enter the story, because, while I was thinking about what topic I would try to give to the subject of Davies' "critical reception," I received a letter from Judith Grant, which, for reasons that will become obvious, instantly caught my attention.[9] Following the appearance of her capacious and richly informative biography, *Robertson Davies: Man of Myth* (1994), Grant has been preparing a two-volume collection of Davies' letters. Our paths first crossed some twenty years ago. I was working on the Twayne World Authors study of Davies (it appeared in 1986), and Grant was about to begin her biography. She had published a short and perceptive monograph on his writing in 1978 and was at work on a couple of collections of his occasional writings. We compared notes about our mutual subject and, at her request, I introduced her to Gordon Roper, who had been one of Davies' valued literary friends in Peterborough in the early 1940s and who, in 1959-60, in his capacity as Head of the Department of English at Trinity College, University of Toronto, had paved the way for Davies, against considerable university opposition, to leave Peterborough for (in the words of Samuel Marchbanks) the fleshpots of "the Ontario Babylon"–Toronto.[10]

The writing of the Twayne book, which I inherited from Professor Roper in 1979, had proved its own kind of struggle for me. It was not just the problem of trying to treat Davies effectively and fairly, with all the academic rigour I could muster; it was that, like Solly Bridgetower in his struggles with his powerful mother, I had to find some space for myself as the author of the study of a major author even as I was doing my best not to disappoint the trust that Gordon Roper had placed in me. It proved a tight and difficult fit. At the same time I also had to struggle to find the necessary time, given my ongoing involvement with two other academic colleagues in a large editorial project involving the search for and publication of the extant letters of Susanna Moodie and Catharine Parr Traill.

What I did not realise as I worked away on the book was the extent of Davies' interest in and anxiety about its appearance. On reflection, since it was the first book-length treatment of his work up to and including *The Rebel Angels*, I should perhaps have realised that he would have been on the *qui vive* about the result. After all, he had been waiting since the late 1960s for Roper's study and here now were further delays and new uncertainties.

I won't include a full account of Davies' responses to the Twayne book, but I will share with you what most surprised me in the comments that he made. Judith Grant assures me that I got off "far more lightly" than she did, though I'm not sure that that is the case.[11]

For the period from 1979, when I took over the book, until 1986 when it appeared, Davies, in the letters I have seen, dwells mostly on aspects of Roper's uncertain health while worrying about the time it was taking to get the book into print. During the interval, as I was working my way through his already large and diverse literary output, I had the chance to interview Davies twice at Massey College, amiably at first, then with some bridling and tension on his part.[12] It was during the latter interview that I tried to engage him in questions that addressed certain of his strongly held views and attitudes: for example, his negative regard for what he called "the Common Man"; his assumption of a sometimes lofty social identity; his defence of wealth and position; his treatment of women in his plays and novels; the instances of bullying that passed for teaching in his narratives; and certain of his readings of the Canadian soul and psyche. It was an interesting experience, but it left me as uneasy as it seems to have left Davies himself.

Here, then, is the way Davies responded as he waited for the book. One undated postcard to Roper, from the early 1980s, bristles with barely contained impatience. "What's with Peterman?" he wrote. "Why is he off in pursuit of old Ma Moodie? Why won't anybody finish ME? I shall write my memoirs and spite you all!"[13] I did, of course, want to "finish" with him, but I wasn't finding him an easy subject. Then, following my interviews with him, which helped me to conceptualise the kind of man and sensibility I was dealing with, came a series of comments–his apparent response to my questions–that describe my "critical method." It was, he wrote in December 1984, a "truly academic [method]– which is to say that at all costs the critic must Know Best about Everything. It is thus that academic reputations are made."[14] While it was heartening to learn that at that stage in my life I actually had a critical method, my approach was clearly not a cause for enthusiasm on Davies' part. Thus, he wrote to Roper on September 2, 1986:

> Glad to hear that the book is to appear at last, after so many vicissitudes. My feeling about Peterman, with whom I had only one talk about the book, was that he belonged to the class of academic who regards authors as candidates for marks, and himself as a stern examiner. I found nothing of appreciation for literature as an art–only a man who applies a system he has learned from others like himself, and which is certainly not "bred in the bone." Nor did we appear to live in the same world; what is precious to me had no meaning for him, or appeared contemptible. My next book [*The Lyre of Orpheus*] will puzzle him a good deal, I think, if, having finished

his academic task on my work, he troubles to read it.[15]

Happily, the ever-kindly Roper spared me these comments.

But what did Davies think of the book once he read it? His fullest response, at least as far as I know, is found in a letter to Doug Gibson at McClelland & Stewart, dated May 29, 1987. Davies let fly with something of his full rancour on that occasion. Describing *The Lyre of Orpheus* to Gibson as "a complex book," he worried that

> I must not make it too complex or ride my hobbies too hard–a fault for which some grave Western critics have been scolding me recently. I am the subject of a Twayne book by one Michael Peterman of Trent University; he is down on me for all the old things–eli[ti]st, given to big words, sloppy construction, too fond of improbable (un-Petermanlike) characters, can't draw women, and flawed, flawed, flawed. All written in the kind of Quaker Oats prose one expects from a Peterborough academic. But I suppose I am an old lion and the asses want to skin me and hee-haw in my shrunken skin.[16]

So there I am, not so much shaken as surprised and bemused by the growl of the old lion. I did not think that, finally, I was nearly as negative as Davies saw me to be; in fact, I greatly admire him as a writer and an important Canadian. Several reviewers of the Twayne book saw me as being more than a little enchanted by my subject, which is apparently a bad thing to make clear, especially among "grave Western critics." But when a man keeps the strict kind of accounts that Davies did, such hostility seems nothing if not fascinating. It is at one with his reaction to the Karsh who resisted what Davies wanted; at one with his mistrust of Judith Grant, who was to him, at least initially, the sort of unscrupulous biographer who insisted upon knowing every secret he had; at one with his cutting opinion of several critics whose perceptions either displeased or gored him; and at one with various disputes or vendettas he carried on during his professional life as editor of the Peterborough *Examiner* and as Master of Massey College. It is most appropriate to contextualise this aspect of himself in his own words, again from a letter addressed to Roper in which he sought to console his friend on the need to find someone else to complete the Twayne book. The letter, written in late March 1979, is both fascinating and insightful:

I felt long ago that the book had become an obsession with you, and that the obsession was not really with the subject (because what there is to say about me can be said pretty briskly and economically) but with some very deep concern about the scholar who lies so deep within yourself. It would be impertinent for me to try to guess what that is, but I suppose it related to your deeply held feelings about Canadian literature, for one thing. And for another, I think it has some roots in your discovery that I am not really the man you think I am or would wish me to be. You have known for many years that many writers are two-sided–good father, faithful husband, en-courager of the young and modest as the violet BUT also raging egotists who would boil their grannies down for soup, rob the blind and kick the crutches from under the paraplegic, and paranoid to a degree that even Freud could not stand–and that they combine all this with a toughness that masquerades as wincing sensitivity. You smelled this in me and–kind and truly good man that you are–it pained you, and you didn't want to write about it. But because you are a scholar, and have forsworn the pleasures of hypocrisy when it is a matter of your work, you felt you ought to give just the teeniest hint. . . . Well, I think Peterman will take the load off your shoulders.[17]

The Davies we see here is thoughtful, sensitive, and forthright with his friend, acutely aware of the dark side of his own writerly ego that kicks out ruthlessly in response to those things that matter most to him. That he would forget such a recognition when it came to what he took to be negative depictions or views that challenged or threatened his carefully groomed, precisely projected image as artist is not in the least surprising. Rather, it makes him more in-triguing. It allows us to see how vulnerable he was behind the composure of his mask. It adds force and edge to the motivations and actions he located in his later protagonists; and it lets us as readers know that, behind the quest to be a more rounded and fully aware individual that stands near the centre of his later work, there lay a primal nakedness and a deep anxiety that knew little restraint. At the same time, in his letters to Roper he worried in a surprisingly vulnerable way about the weaknesses he perceived in each novel as he was writing it, fearful of his capacity to make the narrative work (he agonised, for instance, over how his angel narrators in *What's Bred in the Bone* would be received) and uncertain about whether he could once again sustain the attention of his growing readership.[18] We glimpse here the carpet bag of the ego, as Melville called it, and with Davies we detect a bag well stuffed with masks and costume changes. When we consider Davies closely, it is well not to ignore the "raging" and vengeful egotist, tough, self-serving, and, as he would put it, amoral at the heart's core. The half-darkened face in the stylised photograph, the stinging tail of the manticore, the stone in the snowball were not affectations; they were personal recognitions. It is equally important, however, to emphasise the kindness, generosity of spirit, and openness he could express to a personal friend; this side he seldom showed in public.

My purpose in beginning this way is to situate a complexity. In the midst of not a little carping and resistance from his several or more detractors, particularly in Canada, Davies has achieved an international fame of a kind and breadth that few contemporary Canadian writers have managed or can hope to emulate. Indeed, he has contributed mightily and in many ways to the remarkably improved literary climate and cultural situation that characterised Canada as it neared the millennium. From abroad he seems, in the words of his obituary in *The Economist*, to have been "the novelist who made Canada less boring," as if somehow it were something one could never have expected of a single writer.[19] Here on home ground we are much more aware of the ways in which he slowly and deliberately typed out an impressive and locally indicative career. Since the appearance of *Tempest-Tost* in 1951, his novels have been best-sellers in Canada and, from that modest beginning, have garnered increasing attention in the vast North-American market. Book by book that audience grew. Sadly, at the moment of his greatest reach and popularity as a novelist–*The Cunning Man* sold 80,000 hard-cover copies in the United States alone in 1995–he passed away, allowed too little time, it would appear, to enjoy the widespread acclaim to which he so achingly aspired.[20]

The production of eleven novels over some forty-five years constitutes a major achievement. Still, the figure that invites attention here is not the number of novels but the time span of nearly half a century. A history of that spanning takes us back to a time prior to the Canada Council (an institution that Davies had a significant part in encouraging) when, as a matter of course, young Canadians with artistic aspirations left the country for larger pastures or, in Dennis Lee's memorable words, were busy "continentalizing [their] ass[es]."[21] Davies certainly did both. Though he gave many indications at Upper Canada College and at Queen's that he was well underway in matters of self-presentation, it was at Oxford, where eccentricity had long flourished, that he made himself a remarkable figure. He seemed to a contemporary "the last of the real undergraduate 'figures' in Oxford":

> Any day now you may see the form of Robertson Davies, almost
> Chestertonian in its greatness, proceeding with stately gait up the
> Broad, with a genial nod and a smile to acquaintances, and with a
> deep but dignified bow for the more favoured few. If you are
> fortunate, this important-looking figure will halt to exchange a joke
> with you, and when he laughs, he will shake all over and the roar
> will reverberate from the Broad to the High. Dignity, however, will
> remain. ... Yes "presence," that's the word that sums him up best
> of all, I think.[22]

His debate with his native land, brought starkly home to him when he
returned to Ontario from Oxford and London during the dark days of the Second
World War, became the basis of his fiction and his prose—and a template against
which readers of this country's heartening cultural development since the 1960s
can measure the extent of the progress and the quality of significant achievements. Grant's account of the ways in which Davies made his way on his own
terms—as a journalist, humorist, and a theatre person in the 1940s—is a moving
study in persistence and conviction, as well as of self-assured difference and
superiority. He certainly had financial and familial advantages that ensured his
comfort and often helped pave his progress; and in his essays and fiction he
never was one to criticise the value of such personal advantages. But while he
wore a beard to provide an air of difference and personal panache, and while he
railed privately against the dullness, ignorance, and philistinism that constrained
both his theatrical aspirations and his considerable *joie de vivre* ("you could die
in Peterborough of unrequited jollity," as he once had occasion to recall)[23], he
always got down to work when opportunities presented themselves. In fact, his
need for self-expression was such that he often anticipated such opportunities.
The man was a workaholic with a carefully nurtured sense of balance concerning
the priorities of his life as a whole.

The record of Robertson Davies in Peterborough is compelling.
Returning from Oxford with an attitude that he had carefully cultivated, refined,
and clothed, he found himself relocated in the conservative and, to him, dull life
of eastern Ontario. He found a few kindred spirits—and those he hugged to
himself as gratefully as Robinson Crusoe embraced Friday on that day of
discovery on the desert island.[24] Chafing at the social and cultural constraints
that surrounded him in the 1940s and early 1950s, he was also deeply frustrated

by his failure to make waves with the CBC's drama department, or with Dora Mavor Moore's New Play Society, or with his influential English theatre acquaintances such as John Gielgud and Sybil Thorndike. Predictably, he blamed the former far more than the latter. Despite a range of local successes with his own plays and with other productions in which he was involved– successes that helped lay the groundwork for a lively amateur theatre scene that flourishes to this day in Peterborough–he was forced to a cold and painful recognition, one that came to him in stages: the way things were going, it was becoming increasingly clear that he had little future as a large-scale actor, or director, or, finally and most disappointedly, playwright. Still, as a dutiful son with a young family to look after, he was also building one of his father's newspapers, the Peterborough *Examiner*, into one of the best and most quoted small-city dailies in the country, and he was developing a syndicated audience for his voice of humorous observation and cultural complaint, Samuel Marchbanks. Thus, Robertson Davies paid his dues even as he began to find his voice. He settled slowly into the role of big frog in a small pond and learned to adapt to the limitations of the pond, using those conditions increasingly as a setting for the struggles of his characters and his own relentless quest for recognition.

When we judge Davies harshly, when we make light of or dismiss his achievements as a novelist, we risk losing a great deal. We risk missing, and thus misrepresenting, an important part of Canada's (or at least Ontario's) cultural history, for on one level the eleven novels provide a fascinating map of his imaginative growth and progress. We miss the dramatic example of his struggle not so much to fly by the snares of family, religion, and culture in a colonial country as to grapple with them and to find his own way to a meaningful life of artistic or intellectual expression within that very milieu. Davies had, after all, one essential story to tell–it was his organic story–and he told it over and over because it was so much the inner drama of his own life. He worked very self-consciously and deliberately to locate in the range of his limited personal experiences a psychological depth he knew he must have to make his narratives resonate, and he found that depth, not so much in his sexual and emotional relations with women, which, as the biography reveals, were limited, as in his relations with his strong-minded parents and all that their tethering, controlling ways suggested. And as he developed his modus operandi as a novelist, he nurtured an audience that relished his capacity for social comedy and what he called "grotesquerie," as well as his increasing focus upon individuation and the pursuit of self-knowledge, dark and convoluted as that pursuit might sometimes be.[25]

Notwithstanding his many successes, Davies has persistently had his detractors among literary artists and academic scholars. Sometimes they were his enemies on the cultural battlefield, alienated by his ego, his condescending attitude, his strong opinions, and the space he insisted on filling on the public stage. He was not very successful in keeping private his insistence upon self-importance, especially when it came to rivalries. With the appearance of a good review of *A Mixture of Frailties*, a novel in which he sought for the first time to develop a depth of character that was fully "serious," he confided in his travel diary, "I think & hope that at last I may be getting my rightful place in Canadian letters, as the most SERIOUS writer they have & more truly of the country than the 'sincere' boys–whose sincerity is perhaps more accurately described as naivete."[26] While I can't precisely identify "the sincere boys" (although Hugh MacLennan and Morley Callaghan come to mind), Davies' self-importance and insistent sense of self-worth are inescapable.

That raw ego behind the mask–always dressed for the occasion, hungry for praise, usually aware of its own vulnerabilities and weaknesses but cruel and reductive when affronted or questioned–has aroused several negative, even dismissive responses to Davies. Interestingly, most of these have come from within Canada. One is struck, decade by decade, by the hostility Davies has managed to generate even as the praise mounted and the book sales increased. William Arthur Deacon threw down the gauntlet in a *Globe & Mail* review of *Tempest-Tost*: he wrote that it lacked a "solid core" or a "serious purpose"–and that not-so-velvet glove has been rehurled many times since.[27] I recall the playwright John Herbert, in a 1975 review, making light of Davies' novels, detecting in their pursuit of "psychological profundity . . . a sort of fourth-rate Herman Hesse quality" that approximated "the pain-filled labyrinth of the mind" without achieving anything like it.[28] Writing in the *New Republic* in 1978, that border-figure Joyce Carol Oates disputed Davies' alleged greatness and his newly achieved status as Canada's "leading man of letters." She defined him, with unstinting redundancy, as "a genial storytelling moralizing conservative; or a pompous but charming Tory; or a narrow, exasperating reactionary; or a curmudgeon of the old school whose spite, anger and vanity have been successfully–or nearly so–hidden behind a persona of bemused old-fashioned courtliness." His "colossal ego" seems deeply to have affronted her.[29] And recently, in an article in *Paragraph*, novelist and reviewer T.F. Rigelhof has given Davies a comprehensive dismissal. Having reread all the novels for the review, the exhausted Rigelhof dismisses the overall results with evident satisfaction:

> The novels are unevenly paced, implausibly plotted, shamelessly
> self-aggrandizing. Davies as a novelist didn't grow from strength to
> strength and then fall into decline. His most accomplished fiction,
> *Fifth Business*, was followed by *The Manticore* which is nearly as
> inept as *A Mixture of Frailties*. He reached bottom with *Murther
> and Walking Spirits* and then rose to *The Cunning Man*, his last but
> second best novel. Overtly didactic and deliberately offensive to
> democratic, socialist and egalitarian sensibilities, these novels are
> humorous in the grumpy way of one for whom night life is no kind
> of life and the body is a burden in need of feeding and purging rather
> than a blessing. His books are pervaded by condescending,
> complacent, nostalgic, mostly male intellectuals who aren't
> particularly intelligent but are single, solvent, cerebral and get very
> stiff contemplating the status quo of an Anglo Canada in which
> there is no room for most of us. Quirky more than comic, they are
> diverting. *The Rebel Angels* ranks as one of the most tedious novels
> of the second half of the century but the sub-plot about how old
> violins get restored kept me turning the pages long after I'd ceased
> being even remotely interested in the characters. That's harmless
> enough amusement and I don't begrudge its distraction. Nor do I
> begrudge anyone else the right to gorge themselves on a steady diet
> of Davies. I just don't think these novels offer any reason to be taken
> SERIOUSLY as comic literature.[30]

One can pile up instances of such attacks, though taken together they
begin to sound like variations on a theme–a dismissal of the elegant,
old-boys-oriented, conservative-minded Canada that sprang, if not directly from
the Family Compact, then from some overvalued, class-conscious connection to
United Empire Loyalist stock or Britain. Davies becomes not a novelist who
sought to make and show the way for serious writing in a culturally starved
country, but an apologist for the worst kind of stuffy Anglophilia that Canada
can represent. He is classist, elitist, superior, nostalgic, reactionary, and
male-focused. He is resolutely, pathetically old-fashioned, old-hat.

But other writers see different things, see strengths where we are told
there are only weaknesses. Anthony Burgess, for instance, has praised Davies'
fiction with much enthusiasm, listing *The Manticore* among the one hundred best
novels of this century.[31] John Irving goes further still, calling Davies "the

greatest comic writer in the English language since Dickens."[32] In the *New York Times Book Review,* Michiko Kakatani averred that Davies "has created a rich oeuvre of densely plotted, highly symbolic novels that not only function as superbly funny entertainments but also give the reader, in his character's words, a deeper sense of pleasure–delight, awe, religious intimations, 'a fine sense of the past, and a boundless depth and variety of life.'"[33] No wonder that, for many Americans and for increasing numbers of British readers, Davies was becoming a must-read novelist. (Among the many keen and passionate readers of Davies whom I interviewed in Princeton, New Jersey, and New York City over the winter of 1995-96, I discovered that many were informal disciples, passing copies on from friend to friend and thereby eagerly expanding a circle of devotees.)

Somewhere between the extremes of response we must try to find Robertson Davies. The Davies I admire, a writer (to my mind's eye) beyond the masks and costume, is an Ontario phenomenon born and bred; Ontario is "bred in the bone," and the narratives are always based here and always written from here. I know of few authors (other than perhaps Jane Urquhart, Margaret Atwood, and Hugh Hood) whose experience of the province is so diverse, and certainly there is no other writer who has written about Ontario so well and over so long a span of time. The province was his home for all but a few formative years of his life. His novels give us Kingston, Thamesville, Renfrew, Peterborough, and Toronto in careful detail and as living places. Each of his novels is rooted in a precisely realised Ontario location, so much so that we can chart a kind of cultural history of the province from what he has given us over the years.

We know what he did with the genteel yet stifling ambience of Salterton in his first three novels. And it is worthwhile to remember that he was a writer already labelled as "passé" by some critics and publishers when, after a twelve-year incubation of extraordinary inner fertility, he created *Fifth Business* and brought southwestern Ontario in the form of Thamesville (Deptford) to life on the page. Though he himself turned almost defiantly away from the outdoor life and had no real feel for the experience of wilderness (even of "the cottage") or the extraordinary range of topography and landscape of this province, he was more "truly of the country" (in his own words) than many seem willing to acknowledge or to appreciate. He well knew the sting in the joke about the Canadian who was schooled at home but educated abroad and, while he at first made it seem that the "big spiritual adventures" of his protagonists had to occur abroad, he increasingly rooted those experiences in his native province. *Fifth Business* is Davies' great novel for many reasons, but one of them is surely the way in which he makes his more-than-personal experience of Ontario vividly live and resonate. What Simon Darcourt says of Francis Cornish is emblematic of Davies' central story–that life should be seen as "a great artistic adventure. And a very Canadian sort of adventure, what's more."

Thus, in *What's Bred in the Bone*, Davies tapped into his very painful memories of moving to Renfrew, a rough lumbering town in eastern Ontario, and being the new kid, the privileged outsider, a kind of Little Lord Fauntleroy in a no-nonsense, unforgiving, and conformist place. These were his formative years, the years in which, as many have argued, an artistic sensibility is forged. I still recall from my interview with him how animated and passionate he became when, in response to my question about his apparently low estimate of (what he called) the "Common Man," he spoke fervently about his Renfrew experiences, and how they had hurt and scarred him. As he later told Grant: "Was I wrong? Were my parents wrong? There can be no final decision in such matters. But I saw what I saw, and heard what I heard and when my thoughts turn to Renfrew the sun is never shining in the vision. A child's impressions? Of course, but I think some consideration has to be given to the nature of the child. I was a *very* observant child and my intuitions were acute."[34]

As a very observant child in Renfrew, Davies experienced much that alarmed him about sex and sexuality, cruelty and violence. These actions he identified with the "Common Man." Though he first went on stage in Thamesville, he began to perfect his masks and disguises in Renfrew, because, as his comment to Grant suggests, he needed them. And in *What's Bred in the Bone* he not only tried to write those definitive experiences out of his system but he managed to bring them alive in what may, despite the bantering intrusiveness of his angel narrators, be his second-finest novel. Like *Fifth Business*, it vividly depicts an Ontario we need to know about and remember.

Robertson Davies had a difficult time growing up in Ontario in the 1920s. In his later education, especially at Upper Canada College and at Queen's, he knew many failures and disappointments. As a novelist, however, and without being slavishly autobiographical, he used that education and that sense of personal struggle as the sturdy foundation of his art. As such, though he overreached his range of experience in trying to give Dr. Hullah a Sioux Lookout childhood in *The Cunning Man*, he was extraordinarily successful for the most part in giving body and depth to the world of Ontarians and Canadians, even as that world was changing dramatically from decade to decade. There is indeed an arc of growth in his novels, despite Rigelhof's disclaimer. It peaks, I would argue, with *Fifth Business*, when he surprised a newly aware and self-conscious Anglo-Canadian literary establishment by refusing to be a fossil and by achieving in that novel something wonderfully new and rich, something powerfully resonant and entirely coherent that is arguably as fresh for readers today as it was in 1970. Thereafter, he struggled to hold to this new and high standard. Still, he was never satisfied; he could never be satisfied, given his appetite and need for success. At times, however, the Jungian view of experience, which he definitively espoused much as a newly converted minister becomes evangelical, imposed a perhaps too-rigid grid upon his imaginative energy. In his continuing pursuit of new storylines and approaches, he sometimes, as in the case of *Murther and Walking Spirits*, failed both to control the narrative he chose and to make his material sufficiently compelling. Individually and collectively, however, his novels are an oeuvre of creative achievement and resonant cultural expression. The man behind the mask, the performer of his life, the vulnerable sensibility with a lust to entertain and inform, will, I expect, continue to command wide attention.

## NOTES

1. This letter from Robertson Davies to Gordon and Helen Roper, dated March 9, 1985, is included in the forthcoming *Robertson Davies, For Your Eye Alone, Letters 1976-1995*. This passage, though, is not included in that collection. The letter is part of the Gordon Roper Collection, "Correspondence from Robertson Davies," held by the Bata Library Archives, Trent University, No. 95-015-01.

2. Judith Skelton Grant, *Robertson Davies: Man of Myth* (Toronto: Viking, 1994), 16-17.

3. Ibid.

4. Ibid., 169.

5. Ibid., 169.

6. The story of the portrait sitting at Massey College is not included in Grant's *Man of Myth*. In *For Your Eye Alone*, however, Grant includes a letter to Mordecai Richler (September 12, 1985) in which Davies also recounts his uncomfortable sitting for Karsh

(148-149).

7. Yousuf Karsh, *Karsh Canadians* (Toronto: University of Toronto Press, 1978), 48.

8. The cover of *Liberty* magazine for April 1954 depicted Davies posing as Samuel Marchbanks posing as Davies.

9. I had originally agreed to provide a talk under the very general title, "A History of Critical Reception."

10. Robertson Davies, *The Diary of Samuel Marchbanks* (Toronto: Clarke, Irwin, 1947), 55.

11. Judith Skelton Grant to Michael Peterman, March 11, 1998. Her letter informed me of the passages concerning me that she was planning to include in the published collection of Davies' letters and inquired about my response.

12. The interview took place at Massey College on March 6, 1980. It was an awkward experience in part because I had never done an interview before. Neither was Davies an easy subject. He would not allow me to use a tape recorder, which he said made him uneasy; it was not long after, however, that Grant persuaded him that a tape recorder was an essential component of the interviewing process and the work on the biography.

13. The undated postcard (likely sent in a letter) is a part of the Gordon Roper Collection, "Correspondence from Robertson Davies," held by the Bata Library Archives, Trent University, No. 95-015-01.

14. *For Your Eye Alone* 129. The letter is dated December 1984.

15. Ibid., 160-161. The letter is dated September 2, 1986.

16. Ibid., 183. The letter is dated May 29, 1987.

17. Ibid., 35-36. The letter is dated March 29, 1979.

18. Ibid., 141, for instance.

19. *The Economist* December 9,1995.

20. I spoke to Davies' New York editor at Viking Penguin, Al Silverr
1996. He also reported that Davies had sold out the 900-seat 9?
previous spring and that 400 more were turned away.

21. Though writing of the experiences of the next generation, Dennis Lee identifies a similar preoccupation shared by ambitious young Canadians. See "Cadence, Country, Silence: Writing in Colonial Space," *Open Letter* 4-6 (1973): 41.

22. *Man of Myth* 356.

23. Ibid., 289.

24. Robertson Davies used this memorable phrasing to describe his "discovery" of Gordon Roper in Peterborough at a meeting in the early 1940s. The remark was part of a speech given at Trent University on the occasion of a symposium on Canadian writing held in Roper's honour (March 6, 1976). The symposium papers were published in the *Journal of Canadian Studies* in its May 1976 issue. Davies' postprandial remarks were not included in the issue.

25. *Man of Myth* 356.

26. Ibid., 369.

27. Cited in *Man of Myth* 333-34 (from *The Globe & Mail* November 24, 1951: 11).

28. John Herbert, *The Toronto Star*. My clipping of the review is undated, and the review is not listed in Judith Skelton Grant's bibliography.

29. Joyce Carol Oates, "One Half of Robertson Davies," *The New Republic* (April 15, 1978); reprinted in *Robertson Davies: An Appreciation*, ed. Elspeth Cameron (Peterborough: Broadview Press, 1991), 176-81.

30. T.F. Rigelhof, "The Triumph of Robertson Davies, Novelist," *Paragraph* 18 (1996-7): 11-12. I have removed the dates of publication from the novels that Rigelhof mentions in this passage.

31. Anthony Burgess, *99 Novels: The Best in English Since 1939, A Personal Choice* (Albuquerque: Summit Books, 1984), 130-131.

32. John Irving (33).

33. Michiko Kakatani, *The New York Times Book Review*.

34. *Man of Myth* 92.

# "A Hint of the Basic Brimstone": The Humour of Robertson Davies

FAITH BALISCH

The comic mode is inseparable from Robertson Davies' way of viewing the world; it is the illuminating medium, that "light that plays on the writer's mind, in which all aspects of his work live and take their being."[1] Nevertheless, amidst the considerable body of criticism of his writing, one finds little or no examination of his humour.[2] In his interviews, essays, speeches, plays, and works of fiction, Davies repeatedly reiterates his belief that humour is not incompatible with serious purpose, and that comedy "does not mean simply making people laugh. It is not the art of the stand-up comedian, the wise-cracker. It is a way of looking at life which explores some of the noblest aspects of the human spirit" (*The Merry Heart* 134). Davies has suggested that, initially at least, Canadian critics had difficulty with his idea "of humour as an element inseparable from writing even on serious subjects," and that humour was "not understood and rebuked in my early work. But it was out of the question for me to change" (*MH* 56). Davies says his fictional world is neither a foolish nor a lighthearted one:

> My world is not the cosy nursery retreat of Winnie-the-Pooh. It is a tough world, and it only seems irrational or unreal to those who have not grasped some hints of its remorseless, irreversible and often cruel logic. It is a world in which God is not mocked and in which a man reaps–only too obviously–what he has sown.[3]

This is not to deny the irreverent, irrepressible and perhaps even shocking character of his humour, for it explores the great contradictions and incongruities that are an essential part of human experience. Definition of humour is difficult.[4] In the late 1950s, Davies–as Samuel Marchbanks writing to Mervyn Noseigh, a Ph.D. student studying Marchbanks–says in exasperation:

> Don't you know what humour is? Universities re-define wit and satire every few years; surely it is time they nailed down humour for us? I don't know what it is, although I suspect it is an attribute of everything, and the substance of nothing, so if I had to define a sense of humour I would say it lay in the perception of shadows.[5]

The links between humour and shadows, shadows and the devil, and the daemonic and humour are significant to Davies' concept of humour. Underneath the comic, there is always an awareness of the horrid, the evil, the tragic. He notes this quality in the humour of Stephen Leacock, describing it as "violent as Charlie Chaplin is violent; under the clowning works a vigorous turbulent spirit, whose mellowest productions leave always on the palate a hint of the basic brimstone."[6] Davies' own humour is not lacking in brimstone, stemming as it does from a confrontation between Canada's ostensibly Calvinist gloom, cultural stagnation, utilitarianism, and Victorian prudery, and Davies' own effervescent, determinedly Renaissance spirit. I say "Renaissance" quite deliberately, for Davies devotes much of his work to perplexing twentieth-century readers, brought up in a utilitarian age of scientific scepticism and empiricist materialism, by his insistence upon the significance of the world of "wonders" –the world of the spirit, the imagination, the irrational. He does this most often through yoking together the mundane world of "now" and long-forgotten or dismissed modes of knowing that insist that the world of the spirit is every bit as real and significant as the world of the flesh–all of the flesh, not just the public, visible bits. In Davies' fiction, ambiguity is the essence of humour, and its vehicle is often ideas, actions, or individuals conventionally condemned as worthless or evil. His humour, which begins as relatively straightforward social satire, increasingly relies on the arcane and the symbolic.

Throughout his life, Davies professed himself the enemy of Puritan repressiveness and of the concept of evil as the absence of good. He was a great admirer of the comic genius of the great Renaissance writers Rabelais and Shakespeare, especially of their exuberance and lack of hypocritical re-straint–particularly in matters of the body and the appetites. Great comedies, Davies says, make "us feel, when we have seen them well presented on the stage, that life is great, and that the human spirit is unconquerable. Shakespeare's most splendid scenes of comedy are very often those in which nobody makes a joke" (*MH* 134). And ribald Rabelais? He, even more than Shakespeare, is the inheritor of the medieval confidence in the truth of outrageous laughter. Mikhail Bakhtin reminds us that in the Middle Ages festive laughter, often associated with carnival and parody, was necessary to the maintenance of sanity and social order:

> Laughter created no dogmas and could not become authoritarian; it did not convey fear but a feeling of strength. It was linked with the procreating act, with birth, renewal, fertility, abundance. Laughter was also related to food and drink and the people's earthly immortality, and finally it was related to the future of things to come and was to clear the way for them. Seriousness was, therefore, elementally distrusted while trust was placed in festive laughter.[7]

Although this suggests that laughter is opposed to seriousness, it does not mean that the purpose of such laughter is not serious in its overall effect. In the Renaissance, festive laughter, which was characterised by universalism, freedom from restraint, and delineation of the people's unofficial truth, began to "penetrate the higher levels of literature" and to break through the narrow walls of festivities and to enter into all spheres of ideological life" (Bakhtin 90, 97). This is the laughter that is present–in varying proportions–in Rabelais' *Gargantua and Pantagruel* and in many of Shakespeare's plays. This laughter, Davies believes, encompasses the fullness of life, and this is the laughter that he also believes was forced into exile by the Puritans in the seventeenth century.

In his academic thesis, "Shakespeare's Boy Actors" (1937), Davies points out that

> Before the Restoration, the audience at the playhouse consisted of chiefly two elements: the first of these was the groundlings who were pleased accordingly as the play gratified their simple desire for violent action, broad comedy, flaming words or patriotic drumbeating; the second was the gentlefolk who judged the play by classical standards, or by fashionable standards, if they were wits. Together they did not form an ideal audience for a poet, but they were infinitely preferable to that which was to be his lot when the Puritans began to be theatre goers.[8]

He condemns the Puritan description of plays as "quite contrary to the word of grace and sucked out of the devil's teats to nourish us in idolatry, heathenry and sin," and links the rise of the Puritans to power with the diminishing autonomy of the dramatist to portray the full range of human actions and emotions on stage (10). The gutsy, often ribald, laughter of the groundlings was hived off from the fullness of life, replaced by the hypocritical, more sophisticated, and less subversive laughter of society. Humour, of the kind that Davies admires in Shakespeare and Rabelais, was consigned to the Devil–a diabolical association it continues to have, as he suggests through a discussion among four characters in *World of Wonders* (1975): Ingestree, Jurgen, Ramsay, and Liesl. Jurgen insists, in orthodox Freudian reductiveness, that humour is important as a way of ameliorating the horrors of existence: "Jokes dissemble horrors and make them seem unimportant."[9] Ingestree disagrees, asserting, in Rabelaisian expansiveness, that humour is "absolutely vital to life. It's one of the marks of civilization. Mankind wouldn't be mankind without it" (84). Ramsay transvaluatingly articulates the Puritan distrust of humour, calling it

> One of the most brilliant inventions of the Devil. . . . It diminishes the horrors of the past, and it veils the horrors of the present, and therefore it prevents us from seeing straight, and perhaps from learning things we ought to know. Who profits from that? Not mankind, certainly. Only the Devil could devise such a subtle agency and persuade mankind to value it. (85)

The final word is given, as it so often is in The Deptford Trilogy, to Liesl, whose response is typically ambiguous. She asserts that "humour is quite as often the pointer to truth as it is a cloud over the truth" (85) and promptly invents a legend that the Devil had been thrown out of Heaven for laughing at the Creator's masterpiece, Man, and that he and all the angels who had been unable to suppress their laughter "set up Hell as a kind of jokers' club and thereby complicated the universe in a way that must often embarrass God" (85). The only full point of agreement among them is that humour is usually not associated with God. Magnus Eisengrim had earlier observed: "I don't suppose God laughs at the people who think He doesn't exist. He's above jokes. But the Devil isn't. That's one of his most endearing qualities" (40). Davies' humour, especially his late humour, is frequently dark and requires from the reader a recognition of Evil as an active force in the universe.

Initially, Davies found a compatible theory of humour in Freud's *Wit and Its Relation to the Unconscious*. In *A Voice From the Attic* (1960), he says that Freud not only suggested that humour offered "a way of giving expression to things that would be intolerable if they were said directly," but also offered him a description of the role of the humorist that suited Davies' disgust at the state of Canadian culture:

> The humorist's objective is to strip away, momentarily, the heavy intellectual and moral trappings of adult life, including so many things we regard as virtues, and to set us free again in that happy condition which we enjoyed in the morning of life, when everything came to us freshly; when we did not have to make allowances for the limitations or misfortunes of others; when we dared to call a thing or a person stupid if they seemed stupid to us; when we lived gloriously in the moment, without thought for the past or consideration for the future; when we were, indeed, as the lilies of the field. . . . Humour is daemonic; this is how its daemonism works. As the tragic writer rids us of what is petty and ignoble in our nature, the humorist rids us of what is cautious, calculating and priggish–about half our social conscience indeed.[10]

In his writings from the 1940s and 1950s Davies reveals, reviles, and ridicules the stupidity and repressiveness of a regime as strongly embedded as the bedrock of the Laurentians.

When Davies returned to Canada from England in the early 1940s and began his career as a writer, he found himself in a country that he took to have gone over to cultural Puritanism. His first humorous writing took the form of satire. As Samuel Marchbanks, the garrulous writer of a series of newspaper columns, he is characterised by his irreverent attitude to Canadian sacred cows of every ilk. Marchbanks, for example, rejects the Canadian Puritan work ethic: "I hate work, regarding it as the curse of Adam, and am fully in sympathy with the medieval view that work is an ignoble way of passing the time, beneath the dignity of anyone of fine feelings and intelligence."[11] Although these sketches are often fierce in ridiculing Canadian society, they are also characterised by a lighthearted, sophisticated urbanity that continues to be amusing. That his accounts of his annual wrestling matches with his house demon (the furnace in the basement), and his correspondence with the law firm of Mouseman, Mouseman and Forcemeat over his case against his erstwhile friend Richard Dandiprat continue to amuse is evident in the success of *The Papers of Samuel Marchbanks* (1991), the one-volume edition of the three earlier Marchbanks volumes.

In 1947, Davies denied that the Marchbanks sketches had any underlying seriousness of purpose. In a letter to W.W. Robertson, he says: "I have been writing and publishing this DIARY for 4 years, & in that time I have put everything under the sun into it. . . . The *Diary* is a grab-bag: some like one thing & some another. It has no homogeneity & no plan. . . . In writing the *Diary* I have been guided by one principle & one only–'*Anything for a laugh.*'"[12] But Marchbanks has many sides to him, including one that biographer Judith Skelton Grant describes as "the crusty old curmudgeon, the ribald Rabelais, laying about him in all directions" (268). This is the Marchbanks who reveals the extent to which Canadian Victorian prudery stupidly restricts the freedom of the artist: "Shakespeare," he says, "would never be able to get a job writing for the CBC because he insists on dealing with controversial topics and uses language that would bring a flood of complaining letters from the Holy Name Society of St. Jean de Crabtree Mills (P.Q.) and the Ladies Art, Culture and Poker-work and China-painting Club of Pelvis (Sask.)" (*DSM* 98). In 1950 Hilda Kirkwood put her finger on one of the specific characteristics of Davies' humour when she described Marchbanks as "a sort of displaced person from a less suppressed age" (59). Such displaced persons continue to turn up in all of Davies' works, and their role is generally to facilitate the intersection of opposing, yet related, worlds of flesh and spirit.

Most of Davies' work contains comic confrontations between some characters whose utilitarianism consigns all spiritual matters to oblivion (thereby promoting a kind of Freudian Thanatos complex), and other characters whose joyous rejection of the conventional in religion and social behaviour[13] marks them as striving toward the life force (Eros), the ineffable vigour of which is often found reflected in mankind's great imaginative creations: music, theatre, and art. Much of this humour depends on social satire and frequently involves reversing acceptable Canadian social norms, often by placing Thanatos characters in situations that reveal the inadequacies of their deepest convictions. Increasingly, even in his early writing, Davies directs his readers' attention to the significance of an invisible, artistic, and imaginative world that is co-existent with the empirical or natural one and intersects with it in ways that defy quotidian reason. This, he intimates, is the world in which the spirit finds refreshment and from which great Evil allied to great Good naturally arises. Often, the strange and wondrous paths by which that world of wonders may be reached lie in works of great artistic power and integrity; for spiritual anorexics, the contact may be cataclysmic, as Hector Mackilwraith discovers when he comes under the spell of Shakespeare's *The Tempest*.[14] In *Tempest-Tost* and the other Salterton novels, Davies creates situations that both satirise the Canadian social setting and destabilise orthodoxy. When, for example, Humphrey Cobbler undertakes an impromptu concert with a group of students in the Salterton Cathedral on All Hallow's Eve,[15] it is clear that he is leading them into contact with the nobility of the human spirit to overcome great fear, and not committing the sacrilege that Salterton, as personified in Miss Puss Pottinger, believes. Significantly, Davies' anti-heroic characters are usually those whose rejection of the norms of society consigns them, as it were, to the company of Samuel Marchbanks. Although Davies makes clever use of such familiar character types as Puss Pottinger and Norm Yarrow for purposes of ridicule and satire, he also creates such grotesques as Ma Gall and Giles Revelstoke, whose potent one-sidedness suggests their affinity closer to the humours of Ben Jonson and the grotesques of Dickens than to character(istic)s featured in modern realism. These characters from Davies reveal both the seriousness and complexity of his humour, since their role is often ambivalent and consequently, associated with evil.

To his aggressive wit and social satire, to his grotesques and their fellow citizens, and to the topsy-turvydom resulting from encounters with the larger world of the spirit, Davies adds yet another dimension to his "humour" formed from a knowledge more or less consistent with major insights from Jung.[16] This, he tells us, is a very important string of relation: "It is a psychological string, and some of you may think it is a rather dirty string, but I am unrepentant. In the human psyche the ineffable, the elegant and the praiseworthy are inextricably mixed with the grubby, the commonplace and the reputedly inadmissible. That is what keeps us sane" (*MH* 83). Attuned, as it were, to this "psychological string," Davies becomes increasingly attentive to the workings of Good and Evil in the world, and, redefining his earlier dichotomy of Eros/Thanatos, links humour to the Jungian concept of archetypes. This linking, he explains, accounts for much of his continuing interest in Dickens and Victorian melodrama, for in these he finds the emotional impact of the great archetypes at work in human affairs. Melodrama, Davies asserts, offers the writer "a way of dealing with artistic material that reveals the wonder and caprice of life as well as its undeniable tragedy . . . ; [it is] art in which Good and Evil contend and in which the dividing line between Good and Evil may often be blurred, and in which Good may often be the winner" (*One Half* 213). He goes so far as to say that "even at its worst, [nineteenth-century] melodrama continued to draw on that realm where 'everything was seething with life', and to transfer as much as possible of that psychic vitality to the stage. The plays, so neglectful of the externals of reality, were psychologically convincing because they spoke from those depths to corresponding depths in their audiences" (*OH* 159). These are the same depths to which Dickens speaks so effectively in his fiction: "Dickens explores Evil in a way no literary artist of like comparable stature does, because he contrasts it constantly with Good" (*OH* 215).

By the time *Fifth Business* appeared in 1970, Davies' humour was becoming less dependent on social satire, more entwined with the "psychological string," and, through irony and ambiguity, closer to the topsy-turvy mix of carnival laughter and tragedy.[17] Humour, in the form of 'funny' names, puns (and other verbal devices), parody, slapstick, social satire, and incongruous beliefs and behaviour, continues to be present along with increasingly ironic depictions of discrepancies between appearance and reality and the secrets that dominate the lives of individuals. The comic and the tragic become so intertwined that the reader often sympathises with the very characters that are also the objects of ridicule. The "Rum Old Joker" Satan becomes a real force as Davies' humour stems from the incongruity between the internal and external, public and private worlds of the significant characters, and their confusion about the morality of their immersion in aspects of human experience and knowledge generally shunned or condemned by the modern world. Davies' humour becomes less "realist" and more symbolic, focusing on the role of Good and Evil in the life of the individual and the humour that results from the ambiguity of the two as they continuously act on, and interact with, one another.[18] In Davies' fictional worlds, Evil is powerful and real. He shocks and mocks his Puritan-influenced readers by his reversals of conventional values, since Evil in Davies' fiction is often an agent for good (as it clearly is in *Leaven of Malice*) and the conventionally good is often evil (and like Boy Staunton in The Deptford Trilogy, to be at least pitied as much as condemned). With each novel, Davies leads his readers further into a world of experience they have been trained to denigrate as foolish or insignificant, if not downright evil.

The world of the theatre, which is Davies' earliest agent of spiritual growth, was associated with Satan by the Puritans, and was certainly viewed with distrust in mid-twentieth-century Canada, as were the gypsies, magicians, artists, and foreigners of all kinds who "acted" as spiritual guides. In *Fifth Business*, for example, the world of saints and mythology, being "Papist" and heathen, is clearly demonic to the conventional small-town Protestant Canadian: the Reverend Amasa Dempster describes the veneration of saints as "one of the vilest superstitions of the Scarlet Woman of Rome."[19] Dunstan Ramsay's confusion about saints is linked to his inherited unwillingness to accept the "superstition" associated with miracles. Miracles are, in turn, clearly associated with a "magic" that is equally reprehensible: Amasa Dempster condemns young Dunstable's piteous attempts at magic as the "means by which the Evil One had trailed his black slime across a pure life" (41)–yet his interest in saints and magic ultimately becomes the means of his spiritual growth and Paul's metamorphosis into the great magician, Magnus Eisengrim. In *The Manticore*, David Staunton's journey into his own psyche in the process of undergoing Jungian analysis represents a venture into the great unconscious (which Freud equated with a garbage dump–a place of unmitigated evil), and his venture with Liesl into the bear cave is pure heathenism. Yet for David and Liesl, these are places of great spiritual value. In later novels, Davies' characters are immersed in equally forbidden, sometimes evil, worlds–worlds that require close examination and recognition of "what is of worth in that which is scorned by the unseeing."[20] With each novel, Davies becomes more outrageous in his challenges to conventional ideas about right and wrong, good and evil, and even the relationship of the body and the soul.

As a rule, Davies manipulates interactions between three distinct sets of characters. The first group consists of such rebels as the Ozias Froats of *The Rebel Angels*, who works to discover something of worth in human excrement; and, in The Deptford Trilogy, Liesl, who worships her ancestors in the bear cave in the Swiss Alps and creates the "World of Wonders" magic show; and Padre Blazon, who as a Jesuit is deep in the old man's puzzle, searching for a God for old men. These characters care little for society's ranking, are elitist, egotistical, domineering, and didactic. They are often deformed, outspoken, or eccentric to the point of being ludicrous. At the same time, they are larger than life. They are well aware of the interactions of Good and Evil, and their knowledge gives them strange wisdom. The second group forms the most believable of characters, for these are the seekers, the often introspective souls who recognise their need for spiritual adventure and for more than what the world they ordinarily inhabit offers them. Their contact with a forbidden or rejected world upsets the precarious balance of their ordinary world, enriching their life even as that existence is thrown into sometimes spectacular disarray. They are often confused by the ambiguities that surround them. Finally, there are the inhibitors, characters who are evil, warped by repression, blinded by egotism, and incapable of a rich spiritual life. Their role in the novels is to act as foils to the rebels; and, like them, they are often grotesques of great power somewhat larger than life. They try to restrain the seekers, and are often shown as foolish in their blind loyalty to empiricism. Of this group, the most Evil is Brother John in *The Rebel Angels*, for, unlike most of the inhibitors whose evil lies in their ignorance and repression, he knows he is Evil and relishes the cynicism that characterises his resistance to Good. He is metaphorically the Devil incarnate; and thus when he dies by his own hand at the end of the novel, the reader feels somehow that there is Supreme Justice in the world, that God will not be mocked. In The Cornish Trilogy, Davies pushes his readers further than usual into a world of symbolism when he adds characters who inhabit only the invisible world of the spirit, and who thus possess knowledge denied to ordinary mortals. He uses these spiritual creatures to comment on the incongruities of the human world.

Davies seems to take a mischievous delight in shocking his twentieth-century readers by the detail with which he depicts these ugly, beautiful, contradictory, forbidden, magical, supernatural, filthy, rejected, heavenly, and diabolical worlds and their inhabitants. There is a procession of gypsies, magicians, singers, musicians, artists–true and fake ones–scientists and pseudo-scientists, academics, ghosts, demons, and supernatural movies that pluck a man out of his world into the lives of his ancestors, births, deaths–natural and unnatural–omens, coincidences and other strange twists of fate that Davies insists deserve careful attention, for they have both a real and metaphorical significance in human life. This combination is what makes Davies' work preposterous and fascinating. He repulses, delights, frustrates, or angers us; his works make us laugh, or make us sniff in derision. Taken for all, they reveal–often in a balance of hilarious, shocking, and ugly ways–the foolish inadequacy of conventional concepts of normalcy, and draw the reader deeper and deeper into the world of wonders that is the human comedy.

## NOTES

1. Robertson Davies, *The Merry Heart: Selections 1980-1995* (Markham, Ont.: Penguin, 1998), 56.

2. Criticism of Davies' humour frequently focuses on his satire. This is especially evident in articles dealing with the Samuel Marchbanks volumes and *Tempest-Tost*.

43

Studies include Ivon Owen's "The Salterton Novels" (1958); Hugo MacPherson's "The Mask of Satire: Character and Symbolic Pattern in Robertson Davies' Fiction" (1961); William Solly's "Nothing Sacred: Humour in Canadian Drama in English" (1962); Donna Bennett's "Magnus Eisengrim: The Shadow of the Trickster in the Novels of Robertson Davies" (1976); Patricia Morley's "The Comedy Company of the Psyche" (1976) and "Davies' Salterton Trilogy: Where the Myth Touches Us" (1976); Wilfred Cude's "'False as Harlot's Oaths': Dunny Ramsay Looks at Huck Finn" (1977); Michael Peterman's "Samuel Marchbanks: A Flamboyant Among Drabs," in his *Robertson Davies* (1986); Barbara Godard's "Writing Paradox, the Paradox of Writing: Robertson Davies" (1991), and Martin Hunter's "Magister Ludi: The Mask of Robertson Davies" (1991).

3. Robertson Davies, *One Half of Robertson Davies: Provocative Pronouncements on a Wide Range of Topics* (Toronto: Macmillan, 1977),131.

4. Davies discusses this problem in "Opera and Humour." Here, following Jung, he explains his concept of humour as a "breadth of perception, and what Heracleitus called 'an attachment of opposite tensions, like that of the bow and the lyre.' A reconciliation of opposites indeed" (214). See Davies' *Happy Alchemy: Writings on the Theatre and Other Lively Arts*, ed. Jennifer Surridge and Brenda Davies (Toronto: McClelland & Stewart, 1997), 207-226.

5. Robertson Davies, *Samuel Marchbanks' Almanack* (Toronto: McClelland & Stewart, 1967), 202.

6. Robertson Davies, *Feast of Stephen* (Toronto: McClelland & Stewart, 1970), 43.

7. Mikhail Bakhtin, *Rabelais and His World*, trans. Helene Iswolsky (Bloomington: Indiana University Press, 1984), 95.

8. Robertson Davies, "Shakespeare's Boy Actors," 179.

9. Robertson Davies, *World of Wonders* (Toronto: McClelland & Stewart, 1970), 84.

10. Robertson Davies, *A Voice From the Attic* (Toronto: McClelland & Stewart, 1972), 228-29.

11. Robertson Davies, *The Diary of Samuel Marchbanks* (Toronto: Clarke, Irwin, 1947).

12. Judith Skelton Grant, *Robertson Davies: Man of Myth* (Toronto:Viking, 1994), 265.

13. In *A Mixture of Frailties* (1958), Domdaniel explains the opposition of Eros and Thanatos to Monica: "I'm an Eros man myself, and most people who are any good for anything in the arts or whatever belong to the Eros party. But there are Thanatossers everywhere, the Permanent Opposition" and warns her to beware of false Eros people whose real aim is to "castrate" people (108).

14. Michael Peterman notes that although in *Tempest-Tost* (1980) Davies shows at times his "sensitivity to both the ludicrous and serious aspects of representative social behaviour," his satire of individual characters "is occasionally so overpowering as to be more reductive than amusing" (92). Peterman goes on to suggest that such is the case with his delineation of the misadventures of Hector Mackilwraith. As a man whose emotions have been almost totally repressed, caught by a very powerful anima projection, however, Hector elicits sympathy even as he makes himself increasingly ridiculous.

15. In Robertson Davies, *Leaven of Malice* (Markham, Ont.: Penguin, 1954).

16. See Patricia Monk's various studies of the Jungian influence in Davies' writing, the most comprehensive of which is *The Smaller Infinity* (1982). These studies do not address the ways in which a Jungian spirituality impacts on his humour.

17. Barbara Godard's Bakhtinian studies of Davies' writing, "*World of Wonders*: Robertson Davies' Carnival," *ECW*, 1984/85 and "Robertson Davies' Dialogic Imagination" ECW Press, 1987, are particularly helpful in clarifying Davies' generation of carnival laughter. These articles have been reissued in combined form as "Writing Paradox, the Paradox of Writing: Robertson Davies," in *Robertson Davies: An Appreciation* (1991).

18. In "Painting, Fiction and Faking," in *The Merry Heart* (64-89), his discussion of Mannerist painting, which he describes as "a way of feeling and thinking about life, the way of the moralist who sees and records and reminds but who does not insistently judge" (73), and his comments on the significance of symbolic expression in painting afford further insight into his own creation of symbol–to simultaneously comic and serious effect.

19. Davies, *Fifth Business* 42.

20. Robertson Davies, *The Rebel Angels* (New York: Penguin, 1983), 82.

# Undermining Comedy: Shadows of Determinism in the Salterton Novels

DAVID CREELMAN

> We are not working to banish your shadow, you see, but only to understand it and thereby to work a little more closely with it.
>
> – Davies, *The Manticore*

Robertson Davies' Salterton Trilogy has long played a poor second cousin to the more accomplished and widely studied Deptford novels. But if the first trilogy has garnered less attention than his subsequent fiction, the critics who have examined *Tempest-Tost* (1951), *Leaven of Malice* (1954), and *A Mixture of Frailties* (1958) have spoken with a perhaps surprisingly unified voice. Since Elspeth Buitenhuis explored the transformations of The Salterton Trilogy's main protagonists, commentators have agreed that, in his early novels, Davies develops increasingly careful explorations of the individual's emerging identity. John Mills summarises a commonality of critical opinion when he asserts that the principal characters of the Salterton novels are "conscious in various degrees and at different times of the need to struggle towards freedom."[1] Davies, so Mills suggests, is generally confident that his characters can become more knowledgeable about themselves as they struggle for at least partial release from the family and social structures of a small Canadian city (50).

This now central reading has led to some productive insights. For example, an emphasis on the trilogy's recurring interest in the individual's journey toward maturity and freedom affords readers an occasion to interpret Davies' formal shifts as literary attempts to find an appropriately intimate genre to explore the psychological makeup of his characters. His attention to the individual leads him from the fairly aloof form of satiric/parodic romance in *Tempest-Tost*,[2] to the comedic romance in *Leaven of Malice*,[3] and, finally, to the romantic *bildungsroman* in *A Mixture of Frailties* (Mills 52).

But if Buitenhuis' insights have inspired some productive studies, other critics have overemphasised Davies' sense of optimism and produced reductive readings of the Salterton novels. For example, Patricia Morley overstates the case when she argues that the narratives are "united by a religious myth of achieved freedom and spiritual growth."[4] Such a confident assertion that Davies' protagonists achieve liberty neglects a second important element in the Salterton novels. In his early fiction, Davies is still troubled by a strong sense of scepticism: he is far from sure that complete freedom or self-knowledge can be achieved. Michael Peterman thus develops a more complex position when he asserts that the novels attend to the "individual's struggle and eventual victory, however realistically circumscribed that victory" (83). If we shift our attention from the goals pursued by individuals and examine instead the forces circumscribing humanity as Davies depicts them, a more serious and even grim element in The Salterton Trilogy becomes evident enough.

Attending to the Shadow in the Salterton novels reveals several important aspects of the texts. For example, the recurring tendency in these narratives to refrain from constructing thoroughly happy endings would seem to signify that, even in the early stages in his progress as moralist, Davies was attempting to "bend" the literary forms he had adopted to meet his own purposes. The Salterton novels are certainly anchored in the structures of romance; but Davies is not a formula writer. The satiric impulse and the intellectual curiosity evident in these texts condition the elements of romance and suggest that Davies is working toward the achievement of a genuinely major novelist.

The ways in which the texts' representations of freedom are repeatedly disrupted at key moments also reveal that Davies struggles, consciously or otherwise, with the issue of causality. In many cases, he has drawn flat characters to serve his satiric purposes, and the reader is not encouraged to expect them to change. Such characters as Roger Tasset (*Tempest-Tost*), Matthew Snelgrove (*Leaven of Malice*), and Pastor Beamis (*A Mixture of Frailties*) seem incapable of careful self-analysis, but they nicely perform, or serve, as targets for Davies' wit. In each text, however, Davies does include characters who would like to change themselves or their circumstances, and these figures struggle against powerful constraints. These key characters are so embedded in their immediate and historical contexts, and become more or less free only by commanding such a high degree of personal, emotional, and spiritual strength, that such exertions of the will are infrequently achieved and are rarely represented in a convincing fashion. The narrations frequently hesitate and even falter when the protagonists are brought close to achieving a degree of self-determination. These gaps or textual ruptures, when viewed separately from one another, have been read as the expected and even acceptable weaknesses of apprenticeship writings. But they can also be read as symptoms or signs of a powerful ideological struggle in Davies' early fiction.

When reading the stylistic disruptions of a text to unveil its unconscious structuring–a critical process that sometimes seems prompted by an all-too-determined disposition to peer into dark corners–critics should remember Jacques Lacan's advice:

> Certainly we must be attentive to the "un-said" that lies in the holes of the discourse, but this does not mean that we are to listen as if to someone knocking on the other side of a wall. For if we are to concern ourselves from now on with nothing but these sounds, as some analysts pride themselves on doing, it must be admitted that we have not placed ourselves in the most favourable conditions to decipher their meaning.[5]

But when disruptions recur with such frequency as to establish an uncanny pattern, then such disjunctions signify something of a sublimated struggle. The Salterton texts are driven–consciously, I would argue–by Davies' primarily Tory position, which argues that freedom should be attainable by a worthy few who are also willing to remain faithful to the central tenets of society's best, highest traditions.

The Salterton Trilogy, however, launches an increasingly anxious investigation into the forces for determinism that, logically enough, limit human freedom. This shadow of fatalism complicates and undermines Davies' more readily apparent comedic/conservative vision. His fictional world is not threatened by the kind of raw mechanical and scientific determinism that is more often than not associated with the naturalistic texts of Zola; rather, Davies' characters are caught in a web of psychological forces and spiritual pressures that suggest that freedom is constrained by compulsions that rule the psyche itself. Characters like Solly Bridgetower fascinate Davies, for it seems far from certain that the unwise Solly will be able to overcome his sense of moral and emotional obligation to his mother in order to follow his deepest desires. The Salterton texts are neither the "clever failures" George Woodcock claims[6] nor his most "successful books" as Mills asserts (33). The trilogy, however, does help us to understand how the issue of determinism shadows Davies' work and why the ideas and solutions available in the Jungian frame of things were so fully and happily accepted by Davies before he began The Deptford Trilogy.

Within the satiric world of *Tempest-Tost*, Davies is interested in examining the foibles of Salterton's population. A few special individuals, like Valentine Rich and Humphrey Cobbler, lead free and self-actualised lives, but these "aristocrats of the spirit" arrive fully formed and do not change or vary in the course of the novel (Peterman 92). They contribute little to Davies' exploration of how freedom is actually achieved. The majority of the middle-class Salterton citizens paraded, as it were, through the text are flat characters, devoted to narrow-minded, puritan values or selfish, materialist pursuits. They do not evolve but rather stand as convenient targets for Davies' biting examination of Southern Ontario's provincial culture.

A few of these narrow characters serve a second function as they intimidate and confine the main protagonists. Most threatening are the domineering parents Professor Vambrace and Mrs. Bridgetower, whose limited yet overbearing personalities trap and oppress their children.[7] Driven by his arrogant and critical attitude, Professor Vambrace is the antithesis of the character he plays in the local production of *The Tempest*. Functioning in a parodic imitation of Prospero, his selfishness and egotism limit his daughter and eventually expose her to humiliation. From his overbearing personality, which undermines Pearl's sense of self-confidence, to his refusal to spend more than thirty-five dollars on a ball dress, he has failed in his parental role to smooth her way into the world. In a world in which young females are defined by others as much as by themselves according to their ability to attract the few eligible men, Pearl's failure to allure almost constitutes a failure "to be." If Pearl is true to her name, the narrator also suggests that she possesses an inner beauty. But this inner beauty is not allowed to flourish. Though Mills argues that she "awakens to her enslavement . . . and consciously or unconsciously seeks freedom" (41), in fact she almost completely disappears following the embarrassments of the ball. In her final appearance, during the opening night of the play, she accidentally pinches Bonnie-Susan's neck when Tasset's name is mentioned, which action serves to confirm that she continues to feel a hopeless infatuation with the worthless Roger. Far from making her, as Helen Hoy suggests, the embodiment of "spiritual possibilities extending considerably beyond the deceptively uninspiring physical reality,"[8] Davies ignores Pearl's plight in that last section of the novel as if to suggest that it is beyond resolution.

Solly Bridgetower, Pearl's male counterpart, is similarly oppressed by his mother. "Growing old and set in her ways," Mrs. Bridgetower uses emotional dependence and economic control to enslave her son. In a prolonged passage examining Solly's misery, Davies suggests that if the young lecturer exaggerates his trouble it is only to make "some impression upon the inertia and the immovability of the selfish old."[9] Using an interestingly deterministic turn of phrase, the writer of *Tempest-Tost* consigns the son to an apparently invincible futility: "Solly's writhings in his bonds were necessarily ineffective" (126). Indeed, Solly, like the rest of the cast of *The Tempest*, does not evolve or change in any particularly noticeable way.

Mills criticises Davies for his depiction of the discussions that follow Hector's attempted suicide and argues that the "cheap, callous, callow, wisecracking balderdash" uttered by the characters is inconsistent with their personalities (45). In fact, the various speculations offered by the characters–if insensitive–are adroitly aligned with each of their respective value systems. Freddy and Tom blame "cheap religion," Cobbler blames Hector's "spiritual" and emotional poverty, and Solly blames his inferior education (279, 281). The conclusion emphasises that each of these characters-cum-commentators uses a more or less identical theory to interpret Hector's misery, and thus not one of these is shown to possess that degree of freedom that is necessary to share Hector's experience, to view it from his perspective. The characters are determined by their own philosophic or intellectual positions.

Only with the character of Hector does Davies develop a more thorough analysis of an individual's struggle to free himself from his confining background. Initially depicted as an unimaginative, Prufrockian champion of common sense, Hector lives an emotionally and culturally impoverished life that is described in detail. Hector's ability to attack the bully "Rat-face" and then free himself from his mother's smothering demands confirms that he is able to resist obvious challenges to his sense of integrity. But the son of "misery Mackilwraith" has not been granted the emotional or creative power he needs to lead a full life. When he "decide[s] that he [is] in love with Griselda," he has no map of the emotional landscape he has just entered, and he decides to court her with nothing more than a distorted version of the traditional romance scenario for a guide (133). He eventually recognises that he is handicapped by his lack of "literary education," that "his passions [are] too big for his vocabulary" and that "planning and common sense [are] ... extremely limited servants." These hard-won insights, however, neither prevent his self-indulgent suicide attempt nor seem to have a lasting impact upon him when he awakes (258).

In the final scene, he is "blissfully at rest," still longs to save Griselda's virtue and reveals his desire to return to his common-sense plans of gradual promotion within the Department of Education. Far from affirming that Hector has been able to take what Morley calls "psychological steps towards self-knowledge," "sanity," and "self-understanding" (99), Davies closes with the brief sentence "Hector slept" to confirm that he has returned to his semi-conscious existence (284). Davies' depiction of Hector has much in common with the work of John Hospers, who develops the philosophical position of psychological determinism when he argues that an individual's "desires, volitions, and even deliberations are the product of unconscious forces, compromises, and defenses which are not only not within our control but whose very existence is usually unsuspected by those who are their victims . . . ; a man's will is itself caught up in the flux [of events], itself carried along on the current."[10] As readers, we may feel driven by the conventions of the comedic form to seek a happy and uplifting conclusion, but the language of Davies' first novel and the deterministic images he marshals against his characters suggest that in the first of the Salterton novels, freedom is barely possible for the inhabitants of the backwater Canadian town.

In Davies' second novel, *Leaven of Malice*, the general population continues to function as one-dimensional emblems of human folly for whom change is unlikely, since unwelcome. The members of the lower classes are treated as "comic relief" by the elitist Davies and seem inherently limited by their own base natures (Woodcock 37). George Morphew loves his wife, Kitten, "so far has his nature allowed," but he and his wife are creatures of appetite who are uninterested in the loftier issues of intellectual or spiritual freedom (*Leaven of Malice* 87). Kitten's sister Edith Little is less content with her world, but her desire to transcend her working-class setting and her discovery of Higgins' prank are under-represented in the final chapter, which silences her role in bringing about the happy ending. The limitations and the liberation of the poor are not a major interest of the author.

The parodic portraits of Matthew Snelgrove, Norm and Dutchy Yarrow, and Puss Pottinger further Davies' standard critique of Salterton's self-satisfied, arrogant, and pretentious middle class. As in *Tempest-Tost*, Davies continues to critique Professor Vambrace's selfishness by carefully documenting the absurd and painful lengths to which the man will go to protect his unauthentic self-image. Vambrace eventually ceases to be an overt tyrant and in his final appearance he feels a sense of nobility and peace; but the transformation occurs only as he thinks that "his daughter has been restored to him" (269). The curiously possessive phrasing suggests that he has not entirely relinquished his role as a dominating father. The deluded middle class, like the poor, remain confined in their roles.

But if satire remains a prominent part of *Leaven of Malice*, the quest for self-knowledge and freedom and the resistance to deterministic forces emerge as more explicit themes with the characters Cobbler, Ridley, Solly, and Pearl. Granted a more prominent role than in *Tempest-Tost*, Cobbler is a trickster, a "jovial, antisocial, iconoclastic" individual who tempts the reader to believe freedom is possible as he flaunts social convention and appears to set his own rules.[11] For all his disruptive appearance, Cobbler does not actually do anything to precipitate the crisis. At best, he leads by example. Davies' use of Cobbler as a trickster follows the pattern established in *At My Heart's Core*. In that play, Phelim is corrected and reintegrated into society, and the comic routines of the clown Joey Grimaldi are appropriated by the eminently reasonable Thomas Stewart. Similarly, Humphrey Cobbler is a provocative, unrestricted, and creative character in Salterton; but behind his chaotic image he advocates marriage and children in such a way as to become what Buitenhuis calls a "conservative eccentric" (47). In his final speech to a Solly on the cusp of a major decision, he argues that people cannot change their circumstances and can only "understand . . . [their] trap and make peace with it, tooth by tooth . . . you are not one of the tiny minority of mankind that can grapple with circumstance and give it fall."[12] Even Davies' tricksters sometimes retire stoically into the shade.

If the trickster occasionally appears unchaotic, so the depictions of the quests for identity represented by Ridley, Solly, and Pearl are partially undercut. Gloster Ridley is a newspaper editor who feels beset on all sides and questions his station in life. Longing for absolution for his broken marriage and the pain he has caused his deranged wife, Ridley pins his hopes on an honorary degree from Waverley University as a means of attaining a stable role within the community. Transformed before the final chapter–so Davies tells us in the closing scene–Ridley suddenly becomes a "man released from bondage," a fact confirmed by his decision to decline the honorary degree (275). Two facts–Ridley's sudden release from his past has been achieved only through the mediation of his friend's wife, Elspeth Fielding, whose words are not "extraordinarily wise" though they are "rooted fast in love and womanly tenderness" (234). Davies, of all people, decides to employ this hitherto unknown individual as a *deus ex machina* to assure Ridley that he is a decent and forgiven man–which remarkable rescue suggests that he knows Ridley's problems could not be solved within the traditional schema of cause and effect, which governs so much of the text. While Ridley achieves his desired freedom, the means by which it is attained arguably works to undermine the reader's faith in its plausibility.

The liberation of Pearl and Solly from personal and familial traps represents the first complete and convincing transformation in Davies' novels. Both manage to break from their dominating parents and both present plausible signs that they have started new lives in accordance with the best tradition of the comedic romance. Pearl's break from her father is clean and simple. When he strikes and humiliates her, she is faced with the clear option of unbearable submission to his egotism or a complete emotional severing of their relationship. Pearl wisely, if painfully, decides "that she had lost her father, more certainly than if he had died that night" (148). Armed with clear insight into her family's warped history, yet sustained and soothed by the knowledge that she still loves them, she is able to rename herself "Veronica" and make a clear commitment to Solly as her future partner.

Solly is less fortunate than Pearl, in that Mrs. Bridgetower does not induce a violent rift in their relationship. Even so, once he is armed with a real affection for Pearl, Solly is able to recognise that his mother is "a demon" and he resists her vampiric "yearning for him" (228). He, too, confirms his transformation as he gives up his oppressive critical study of Heavysege and plausibly reorients his own career as a creative writer. The text closes with a notice of their forthcoming marriage; were it not for the fact that Davies returns to their relationship in his next narrative and chronicles its near destruction, we might think he is constructing a complete celebration of their free and happy future.

The malicious "dead hand" of fate descends quickly on Solly and Veronica Bridgetower in the opening scenes of *A Mixture of Frailties*.[13] The death of Solly's mother might reasonably be expected to signal his release from his "hell of dependency" (22), but the "grisly practical joke" of Mrs. Bridgetower's will continues to bind the young couple to her malicious spirit until they produce and name a male heir. Forced to remain in his mother's home, and inadequately supported by his wee income, Solly is gradually warped by the conditions he is unable to alter or undo. Critics have often noted that the framing narrative of the Bridgetowers' struggles feels strained and heavy compared to the story of Monica's metamorphosis, but their hardships act as a balance to the apparent freedom of Monica's sojourn in Europe. Veronica watches in despair as Solly, "who had been high spirited and amusing in his ironic, undergraduate way before their marriage, had become more and more like his Mother since his Mother's death. A severity, a watchfulness had grown on him" (271). Solly gives himself over to the Thanatossian forces in his life as he concludes that people should "give up caring too much about anything" (367). Solly eventually forgives his mother and prays for her soul after Veronica has given birth to a son who will free them. They have won their liberty, but only on the terms defined by his mother. Complete self-determination is not an option in a life circumscribed by malicious resolutions and blind chance.

Monica's life initially seems antithetical to Solly's. Smiled on by fortune, she is given the opportunity and the appropriate guides to remake her identity. Raised in the kind of puritan, fundamentalist, working-class community that Davies so likes to satirise, Monica seems to be able completely to abandon her past and to refashion herself into a diva. As Peterman points out, Davies' apparent argument that it does not matter "what shape the vessel originally takes" becomes a "major blind spot in the novel" (113). Davies can develop characters who are either imprisoned or untouched by their histories, but he continues to find it hard convincingly to depict an individual as an active agent renegotiating her immediate contexts. Indeed, the two stylistic ruptures that mar the otherwise accomplished tale of Monica's transformation occur at those moments when she herself must choose her own fate: the instant she responds to Giles Revelstoke's suicide and her final decision to marry Domdaniel at the end of the book.

Critics have frequently examined Revelstoke's role as an aptly named powerful trickster figure who initiates Monica into the Dionysian world of the artist's life. Given that Davies usually reins in his disruptive figures before they subvert the essential elements of society, it is not surprising that the excessive Revelstoke is killed off. Buitenhuis notes that Revelstoke is a force "beyond even

Domdaniel's control" (50); Hugo McPherson observes that his death figures as a "final step in Monica's artistic development" (29); and Peterman observes that his death "teaches her about moral complexity and complicity" (110). Revelstoke's death, which makes perfect sense within the thematic order of the novel, is nonetheless represented in what seems a most awkward fashion. The five separate confessions by the various characters who feel responsible for Giles' death sign Davies' troubled attempt to use comic effects to draw attention away from the fact that the most radically free figure yet seen in his fiction has been extinguished. As Giles himself dies, Monica facilitates his demise by retreating to the self-centred, puritan, inhibited, fearful visions of respectability that defined her character back in Salterton, as if to confirm that Monica is not as capable of deep change as the narration first suggested.

Domdaniel's proposal to Monica and her assumed acceptance form a second textual rupture. Once again the colonialist/elitist side of Davies is sensitive to the thematic importance of wedding youthful Canadian talent and seasoned European artistry (Morley 102). But Davies does not risk depicting Monica's actual acceptance, much less including a scene of the newlyweds on their honeymoon. The couple's engagement does not bathe the conclusion in the light of love, for Domdaniel, the old, middle-of-road and vaguely manipulative teacher, seems to have been shaping Monica from the outset, undercutting the text's larger celebration of the singer's self-determination. Until the very end, Davies is fighting a sense of fatalism, the sense that forces beyond our control shape and move us.

Given Davies' constant and sometimes unsuccessful struggle against determinism in The Salterton Trilogy, it is not surprising that he should use and rely on the affirmative structures of the Romance to guide his texts toward happy endings, even when such conclusions resist some of the very impulses of the texts themselves seem to indicate. No wonder that the Davies of Salterton shows "little formal originality," for his explorations of individuality are tentative enough without disrupting their underpinning formal structures (Woodcock 37).

Given his recurring and unconscious hesitation to break free from an underlying determinism, it is not surprising that he should turn to Jung with such overwhelming enthusiasm in his next trilogy. From Jung, Davies learned that he could take the external forces that so threaten his Salterton heros and heroines—the monster mothers, malicious tricksters, uncanny turns of fate—and rewrite them not as external forces but as manifestations of the psyche's own needs and desires. In the Deptford series, Davies finally begins to overcome the external forces by converting them into aspects of the internal. And if his resulting use of and gratitude to Jung sometimes overwhelm his fiction, as in the case of *The Manticore*, it is only because the longstanding tension in his early fiction has finally been eased.

## NOTES

1. John Mills, *Robertson Davies* (Toronto: ECW, 1985), 41.

2. Hugo McPherson, "The Mask of Satire: Character and Symbolic Pattern in Robertson Davies' Fiction," *Canadian Literature* 4 (1960): 18; and Helen Hoy, "Poetry in the Dunghill: The Romance of the Ordinary in Robertson Davies' Fiction," *Ariel* 10 (1979): 72.

3. Michael Peterman, *Robertson Davies* (Boston: Twayne, 1986), 83.

4. Patricia Morley, "Davies' Salterton Trilogy: Where the Myth Touches Us," *Studies in Canadian Literature* 1 (1976): 96.

5. Jacques Lacan, *Écrits: A Selection* (New York: Norton, 1977), 93.

6. George Woodcock, "A Cycle Completed: The Nine Novels of Robertson Davies," *Canadian Literature* 126 (1990): 40.

7. Elspeth Buitenhuis, *Robertson Davies* (Toronto: Forum House, 1972), 47.

8. Hoy 75.

9. Robertson Davies, *Tempest-Tost* (Harmondsworth: Penguin, 1951), 126.

10. John Hospers, as quoted by Richard Taylor in "Determinism and Modern Psychiatry," *The Encyclopedia of Philosophy*, ed. Paul Edwards (New York: Macmillan, 1967), 368-9.

11. Russell Brown and Donna Bennett, "Magnus Eisengrim: The Shadow of the Trickster in the Novels of Robertson Davies," *Modern Fiction Studies* 22 (1976): 350.

12. Robertson Davies, *Leaven of Malice* (Toronto: Clarke, Irwin, 1972), 192-3.

13. Robertson Davies, *A Mixture of Frailties* (New York: Scribner, 1958), 22.

# WORKS CITED

Brown, Russell M., and Donna Bennett. "Magnus Eisengrim: The Shadow of the Trickster in the Novels of Robertson Davies." *Modern Fiction Studies* 22 (1976): 347-363.

Buitenhuis, Elspeth. *Robertson Davies*. Toronto: Forum House, 1972.

Davies, Robertson. *Leaven of Malice*. Toronto: Clarke, Irwin, 1954.

–. *A Mixture of Frailties*. Toronto: Macmillan, 1958.

–. *Tempest-Tost*. Markham, Ont.: Penguin, 1951.

Hospers, John. Quoted by Richard Taylor in "Determinism and Modern Psychiatry." *The Encyclopedia of Philosophy*. Ed. Paul Edwards. New York: Macmillan, 1967.

Hoy, Helen. "Poetry in the Dunghill: The Romance of the Ordinary in Robertson Davies' Fiction." *Ariel* 10 (1979): 69-98.

Lacan, Jacques. *Écrits: A Selection*. New York: Norton, 1977.

McPherson, Hugo. "The Mask of Satire: Character and Symbolic Pattern in Robertson Davies' Fiction." *Canadian Literature* 4 (1960): 18-30.

Mills, John. "Robertson Davies." *Canadian Writers and Their Works*, vol. 6. Ed. Robert Lecker, Jack David, and Ellen Quigley. Toronto: ECW, 198

Morley, Patricia. "Davies' Salterton Trilogy: Where the Myth Touches Us." *Studies in Canadian Literature* 1 (1976): 96-104.

Peterman, Michael. *Robertson Davies*. Boston: Twayne, 1986.

Woodcock, George. "A Cycle Completed: The Nine Novels of Robertson Davies." *Canadian Literature* 126 (1990): 33-48.

# Magic in the Web: Robertson Davies and *Shamanstvo*

TODD PETTIGREW

| | |
|---|---|
| Othello: | To lose't or give't away were such perdition |
| | As nothing else could match. |
| Desdemona: | Is't possible? |
| Othello: | 'Tis true. There's magic in the web of it. |

*Othello* 3.4.67-69

Robertson Davies published books in seven different decades, books ranging from literary criticism to popular journalism to drama, and, perhaps most importantly, to novels. My edition of *Happy Alchemy* advertises thirty-two books by Davies–and that list does not seem to include all the plays. The task of coming to terms with the whole of Davies' oeuvre is a daunting one.

To complicate matters, scholarly opinion about Davies' work, perhaps inevitably, is more complicated and varied than the work itself. Criticism about Davies seems to include hyperbolic praise and openly hostile attacks in equal measure. John Irving has called him "the greatest comic novelist in the English language since Charles Dickens,"[1] and John Kenneth Galbraith, in a passage that Davies' publishers are fond of citing, claimed that Davies' works were among the "very best work of this century."[2] At the same time, Joyce Carol Oates has been anything but edified by Davies' reputation as a "leading" figure in Canadian literature, calling him "a symbol of all that younger Canadian writers and artists have been struggling to accommodate, or repudiate, or transcend, or forget."[3] Other critics have tasked Davies for his morality and moralising, finding him sexist, elitist, and, says Linda Lamont-Stewart, "dangerous."[4]

How did Davies engender, as it were, such radically different responses? Is there something about his writing that lends itself to polarised responses? How is it that one writer could lead intelligent readers down paths leading in exactly opposite directions?

To explain the complexities of reactions to Davies, I come at last to the somewhat exotic word that I have borrowed for my title. Davies' thought and style, and, consequently, the responses generated in his readers can be characterised by a term that Davies himself used to characterise a significant writer's thought and style: *shamanstvo*. Davies, of course, borrowed the term from Nabokov; and we find him using it to describe the writer's craft as early as *A Voice from the Attic* (1960). In 1992 the idea is still on his mind, and it becomes the basis for his discussion of good writing that forms the second half of his *Reading and Writing*.

Davies translates *shamanstvo* as "enchanter-quality," and it is a quality central to his work. Enchantment emerges not only as a "literal" plot element with, for example, the narrative enchantments of Eisengrim and the gypsy magic of the Cornish novels, but also as a formal, stylistic characteristic of Davies' writing. But what makes for effectual literary enchantment? Ensnarement, for Davies, is one key to *shamanstvo*. In *Reading and Writing*, Davies explains,

> You cannot weave a spell without words. But words alone are not enough. A story is not enough. To weave the spell the writer must have within him something perhaps comparable to the silk-spinning and web-casting gift of the spider; he must not only have something to say, some story to tell or some wisdom to impart, but he must have a characteristic way of doing it which entraps and holds his prey, by which I mean his reader. (62)

The metaphor is provocative, outrageous even though consistent with the radical sense of "text" as weave, for it places the writer in an undeniable position of potentially deadly power.[5] The writer not only controls the reader's reading, his imagination, but, in Davies' metaphor, his very life, for the reader is reduced to "prey." The reader/fly, entrapped in the author/spider's web is helpless to control his sensations and is at the mercy of the stronger, more cunning power that will determine his eventual fate. No wonder, then, that Davies has been criticised for his "monologic" approach to writing. Stephen Bonnycastle, for example, questions what he sees as Davies' tendency to preach, to lecture, and to dazzle rather than to collaborate, to co-operate, and to engage in a conversation. "The most serious deception" in The Deptford Trilogy, says Bonnycastle, "is that in which form and content come together to suggest that monologue is the summit of human discourse."[6]

If *shamanstvo* involves the monologic domination of the reader, its fictional embodiment, the thematic representative of *shamanstvo* in the novels, is Magnus Eisengrim. Eisengrim's life is about domination–witness his days in the circus–and it is domination that he finds fulfilling in and about live Concert. Indeed, Eisengrim finds screen-acting tiresome, for on television, he says, "I can't see my audience, and what I can't see I can't dominate. And what I can't dominate I can't enchant" (557). If his audience members are partners, they are only partners, according to Eisengrim, "in their own deception" (557).

Eisengrim, the wolf-spider, as it were, seems to embody Davies' ideal of storytelling, for much of the account of his life involves a design designed to ensnare Roly Ingestree, to crush him in revenge for his shabby treatment of Sir John at the Irving memorial. But if Roly is Eisengrim's prey, he is not the first. Roly is understandably harsh on this point: "You ate poor old Sir John. You ate him right down to the core."[7] There is no reason to suppose Roly is imagining the magician as a spider, but the metaphor works: spiders can only ingest liquids and consequently inject their prey with digestive juices and then drain their victims from the inside. However Eisengrim conceives himself, he admits to Ramsay that ultimate domination was his goal with Sir John: "In my inmost self I wanted to eat him, to possess him, to make him mine." Roly was right: "He had seen what I truly thought I had kept hidden" (855).

Despite Eisengrim's status as a predator, he is not a fully realised enchanter, for domination is not the only aspect of *shamanstvo*. Indeed, ensnarement is slightly misleading, since Davies conceives of the ensnarement in an unusual way. Taking the second part of Goethe's *Faust* as the single greatest literary embodiment of the enchanter quality, Davies notes: "I know of no instance of this quality more concentrated or more powerful than" in this work "where a world of insight and wisdom and spiritual enlargement is given form."[8] The enchanted reader must give himself over to the writer, be dominated for the sake of art. But for Davies, it is precisely that sacrifice of the reader, the willingness of the reader to set down on the web of a novel or a trilogy and be trapped there for a time, that makes important and interesting literature possible. It is at this point of intellectual vulnerability that the reader can achieve real intellectual discovery in the world according to Davies.

Davies, claiming that the writer conveys to readers a particular and striking mode of thought, develops the implications of *shamanstvo* in *Reading and Writing*: "He is telling them things that they recognize as soon as they hear them . . . but which they have not been able to seize and hold and put in language themselves" (63). At its best, a novel may be a direct revelation of reality that, when it "comes, leaves us enlarged and in possession of some new ground in the exploration of ourselves" (64). By willingly submitting to the will of the author, the reader takes from the author whatever unique intellectual gifts he may possess. The fly is not consumed but is liberated to a degree, free to explore the web though constrained to follow the paths the spider has set out. Dunstan Ramsay is pleased to fall into such a trap when he first reads Coleridge's "Kubla Khan" and "almost jumped out of [his] skin" with the aptness of the famous ending lines (*The Deptford Trilogy* 82).

Spiders spin more than one kind of silk for their webs. The spiral threads are sticky and entrap the insects that provide sustenance; the radial support threads are not sticky, allowing the spider to move about its own web without getting caught. But in the admittedly bizarre metaphor I have set out, it is the prey who benefits from the privileges of the radial strands, and it is the critics who can observe readers navigating the web.

One radial strand of The Deptford Trilogy that critics have found especially interesting is aligned with the question of Ramsay's identity and the degree to which he attains self-knowledge. The issue has polarised critics. David Williams all but accuses Ramsay of deliberate falsification and thus implies that Davies has given us an unsatisfying, unacceptable hero. *Fifth Business*, says Williams, is Ramsay's "final work of conjuring a saintly new persona, and he does it much better than he ever could 'secure and palm six half crowns.'"[9] Michael Peterman's monograph on Davies takes a polar opposite position, arguing as it does that before one can doubt Ramsay's narrative, one must observe "a patterned discrepancy between autobiographical assertion and actual fact." He contends that this is not the case in the Deptford novels: "Neither *Fifth Business* nor its successors provides sufficient grounds to doubt Ramsay's perception or integrity."[10]

Nancy Bailey calls *Fifth Business* a story of a "re-birth that failed" and claims that far from coming to an increased awareness of himself, Ramsay "remains in the same darkness of illusion with which he charges Boy Staunton."[11] Wilfred Cude, while praising Ramsay for his "comprehensive grasp of reality," insists that he is "very wrong about being Fifth Business."[12] Instead, Cude suggests that his true identity is that of a modern day St. Dunstan, and the article ably demonstrates the ways in which Davies' character parallels the historical saint (109). The tendency to gainsay or endorse Ramsay's attempts at self-discovery are taken a step further by Dennis Duffy when he berates the novel for not espousing a single consistent vision of truth. Duffy asks, "How can *Fifth Business* hold, on one hand, a view of truth so relative and so inextricably bound up in praxis, and, on the other, usher readers into a chamber filled with Jungian archetypes visible only to the elite?"[13]

Duffy's question is provocative, and I do not intend even to begin to answer it definitively. I will say that, in my understanding, Davies' "view of truth" is perhaps different from that of Duffy. The episode in which Boy demotes Ramsay from the post of Headmaster at Colborne is sometimes cited as an example of Ramsay's lack of self-knowledge. Boy's description is surprising, since, until that point, apart from his war wounds, there is no indication that Ramsay's physical appearance or demeanour is at all extraordinary. On the contrary, Ramsay implies that his presence was pleasant: "I was classy," he says, "I was heavily varnished, and I offended nobody" (186). But Ramsay has vowed not to "posture" in his account, and so writes "only of what I knew when it happened" (71). The obvious implications of the demotion incident are not that Ramsay is unaware of his appearance and its effect on people but that he was not aware of it until that time. Davies, as the master-enchanter of the trilogy, has structured his tale so as to give the reader virtually the same shock as Ramsay himself experienced that day in 1947. Ramsay's narrative is undoubtedly one of self-revelation or, more aptly, the revelation of selves. The revelation, though, is not straightforward or easy. Its truths are multiple: as Ramsay himself notes, "I cannot remember a time when I did not take it as understood that everybody has at least two, if not twenty-two, sides to him" (76). These multiple truths of Ramsay's identity, these paths we can label as "Dunstable," "St. Dunstan," "Gyges," "Fifth Business," and so on, are devised so that if we do not follow them carefully, we may get stuck. We may become immobilised on the web; and, seeing only that point at which we have stopped, we may lose sight of the complexity of its construction.

In The Cornish Trilogy, the reader is again at risk of being ensnared.

The Cornish novels take wisdom as a central theme, particularly the search for such sources from which it can be drawn. The Cornish novels offer the reader the opportunity to view the university as a place primarily concerned with truth, and university professors as custodians of wisdom. Simon Darcourt, however, finds his most fulfilling conception of self not at the university table, but in Mamusia's reading of Tarot cards. Mamusia–Maria's gypsy mother–is hardly a figure of conventional wisdom and decorum. She steals from the grocery store; she cooks up love potions from feminine hygiene products; she restores violins with manure. Nevertheless, one follows the thread a little further and realises that she, as much as anyone in Davies, represents a genuine understanding of oneself and one's place in the world. Darcourt, indeed, feels himself redefined by her reading of the Tarot cards he is dealt: "The Fool. You see he is going on a journey and he looks very happy. He is always going some place is the Fool. And he has a good fool's dress, but see, the pants are torn at the back. Part of his arse is showing. . . . And what does the little dog do with the bare arse? Maybe he is nipping at it."[14] The Fool is someone with direction and energy. He is, Mamusia explains, "going just as fast as he can to something he thinks good" (981).

Darcourt is inspired by the freedom and spirit that figured in the Fool and embraces the symbol at once. That embracing represents a kind of rebirth for him. Moments after the revelation, he is "exhilarated as he had not been in many years" (982). Moreover, on reflection, the image becomes increasingly compelling. Where he had thought of himself as a "servant, a drudge, not without value, but never an initiator or an important figure in anyone's life but his own," he comes to realise that "Mamusia had declared as true what he had for some time felt in his bones. He was something better" (987).

And we can follow this thread even further, to the amusing account of Yerko's claque, near the end of *The Lyre of Orpheus*. Where Yerko had been mostly noted for his pungent farting, he emerges as a model of high culture by leading his group of planted opera audience members who laugh and cry and applaud at all the right times. Early in the Concert of *Arthur of Britain*, for example, the Canadian audience applauds the scenery, raising the ire of both Gunilla and Geraint, but Yerko's claque puts the rest of the audience in its place with well-apportioned shushing (1115). By this point, Yerko has become the norm of civilised behaviour, illuminating relatively boorish Canadians. In the end, however, Darcourt redeems his countrymen and women, by pointing out that any modern audience should applaud the scenery of *Arthur of Britain*, for "it was outlawed sixty years ago when there was all that blethers about letting the audience use its imagination" (1115). But then Darcourt, for a time, becomes the voice of traditionalism. And so it goes. One idea leads to the next, characters play one role and then another, of satiric butt and satiric norm, all caught in *shamanstvo*, the magic of the web. This complex of interconnected ideas gives the works their imaginative range and strength, since the complexity of the narratives demands intense mental engagement.

It has been my aim to afford some insight into Davies' body of work as a whole, but, perhaps inevitably, I have only been able to follow a few of its threads. I have dwelt on Deptford, but I have said nothing about the Salterton novels, although there is surely much there connected with *shamanstvo*. Similarly, I have been silent as to the later novels, though both *Cunning Men* and *Walking Spirits* have obvious connections to enchantment. I have said nothing about how *Fortune, My Foe* anticipates the intellectual ensnarement of the Cornish novels; but surely Franz Szabo has much to say to Mamusia–and that still leaves a considerable stack of plays untouched.

And what of the mass of critics I promised to make some sense of? Anthony Dawson, who has recognised the weblike structure of *Fifth Business*, suggests that the novel is full of clues that can be probed for their significance in the overall pattern. Thus, argues Dawson, critics "seeking to *explain* Davies' texts, are in a way doomed to *perform* them" (156; his emphasis). Dawson's use of the word "doom" recalls the spider/prey image. But I would suggest that it is just as apt to say that critics, and readers for that matter, are free to perform *in* Davies' texts as much as they are doomed to perform the texts themselves. Davies' vision of the world is a complex one, and the web that he creates is designed to allow for a variety of possible interpretations and perspectives. The remarkable range of critical reaction to Davies' work arises from this basic principle of Davies' fictional structures. The reading that one generates depends on the point at which one arrives in the net, and the turns one takes in moving around in it. The nature of such turns is complex and involves one's ideological predispositions as well as one's tastes–one's store of knowledge and one's expectations about reading and writing.

Have I arrived–and it would no doubt be embarrassing if I had–at the very simple conclusion that my own reading of Davies and his critics was meant to avoid? Have I been saying that it is simply a matter of accepting Davies' morality or not? I don't think so. That sentiment implies that Davies' ideas about the world, its people, and its writing are monolithic, static, and simple; I have tried to suggest that they are just the opposite. Further, the for-or-against view implies that there are few points in between, that one must reasonably reject Davies and his ideas wholesale or swallow them without relish, like political leaders (*DT* 169). The image of the web gives us a more complicated Davies, conservative, elitist, sexist along some strands, radical, populist, sexually adventurous among others, with abundant possibilities that connect, dart between, or run parallel to these strands.

The meaning of Davies' work lies not in a particular didactic intent, but in the way in which Davies patterns ideas. In *The Merry Heart*, Davies writes of his oeuvre that it works indirectly "in the direction of new discovery, the new conquest, the new great adventure. That is, if you want to call it by an ambiguous name, the artist's 'magic, his enchanter quality.'"[15] "Is't possible?" Desdemona asks Othello. " 'Tis true. There's magic in the web of it."

## NOTES

1. John Irving, "The Magic Touch of a Revered Storyteller," *Maclean's* (December 18, 1995): 90.

2. John Kenneth Galbraith, "The World of Wonder of Robertson Davies," *Robertson Davies: An Appreciation*, ed. Elspeth Cameron (Peterborough, Ont.: Broadview, 1991), 41.

3. Joyce Carol Oates, "One Half of Robertson Davies," *Robertson Davies: An Appreciation*, 181.

4. Linda Lamont-Stewart, "Robertson Davies and the Doctrine of the Elite: An Ideological Critique of the Cornish Trilogy," *Robertson Davies: An Appreciation*, 291.

5. Anthony B. Dawson notes how *Fifth Business* is a novel "which unwary critics have wandered into, like flies into the spider's parlour" ("Davies, His Critics and the Canadian Canon," *Canadian Literature* 92 [1982]: 154-55).

6. Stephen Bonnycastle, "Robertson Davies and the Ethics of Monologue," *Robertson Davies: An Appreciation*, 171.

7. Robertson Davies, *The Deptford Trilogy* (New York: Penguin, 1983), 759.

8. Robertson Davies, *Reading and Writing* (Utah: University of Utah Press, 1992), 63.

9. David Williams, "The Confessions of Self-Made Man: Forms of Autobiography in *Fifth Business*," *Journal of Canadian Studies* 24 (1989): 98.

10. Michael Peterman, *Robertson Davies* (New York: Twayne, 1986), 123.

11. Nancy Bailey, "The Role of Dunstan Ramsay, the Almost Saint of Robertson Davies' Deptford Trilogy," *The Journal of Commonwealth Literature* 19 (1984): 38.

12. Wilfred Cude, "Miracle and Art in *Fifth Business*," *Robertson Davies: An Appreciation*, 97, 98.

13. Dennis Duffy, "To Carry the Work of William James a Step Further: The Play of Truth in *Fifth Business*," *Essays on Canadian Writing* 36 (1988): 10.

14. Robertson Davies, *The Cornish Trilogy* (New York: Penguin, 1990), 980.

15. Robertson Davies, *The Merry Heart: Selections 1980-1995* (Toronto: McClelland & Stewart, 1996), 143. Readers may recall that in *Reading and Writing*, Davies refers to the enchanter quality as "a direct revelation of reality" (64). There, Davies is referring to the provocative power of *shamanstvo* in general rather than to his particular aims as a writer/enchanter. I therefore take "indirectly" as a more appropriate statement about Davies' writing.

# The Leaven of Wine and Spirits in the Fiction of Robertson Davies

K.P. STICH

"**V**isited a friend this evening who had procured a bottle of a very special tonic called *Noilly Prat*; in the interest of temperance, we experimented to see how much of the tonic it was necessary to put with a jigger of gin in order to kill the horrid taste. After several tries we got the measurements exactly right." So says Samuel Marchbanks in his *Diary*.[1] Whether Davies himself liked martinis is of no concern here. My subject is his fondness for literary references to alcohol; they are as readily evident in his Marchbanksian ventures as in all of his novels and stories. Gin, brandy, cognac, rye whisky, scotch, and wine flow freely there. The writings of Davies also include reference to a variety of other drinks, including sherry spiked with either gin or brandy,[2] hot toddies (*Leaven of Malice* 173), armagnac,[3] aquavit (*Lyre of Orpheus* 200), pink gin,[4] champagne cider,[5] nostrums,[6] ordinary beer (*World of Wonders* 61), and plonk, "an insidious mixture of stout, brandy and coarse-ground poppyheads" (*LM* 17) for that imagined extra kick. In other words, his fiction, Marchbanks' papers included, appears to come equipped with well-stocked cellars and an implicitly open invitation, long before *The Lyre of Orpheus*, for the judicious reader to descend into the mythic cellar or underworld of Dionysus.

Alcohol as a literary motif, however, has traditionally struck contemporary critics as embarrassing or, in any case, trivial,[7] and they have left it largely neglected in their criticism of Davies' fiction as well. Heeding Davies' caution against taking anything to be trivial,[8] I intend to juggle and measure the alcohol motif in its role as liquid "Fifth Business," an obvious stimulant for his attack on intemperate temperance or prohibitionism of any sort and also an agent with less obvious connections to his psychological and mythic explorations.

In 1916, just three years after the birth of Robertson Davies, the Ontario Temperance Act made it illegal to sell beverages that exceeded 2.5 percent alcohol per volume; the sale of so-called "native wine" remained legal, as did the vending of any alcohol for "medicinal, sacramental, industrial, or scientific purposes."[9] The consequences for a local physician (especially if he were also the local pharmacist) could have been particularly taxing personally, even as they underlined the dangers of intemperate temperance laws. Davies certainly thinks so in his portrayal of Dr. Ogg as "a drunk and a failure" who earns his living "chiefly by writing prescriptions for bottles of gin, whisky, and brandy, required regularly by the few hundred citizens of [his] village for ailments that Dr. Ogg identified" (CM 26-27). The Ontario Temperance Act was repealed in 1927 and replaced by the Liquor Control Act (Ontario), which was authorised together with the Liquor Control Board of Ontario to run the province's liquor stores (Single 141). For many years, the regulations of the LCBO were far from user-friendly, which fact explains Marchbanks' reference to "the Government Alcoholic Discouragement Board."[10] Every personal purchase, for instance, required one first to have obtained an "Individual Liquor Permit."[11] The need for such permits ended only in 1962. Just seven years later, the LCBO opened its first self-serve outlet; and within a decade, two-thirds of their stores had followed suit (Single 153).

It is surely a matter of coincidence rather than synchronicity that Davies' life roughly spans Ontario's rise from being intoxicated with Prohibition ideals to having the LCBO become, by early 1997, "the largest purchaser of alcohol in the world."[12] Yet, it is hardly accidental that Davies, given his early and lasting attraction to satiric writers like Rabelais and Sinclair Lewis,[13] should have been ready to defend in his own writing the time-honoured place of alcohol in Western culture. His defence is directed against puritanical interest groups' fear of alcoholic spirits and the subsequent tendency severely to restrict their availability. Davies sees such prohibitionism as a vain attempt to mask the fear of any form of literal or symbolic intoxication, with alcohol simply being the easiest intoxicant to single out because of its perceived liberating influence on the libido (in the Freudian as well the Jungian sense of that notion) and the creative imagination. Indeed, from as far back as the early days of the North American temperance movements in the 1830s, total abstinence advocates have tended to connect the writing and reading of literature with the drinking of alcohol.[14] Davies sees such connections more positively than negatively, especially with regard to authors he likes, such as Evelyn Waugh and E.T.A. Hoffmann. Waugh's "terrible dosings [of alcohol]" Davies passes off as "little frills and arabesques,"[15] and Hoffmann, he says, wrote his best stories when "more than half-drunk."[16] (This idea comes up again in *The Lyre of Orpheus* when, speaking from Limbo, Hoffmann himself confirms, as it were, the inspirational rather than stupefying effect of vinous intoxication on his imagination, preferably in the company of women [*LO* 217].) Davies' irreverent praise of a half-drunk genius occurs intemperately, some might say, in the 1954 Christmas issue of *Saturday Night* in which Davies reviewed a collection of Hoffmann's stories of the uncanny and the grotesque; he recommended the collection for "congenial" year-end enlightenment.[17] Moreover, as one of the magazine's editors, Davies may also have helped round out his review with a complementary advertisement for a cognac–not brandy–that promises to be "Always in Good Taste."[18]

It comes as no surprise that in his own fiction from the 1950s onward, Davies is, at least on the surface, very much closer to the alcoholic humour of Rabelais, the anti-Prohibition satire of Sinclair Lewis, and the remarkably "wet" sunshine of Leacock than to initiations into the realm of the unconscious by means of the intoxicating imagination. Although he does not explicitly welcome his audience as "most noble boozers" or "indefatigable boozers," as does Rabelais,[19] Davies, it seems to me, presupposes his friendly reader not to be a teetotaller. In fact, teetotallers do not fare so well in his fiction–the cases of Professor Pfeiffer in *The Lyre of Orpheus* and Boy Staunton's parents in *Fifth Business* immediately come to mind. Inveterate drinkers, meanwhile, are treated sympathetically–as evinced by Cecil Athelstan in *Fifth Business*, David Staunton in *The Manticore*, Harry Kinghoven in *World of Wonders*, John Parlabane in *The Rebel Angels*, Dr. Ogg and the Anglican priest Charlie Iredale in *The Cunning Man*. Of course, there is also Francis Cornish's older brother, a victim of severe fetal alcohol syndrome, reminding the reader that Davies is not blind to alcohol abuse. It is the moderate and occasionally immoderate drinkers, however, who abound–characters like Samuel Marchbanks, Solly Bridgetower, Valentine Rich, Humphrey Cobbler, Dunstan Ramsay, Liesl Vitzlipützli, Hamish McRory, Simon Darcourt, Maria Magdalena Theotoky Cornish (except when pregnant), Gunilla Dahl-Soot, and Jonathan Hullah. They provide Davies' writing with memorable moments of sunshine, if one cares to see alcoholic humour that way and is inclined to believe in the convivial or relaxing or invigorating or otherwise allegedly beneficial effects of well-tempered drink.

Such moments may be brief or they may linger, as the following examples will show. "Have a drink and let us cheer you up,"[20] says Maria Cornish to Darcourt, who likes to cheer up that way. So does Mrs. Bridgetower: "I think I could take a glass of sherry. Perhaps with a little something in it" (*LM* 152), she says to her son Solly, who prefers to treat himself to a glass of rye and water in his room (*Tempest-Tost* 46, *LM* 141). Alcohol becomes part of Jonathan Hullah's well-being when, at the age of nine and deathly ill, he learns the "'medicinal' and only accidentally pleasurable" propensities of wine, and thus begins his lifelong love of vintages and respect, as a physician, for alcohol's place in society even in the treatment of alcoholics (*The Cunning Man* 32, 429). Samuel Marchbanks, meanwhile, attests to the difficulties of occasional abstinence. In the very first entry of his diary, which was for "Sunday & New Year's Day," he writes: "Woke early this morning, and thanks to my discretion last night, my tongue was as red and shiny as a piece of Christmas ribbon, and my breath was like a zephyr from a May meadow. . . . Wasted no time on New Year's resolutions, for I outgrew such folly long ago. Any betterment in my character will be the outcome of prolonged meditation, and slow metabolic and metaphysical reform . . ." (*DSM* 2). In other words, he is not ready to maintain his discretionary abstention from alcohol on New Year's Eve for very long. Indeed, in his entry for the last day of the year, he admits how incapable he has been of watering down his consumption (*DSM* 202).

Marchbanks' observation serves as a basic reminder to read Davies' alcoholic humour in the context of Ontario's history of prohibitionism and the gradual loosening of liquor restrictions. Indeed, *The Diary of Samuel Marchbanks* draws on Davies' 1945 and 1946 Marchbanks columns from the Peterborough *Examiner,* the newspaper of which he had become editor in 1942 (Grant 240, 264). These facts matter because in "public (not in private) Peterborough was dry" at that time, and Davies "was editorially in favour of liberalizing the liquor laws" (Grant 243). This, by the way, is one of Grant's very rare references to the subject of alcohol. It was in 1946 that the Liquor Licence Board of Ontario (LLBO) was created to oversee the liberalizing of on-premise drinking; it was also in that year that cocktail lounges were established in Ontario (Single 141). Thus, when *The Diary* was published in 1947, followed in 1949 by *The Table-Talk of Samuel Marchbanks*, the possibility of civilised sipping in public places was such a topical issue that Marchbanks could speak satirically of "Ontario's Bacchic Refinement" as found

> In the Cocktail Lounge of a large Toronto hotel. Although it was full
> of people, an awesome hush hung over the place, and there were
> three superior waiters at the door, to make sure that no undesirable
> guest (the kind of person, for instance, who shouts, "Well, here's
> looking up your address!" to his female companion whenever he
> takes a drink) gained admission. . . . My drink was not as good as
> I could have made at home, but it was worth the money to sip it in
> surroundings of such mortuary restraint.[21]

The lounge's "awesome hush" and "mortuary restraint" are reminiscent of
Leacock's well-known "Mausoleum Club" and of his uncannily silent and
suggestively named "A Study in Still Life–The Country Hotel." (In the latter,
Leacock satirises the turn-of-the-century liquor laws that would give a licensed
establishment "on the sunny side of Main Street" a mausoleum-like ambience.)[22]
"How long will it be," asks Marchbanks forty years later, "before they [the
government] learn to treat liquor sensibly in this country?" The question surfaces
after a visit to his local LCBO store, where he "hobnobbed with high and low,
rich and poor, clergy and laity for twenty minutes while waiting [his] turn"
(*DSM* 63), where alcohol would be considerably cheaper and, consequently,
better than at a cocktail lounge, and where natural aristocrats and democrats
seem to meet as if in defiance of both bourgeois small-mindedness and the
misplaced temperance snobbery of affluent drinkers like David Staunton.[23]
Marchbanks' humorous as well as serious notion of the liquor store as "that
mighty democratic institution" (*DSM* 63) presents the LCBO as having a
potentially civilizing influence, especially when compared to the uncivil effect
of the dry Prohibition years. Only wealthy people with foresight or illegal
connections were then able to afford legal private stocks, particularly (for
obvious reasons) with regard to wine. The cellars of Senator McRory and of the
Cunning Man's father are two good examples. At the same time, by being in the
hinterland worlds of Blairlogie and Sioux Lookout, respectively, these cellars
seemingly amplify alcohol's civilizing capabilities.

   The cultural importance of the liquor store in the mid- and late 1940s
carries over into the world of Salterton in *Tempest-Tost* (1951), the LCBO
joining forces with another Davies civilizing agent, the theatre. The Salterton
Little Theatre undoubtedly owes much to Davies having become directly
involved in 1948 in the running of the Dominion Drama Festival, which had
celebrated its revival a year before (Grant 300). From its early days in the
1930s, the Festival's future was said to be linked to its "'hav[ing] been founded

on love and whisky,'"[24] with the latter flowing exceptionally freely and openly in the 1950s in the form of financial backing from Canadian distillers of whisky (Lee 136). Such sponsorship withstood widespread protest, mostly from church leaders and organisations like the Women's Christian Temperance Union (Lee 156, 157).[25] When Robertson Davies wrote the Foreword for *Love and Whiskey* (1973), Betty Lee's provocatively titled history of the Dominion Drama Festival, the subtext of love, plenty of good cheer and jabs at Prohibition-mindedness in his *Tempest-Tost* could not have been far from his mind.

So far, I have engaged something of the social and cultural roles of alcohol in Davies' fiction. Whether with reference to male or female characters, his emphasis is on the sunny rather than the sinister side of drink. His choice of situations is most often comic and theatrical. The stage may be, for instance, a bed, as in the case of Solly having hot toddies with the Cobblers, or of Eisengrim, Liesl, and Dunstan enjoying their nightcaps together in their quasi-mystical marriage (*LM* 173; *WW* 337); it may be a demure living room like the Forresters', where the Salterton Little Theatre organisers have their seasonal foundation drinks, or the splendid Round Table gatherings of the Cornish Foundation (*TT* 53; *What's Bred in the Bone* and *LO*); it may be St. Nicholas' Cathedral for Humphrey Cobbler's All Hallows' Eve prank (*LM* 51-52); or it may be the Upper Library at Massey College on special after-dinner occasions such as the visit of Dr. Theophrastus von Hohenheim, when port, Madeira and cognac are never in short supply.[26] Whatever the scenario, it is part of what Davies has Jonathan Hullah call "the Great Theatre of Life" (*CM* 469) and in which wines and spirits, so it appears, heighten one's perceptivity with regard to the outer- or inner- or underworld. Here are a few straight-up eye-openers: for Jonathan Hullah "a heartening drink" serves literally to strengthen the heart while also opening up its symbolic depth; his friend Hugh McWearie is only half joking when linking "excellent whisky" to increased "intuition" (*CM* 447); Harry Kinghoven's inveterate drinking seems indispensable to his genius as a cameraman (*WW*); Senator McRory's well-stocked cellar appears to be connected to his leisurely pursuit of "sun-pictures" (*BB* 167); and Simon Darcourt, his mind "inspired by wine" and the anticipation of finding in the pages of *Vogue* "some pictures of women with very few clothes on, or perhaps none at all" (*LO* 59-60), is ready to see a cosmetics ad as a Francis Cornish drawing and to turn this discovery into a breakthrough for his Cornish biography.

While Darcourt's explicit interest in wine and women may not afford us the best insight into his "lively but controlled imagination" (*LO* 107), the implicit link between his imagination and his lively and controlled drinking opens up the Dionysian subtext of not only Darcourt's interweaving of theology, psychology, mythology, and the theatre, but also Davies' pursuit of the alcohol motif beyond situational comedy and social satire. I do not use the term "Dionysian" naively here as either a synonym for bacchanalian or the antonym of Apollonian; I have in mind the god Dionysus and "the polymorphous nature with which the Greeks so amply endowed him."[27]

"Greek religion," it is worth remembering, "had no formal theology, no priestly class of interpreters. . . . Greeks experienced religion through ritual and myth and the myths . . . were endlessly changed and re-imagined for every generation by its artists and poets."[28] Dionysus, one could say, personifies a mythic platter of plenty with offerings of his multiple names, identities, and cultic associations.[29] Euripides, in his *Bacchae*, alludes to this adaptability from the beginning when he calls Dionysus also Bromius and Bacchus. (It was Roman culture, incidentally, that later turned Bacchus into the over-simplified god of drunkenness.) Dionysus can appear as "at once masculine and effeminate, bearded and youthful, sober and intoxicated, tragic and comic, ephemeral and timeless, an embodiment of life as well as death, thus incorporating the whole spectrum of human experience," according to Albert Henrichs, one of today's authorities on Dionysian mysteries. Henrichs stresses Dionysus' major masks as the god of the grape and of the theatre and as an inspirer or guide of women and the spirits of the dead (13-14). "Dionysus and his followers," concludes Henrichs, "can be seen as abandoning, shifting, or transcending the limits of everyday experience through their association with exalted or anomalous conditions such as intoxication, masquerade, illusion, trance or madness. They are thus linked with an expansion of physical and mental faculties—one that leads either to states of heightened self-awareness or to destructive disruptions of the personality and even to the annihilation of life" (14-15).

From *Tempest-Tost* to *The Cunning Man*, the theatrical world of Davies' fiction readily accommodates the masks of Dionysus. For the purpose of this essay, I will now focus my attention on *The Lyre of Orpheus*. My reason is pragmatic: as a fundamentally "epiphanic god" (Henrichs 17), Dionysus would grant "deliverance" and does so most remarkably when he blends into the figure of Orpheus.[30] That is to say, the Dionysian underworld is interconnected with the underworld or Hades of Eleusinian and Orphic mysteries and shares their inherent message of "death as the way to real life" (Graf 242-43).

The lyre, which in Davies' novel, "opens the door to the underworld"

(37), is said to belong obviously to Orpheus. Davies accredits Hoffmann with this notion, and the source is, I think, Hoffmann's review of Beethoven's *Fifth Symphony*, where the lyre of Orpheus serves Hoffmann as a metonymy for the power of music to open up "an unknown realm, a world which has nothing in common with the external senses," an archetypal world of "the inarticulate" and "the infinite" (234-35). Yet to hear this lyre is also tantamount, in Euripidean drama, for instance, to experiencing the power of Dionysus through the music commonly associated with him.[31] It is therefore reasonable to suggest that Davies' allusion to Orpheus includes Dionysus. The original inventor of the cithara or lyre, meanwhile, is said to be Hermes (Zeitlin 179)–the same Hermes who, in iconography, is often seen as delivering the infant Dionysus to the care of the nymphs of Nysa[32] and who is also often depicted in the company of the god.[33] Given his multiple identities and his association with Hermes (trickster, joker, Trismegistus, god of letters, medicine, and magic), it is not surprising for Dionysus to take on the makings of "a divine magician" (Henrichs 35) and for Pentheus, in Euripides' *Bacchae*, to refer to him as "a conjurer of sorts" and "some stranger" because of his many guises.[34]

Thomas Mann, in his 1912 novella *Death in Venice*, was one of the first modern novelists to perceive Dionysus as the archetypal stranger, or Other, in the contemporary context of depth psychology (Henrichs 32). The prevalence of the motif of the stranger in his fiction would have caught the attention of Davies, who was not only drawn to Mann but would also have readily recognised the affinities between the Dionysian stranger and the Jungian archetypes of the Persona and the Shadow. Yet because of his androgyny and pivotal role in the mythic world of the unconscious, Dionysus is also closely affiliated with the archetype of the Anima and the corresponding goal of "an increase of consciousness through 'integrating' the anima."[35] By combining the archetypal realities of the Persona, the Shadow and the Anima, the Dionysian imagination seems to promise an enticingly magnanimous initiation into the mysteries of individuation–Know yourself. That is Dionysus' implicit message in the *Bacchae* (30). I suggest that it is promptings of Dionysus that guide not only Davies' allusions to alcohol but also, as Patricia Köster has shown, his interest in "a natural religion derived from the depths of character."[36]

While Jung, Mann, Hoffmann, Henrichs, and my other sources add weight to my notions of the psycho-mythic importance of Dionysus to Davies, and while the alcoholic ambience of *The Lyre of Orpheus* seems to consolidate that importance, albeit in a deceptively lighthearted way, I nevertheless wish I had more than circumstantial evidence and analogies to rely on. I have counted only two explicit references to Dionysus; both are complementary. One occurs, most appropriately, in *High Spirits*, where "Dionysian forces" are said to coexist with Apollonian ones at Massey College (83); the other, also appropriately, comes up near the end of *Murther and Walking Spirits*: "Apollonian scintillant perspicuity, if taken too far, is apt to turn into Dionysian grossness of folly" (374). One may find this Apollo-Dionysus polarity everywhere in Davies' fiction. One should not, however, interpret it as inherently in favour of the Apollonian side, especially not in *The Lyre of Orpheus*, where Simon Darcourt loves to pursue folly over cultural fences meant to protect against grossness and otherness.

Darcourt wears many masks (*personae*): he can be, for instance, a couth and an uncouth tippler, a voyeur (in the pages of magazines and in his social life [see *LO* 124]), a thief, "a priest of the type of the mighty Rabelais" (*LO* 297), and a designing server of drinks: "Let's tank her up and see what happens," he says to himself in response to Gunilla Dahl-Soot's imposing presence at a Cornish Foundation dinner party (*LO* 125). He is also ready to combine his many sides under the mask of the archetypal Fool who feels "urged onward by something outside the confines of intellect and caution" (*LO* 296), something Orphic and Dionysian for which wine and spirits tend to be triggers. Darcourt is certainly not a pretentious, know-it-all fool like Pentheus, who wanted to put Dionysus in chains (Euripides 30). Moreover, as a professor of New Testament Greek, Darcourt's knowledge of the language presupposes, I should hope, some familiarity with Euripides' plays; as a priest with unorthodox Gnostic affinities, he would have known that the Dionysian mysteries were taboo in the (as Jung puts it) "predominantly Apollonian cult and ethos of Christianity."[37]

According to Grant (531), Davies read with great interest the 1968 edition of Jung's *Psychology and Alchemy*, in which he would have come across Jung's conclusion that willful disregard of the latent mythic power of Dionysus in Western society "has served to throw the gates of hell wide open" (143). Davies is trying to make us hear the music of Dionysus again through the lyre of Orpheus, which, instead of engulfing folk in a hellish inferno, guides them into the archetypal underworld of the collective unconscious. In *What's Bred in the Bone* and *Murther and Walking Spirits*, Davies prefers to see that world of the psyche or soul as the Realm of the Mothers; there, in Dionysian sub-, or interior contexts, one is bound to meet the Great Goddess personified variously, for example, as Eurydice, Demeter and Persephone.[38]

The mysteries of Dionysus, Demeter and related divinities, however, "were a personal, but not necessarily a spiritual, form of religion" (Burkert 87); they were fraught with variations, paradoxes and enigmatic initiations, yet they provided individuals with "doors to a secret that might open up for those who earnestly sought it" (Burkert 114), doors that have been used for a long time by creative writers exploring the infinitude of the individual psyche. That is why such writers are among the best answerers to the inevitably open questions about Dionysus (Henrichs 42). Davies, as I have tried to show, is one of them. Since his answers are conveniently predicated on his fondness for literary alcohol, they, not surprisingly, also include the occasional whiff of hellfire and brimstone, of alcoholism, crime, and dangerous otherness. I am thinking, for instance, of the boozing Padre Blazon, the murderer Charlie Iredale, the murderer and suicide John Parlabane, and, reluctantly, Darcourt, for whom the roles of servant to Dionysus and Devil's advocate seem somewhat interchangeable. The symbolism of *demon rum* and the *good creature* is inevitably ambiguous business, and the old adage *in vino veritas* is slant enough even at the most cordial of times. It is perhaps worth remembering that the career of Thomas Mann's confidence man Felix Krull, a favourite with Davies, began in his father's wine cellars but ended in prison, and that Francis Cornish thinks of his final experience of physical death as "transporting wine" (*BB* 523), a decidedly provocative analogy to the barrels of wine in which his faked masterpieces were smuggled out of Germany into England.

In today's Ontario, of course, the motif of alcohol may be losing much of its "generative magic"[39] as a symbol, not only because of the easy availability of wines and spirits but also because of considerable agitation for a new temperance movement in North America, this time under the auspices of standardised health rather than standardised religion.[40] Thus, Davies' symbolic Dionysian sunshine, although an intricate part of his defence of the unstandardised Menippean imagination in the lives of both men and women, will likely remain culturally problematic. His rhetoric of alcohol, however, is far from empty, and to see that does not, I think, require first "a reasonable consumption of port and Madeira" with the High Table select at Massey College (*High Spirits* 43). What may appear to be rhetorical empties on his Dionysian platter of plenty are, in most cases, teasing and still fermenting specimens of what Davies routinely calls the "tricky bits in [his] books."[41] They may be as deceptively simple as Zadok Hoyle's mantra, "Life's a rum start" (*BB* 166 and elsewhere), as seemingly sober as Sir Benedict Domdaniel's *bon mot* that "experience is wine and art is the brandy we distill from it" (*MF* 137), and as capricious as Jonathan Hullah's aside about the way "the Government of Ontario used to sell spirits–usually rye or scotch–in three sizes of bottles: the Baby Bear (12 oz.), the Momma Bear (24 oz.), and the Daddy Bear (40 oz.)" (*CM* 421). There is, in my mind, no quirkier passage than Hullah's to show Davies' readiness to take the mickey out of the kind of critic who might write intemperately to the LCBO for clarification on "Bears" and the kind who is unprepared to see, as it were, the golden locks and other masks of Dionysus in his fiction.

## NOTES

1. Robertson Davies, *The Diary of Samuel Marchbanks*. 1947. *The Papers of Samuel Marchbanks* (New York: Viking, 1986), 192.

2. Robertson Davies, *Leaven of Malice*. 1954. (Markham, Ont.: Penguin, 1980), 52; and *A Mixture of Frailties*. 1958. (Markham: Penguin, 1980), 13.

3. Robertson Davies, *The Lyre of Orpheus*. 1988. (Markham, Ont.: Penguin, 1989), 242.

4. Robertson Davies, *World of Wonders* (Toronto: Macmillan, 1975), 184.

5. Robertson Davies, *Tempest-Tost*. 1951. (Harmondsworth: Penguin, 1982), 5.

6. Robertson Davies, *The Cunning Man* (Toronto: McClelland & Stewart, 1994), 32.

7. Thomas B. Gilmore, *Equivocal Spirits: Alcoholism and Drinking in Twentieth-Century Literature* (North Carolina: University of North Carolina Press, 1987), 3-7.

8. See Robertson Davies, *Murther and Walking Spirits*. 1991. (Markham, Ont.: Penguin, 1992), 293, 389.

9. Eric Single et al. "The Alcohol Policy Debate in Ontario in the Post-War Era." *The Social History of Control Policy in Seven Countries* (Toronto: Addiction Research Foundation, 1981), 140, 141, 147. Currently, most beers and wines sold in Ontario contain five and twelve percent alcohol, respectively; whisky and other distilled spirits contain forty percent. "Native wine" was wine made solely from "Ontario grown grapes or cherries and sugar" (see below, F.P. Brennan's *The Liquor Control Act*).

78

10. "Marchbanks's Garland," *Papers*, 385-538.

11. F.P. Brennan, *The Liquor Control Act. Ontario. Annotated* (Toronto: Canada Law Book Company, 1928), 144.

12. Carolyn Abraham, "Liquor Profits Make Tories Reconsider Privatizing LCBO," *Ottawa Citizen* (20 May 1997): F1-F2.

13. Judith Skelton Grant, *Robertson Davies: Man of Myth* (Toronto: Viking, 1994), 535, 239.

14. Nicholas O. Warner, *Spirits of America: Intoxication in Nineteenth-Century American Literature* (Norman: University of Oklahoma Press, 1997), 26-27.

15. Robertson Davies, *One Half of Robertson Davies* (Toronto: Macmillan, 1977), 175.

16. Regarding his own writing, Davies says, "I don't write any better for a few drinks" (see Roper 28).

17. Robertson Davies, "A Classic at Christmas," *Saturday Night* (December 25, 1954): 10-11.

18. In a comparable situation, the last page of Davies' essay "Keeping Faith," the final contribution in the "One Hundredth Anniversary Issue" of *Saturday Night*, is followed by a whole-page advertisement for Crown Royal whisky.

19. François Rabelais, *Gargantua and Pantagruel*, trans. J.M. Cohen (Franklin: The Franklin Library, 1982), 37, 601.

20. Robertson Davies, *What's Bred in the Bone*. 1985. (Markham, Ont.: Penguin, 1986), 5.

21. Robertson Davies, *The Table-Talk of Samuel Marchbanks* (Toronto: Viking, 1986), 259-60.

22. Stephen Leacock, *Literary Lapses*. 1910. (Toronto: McClelland & Stewart, 1957), 99.

23. See Robertson Davies, *The Manticore* (Toronto: Macmillan, 1972), 18-19.

24. Betty Lee, *Love and Whiskey: The Story of the Dominion Drama Festival* (Toronto: McClelland & Stewart, 1973), 251.

25. See also Mary Hallett and Marilyn Davis, *Firing the Heather: The Life and Times of Nellie McClung* (Saskatoon: Fifth House, 1993), 282.

26. Robertson Davies, *High Spirits* (Harmondsworth: Penguin, 1982), 115-126.

27. Albert Henrichs, "'He Has a God in Him': Human and Divine in the Modern Perception of Dionysus," *Masks of Dionysus*, ed. Thomas H. Carpenter et al. (Ithaca, N.Y.: Cornell University Press, 1993), 13.

28. Helen P. Foley, *The Homeric Hymn to Demeter* (Princeton, N.J.: Princeton University Press, 1993), 84.

29. See Thomas H. Carpenter and Christopher A. Faraone, editors of *Masks of Dionysus* (Ithaca, N.Y.: Cornell University Press, 1993). N.F. Richardson, in his introductory comments to *The Homeric Hymn to Demeter*, allows for a connection between Dionysus and a cornucopia or horn of plenty (26, 27).

30. Fritz Graf, "Dionysian and Orphic Eschatology: New Texts and Old Questions." *Masks of Dionysus* (Ithaca, N.Y.: Cornell University Press), 242-243.

31. Froma I. Zeitlin, "Staging Dionysus between Thebes and Athens." *Masks of Dionysus* (Ithaca, N.Y.: Cornell University Press), 178.

32. François Lissargue, "On the Wildness of Satyrs," *Masks of Dionysus* (Ithaca, N.Y.: Cornell University Press), 215.

33. Larissa Bonfante, "Fufluns Pacha: the Etruscan Dionysus," *Masks of Dionysus*, (Ithaca, N.Y.: Cornell University Press), 231-32.

34. Euripides, *The Bacchae*, trans. Michael Cacoyannis (New York: Meridian, 1987), 15.

35. James Hillman, *The Myth of Analysis* (New York: Harper Perennial, 1992), 295.

36. Patricia Köster, "'Promptings Stronger' than 'Strict Prohibitions': New Forms of Natural Religion in the Novels of Robertson Davies," *Canadian Literature* 111 (Winter 1986): 77.

37. Carl Gustav Jung, *Psychology and Alchemy*, vol. 12, *The Collected Works of C.G. Jung: Second Edition*, ed. Herbert Read et al., trans. R.F.C. Hull (Princeton, N.J.: Princeton University Press, 1968), 143.

38. Barbara G. Walker, *The Woman's Encyclopedia of Myths and Secrets* (San Francisco: Harper Collins, 1983), 218-19.

39. I have borrowed this term from William Covino, who suggests that "magic can be generative or arresting, a mode of creating novel possibilities for action or a mode of constraint" (21).

40. David J. Pittman, "The New Temperance Movement," *Society, Culture, and Drinking Patterns Reexamined*, ed. David J. Pittman and Helene Raskin White (New Brunswick, N.J.: Rutgers Centre of Alcohol Studies, 1991), 775-90.

41. Elizabeth Sifton, "Interview with Robertson Davies," *Robertson Davies: An Appreciation*, ed. Elspeth Cameron (Peterborough, Ont.: Broadview, 1991), 24.

## WORKS CITED

Burkert, Walter. *Ancient Mystery Cults*. Cambridge: Harvard University Press, 1987.

Carpenter, Thomas H. and Christopher A. Faraone, eds. *Masks of Dionysus*. Ithaca, N.Y.: Cornell University Press, 1993.

Covino, William A. *Magic, Rhetoric, and Literacy: An Eccentric History of the Composing Imagination*. Albany: State University of New York Press, 1994. Davies, Robertson. *The Rebel Angels*. Markham, Ont.: Penguin, 1983.

Hoffmann, Ernst Theodor Amadeus. Review of Beethoven's *Fifth Symphony, Opus 67*. 1810. *Music Through Sources and Documents*. Ed. Ruth Halle Rowen. Englewood Cliffs, N.J.: Prentice-Hall, 1979.

Mann, Thomas. *Confessions of Felix Krull, Confidence Man*. Trans. Denver Lindley. New York: Vintage, 1969.

# Metadrama and Melodrama: Postmodern Elements in the Plays of Robertson Davies

## LOIS SHERLOW

Robertson Davies' first play, *Three Gypsies*, a romantic comedy set in Wales, was written during Davies' final year at Oxford (1937-1938), just before his brief first career as a theatre professional.[1] Davies did not apply himself seriously, however, to becoming a playwright until 1944, when he could foresee a post-war resumption of theatrical activity both in Europe and Canada. He developed his craft in what he himself later called "the primitive era of Canadian theatre."[2] In the 1940s and early 1950s in Canada, opportunities for professional production of new plays were almost non-existent; the only critics available to assess and promote Davies' early works were the adjudicators of the Ottawa Drama League and the Dominion Drama Festival, who, to their credit, did advance the cause of Canadian drama by awarding him several prizes for playwriting.[3] But, more to the point, Davies was staging his early plays for Canadian audiences that had no conception of indigenous dramaturgy: their theatrical sense was based on European tradition. "Audiences were not warm to Canadian plays," he later recalled, citing a remark overheard before an early performance of *At My Heart's Core*: "'I suppose this is another of those damned Canadian plays that we have to encourage.'"[4]

On the other hand, as a beginning playwright, Davies did not know who his audience was, and he had to struggle to find out. At first, he did not regard himself as a specifically Canadian playwright. Instead he hoped to find his audience in England, where he had made influential theatrical contacts before the war. *The King Who Could Not Dream* (1944) and *Benoni* (1944) were read–but

82

refused production–respectively by John Gielgud (with whom Davies had worked while still a student at Oxford) and Sybil Thorndike (who had received Davies' script from Tyrone Guthrie) (Stone-Blackburn 11). In 1947, Davies sent Gielgud a play derived from Geoffrey of Monmouth: the protagonist was King Cole, whom Davies depicted as a fertility god, and his antagonist an archdruid, Cadno. Gielgud refused the script on two counts: because "the mystical era was difficult to realize in the concrete form of theatre" and because "people would probably think it was about Churchill and Clement Attlee" (48). Ironically, however, *King Phoenix*, deemed too obscure or too susceptible to misinterpretation for London–or indeed, as a beginner's play, not well enough written–was neither rejected, nor withheld, on any such grounds in script-starved Canada. Herbert Whittaker took on the play and, in 1948, directed it with a cast of Toronto amateurs; Davies himself presented it to his home audience in Peterborough in 1951.

At the same time that Davies was hoping to succeed on the London stage with his more mythical plays, he was also dramatizing, in *Hope Deferred* (1945) and *Overlaid* (1946), the specifically Canadian subject of cultural impoverishment and repression, which found further expression in *Fortune, My Foe* (1949) and *At My Heart's Core* (1950). Despite the topicality of these four plays, their critical successes and their frequent performances by Canadian amateur groups, it is arguable that their author never really understood his Canadian audience. Unlike his theatrical contemporary, Gratien Gélinas, for instance, and unlike the creators of the later alternative theatre, Davies did not cultivate elements of realism or populism in his drama, preferring instead to convey his cultural polemic in romantic and satirical modes, usually with a strong literary tone. The abstractness of *Question Time* (1975), that later elaborate allegory of Canadian identity, destiny, and moral responsibility staged at the St. Lawrence Centre in 1975, seems to affirm that Davies had cultivated an egotistical separateness from the new Canadian audience that developed with an emerging professional theatre that was making a break from the international canon. Indeed, Davies maintained a strong resistance to most influential contemporary movements in theatre.

In *A Masque of Mr. Punch* (1962), Davies uses Punch to represent an old-fashioned theatricality that, to his mind, affronts and confounds all the playwriting styles and critical criteria of the time. A playwright called Samuel Bucket, author of "the drama of Nothingness," comes under more fire than most in the masque.[5] In *Fortune, My Foe*, Davies satirises left-wing ideologists who would use theatre to purvey political "messages."[6] Davies consistently wants to value theatricality above ideology, just as he values romance over realism. He often idealises the notion of a theatre of feeling, not intellect: hence, his fondness for melodrama and myth. Although he often asserts that humour is the natural vehicle for his sense of the vital spirit, his plays, even when they are trying to be uproarious, are overburdened with moralizing messages: most of the characters sound like the playwright, and most are as articulate.[7] Patricia Monk goes beyond the moralizing tone of the plays to their form and their possible precursors. She convincingly argues that Davies' drama has much in common with medieval morality plays, even though they propound "individual morality" instead of Christian doctrine.[8] It appears to be that as a theatrical moralist, Davies, to the last of his plays (*Pontiac and the Green Man* [1977]), takes perverse pride in resisting late-modern dramatic forms on the grounds that they are, in his view at least, either nihilistic or propagandist. Equally, he shows resistance in his plays, as elsewhere, to all current political and scientific discourses.

It is hardly surprising, then, that there has been no real critical attempt to relate Davies' plays to developments in Canadian theatre. Only Mavor Moore, in his monograph *Four Canadian Playwrights* (1973), seems to recognise the importance of making such a relation in that he presents Davies in the company of his contemporary Gratien Gélinas, as well as James Reaney (whose preoccupations and style would bear some comparison with those of Davies) and George Ryga (who could be considered the polar opposite of Davies in early contemporary Canadian dramaturgy). Susan Stone-Blackburn, thorough though she is in her analysis of the plays themselves, is too eager to dismiss the relevance of the contemporary dramatic context. When she sets out to account for the failure of the Jungian Casanova play *General Confession* (1956) to be produced, she ironically and dismissively generalises the aims of modern drama in order to make exaggerated claims for her subject's dramaturgical stature: "[The play] is not about the trapped and limited twentieth-century everyman who apparently defines and reflects the limits of human aspiration today; accordingly its style is not restrained, but flamboyant. . . . These are . . . sins against current fashion, not against criteria for a dramatic masterpiece" (151-52). Their literariness, as well as their author's literary success, has led to the viewing of Davies' plays as literature in dramatic form rather than as theatre. They are certainly not part of the evolution of the new (and strongly anti-literary) theatre that came into being in the 1960s. Davies was not comfortable with the new theatre and, in the 1980s, unapologetically declared his own plays "old-fashioned" (Perkyns, foreword). Theatre itself, however, has evolved beyond both absurdism and the populism common in the 1960s and 1970s to new forms. Classical literary texts and cultural history have become indispensable elements in the postmodern dramaturgy of recent years. I should like to propose that, although Davies' dramaturgy did not harmonise with the alternative theatre movement of the 1970s, it does demonstrate, on the other hand, some fundamental features in common with the Canadian theatre of the 1980s and 1990s.

The similarity to postmodern–and equally for the purposes of this argument, postcolonial–theatre is suggested above all by the extreme metatheatricality of Davies' work. What qualifies as metatheatre–or metadrama–has been variously defined. Broadly, as Richard Hornby puts it, "it occurs whenever the subject of a play turns out to be in some sense, drama itself . . . a playwright is constantly drawing on his knowledge of drama as a whole (and ultimately culture as a whole) as his 'vocabulary' or his 'subject matter.'"[9] Hornby goes so far as to suggest that "*all* drama is metadramatic, since its subject is always the drama/culture complex." Metadrama, in the form of a play within a play and many other devices, acts as a form of estrangement: Brecht's *Verfremdungseffekt* is a familiar example (31). Joanne Tompkins theorises a specifically postcolonial version: "If metatheatre 're-uses' or 're-cycles' theatre, then in the postcolonial context it should be possible to see [it] as a strategy of resistance . . . often a self-conscious method of re-negotiating, re-working–not just re-playing–the past and the present."[10] The relevance of the theories of Hornby and Tompkins to Davies' theatre is readily apparent: from the beginning of his career he demonstrates a strong tendency to enjoy the self-referentiality of theatre and to manipulate the drama/culture complex as far as his invention allows–and not only in his plays–in the interest of estranging unexamined habits of perception common in Canadian society.

Davies became a playwright after several years of both scholarship and theatrical practice at the heart of the British cultural establishment. He had moved back from the centre of the old English-speaking world to unmapped cultural territory. Canada in the 1940s has been defined by Robert Kroetsch as already a postmodern country, by virtue of its marginality: "The centredness of the high modern period . . . made us irrelevant to history. . . . Canada was invisible."[11] As European domination gave way to that of the United States and the USSR in the post-war period, other countries were forced to find a position in the new order; and so, according to Kroetsch, a "willingness to refuse privilege to a restricted or restrictive cluster of meta-narratives [became] a Canadian strategy for survival" (23). When Davies wrote *Fortune, My Foe* in 1948, he was not merely satirizing the philistines of Kingston, as has sometimes been supposed, but also engaging with much more awesome forces–the metanarratives of the two world powers that threatened to overwhelm the artistic traditions of Europe. The refugee puppeteer of the play, Franz Szabo, is significantly Czech: the threat posed by Canadian philistines is nothing to him compared with the ideological and political forces that have already impinged on his culture and art. The anti-artistic forces of the new world order (the twin threats of American and Russian ideological dominance) intermingle with those present in the local culture at Chilly Steele's "equivocal establishment" at the margins of Kingston (13). All parties are brought together there to witness the windmill scene from a puppet play of Don Quixote, presented by Szabo.

The performance causes the bar to become an ideological battleground. Davies here employs what Tompkins calls "counter-discursive metatheatre," which "re-writes (or re-presents) a classical text or part thereof" and thereby "assists in the re-reading and re-structuring and re-situating of the larger 'base' play" (42-45). In the third act of *Fortune, My Foe*, Davies' audience must watch two plays at once. In the outer play, a young academic, Nicholas Hayward, is considering seeking employment in the United States, as he believes, to satisfy his girlfriend Vanessa; his older friend Idris Rowlands, also an academic, counters the young man's idealism with an embittered pragmatism born of hard experience. The "windmills" of the outer play are the would-be communist propagandist Ursula Simonds and two local pseudo-artistic mediocrities, Orville Tapscott and Mattie Philpott, all of whom have been invited to see the puppet play with a view to offering its presenter paid employment and exposure. Simonds finds the play "no good because it has no message," while Tapscott and Philpott are appalled by what they perceive to be immoral and indecent attitudes implicit in the action (90-92). These responses are intrinsic to Davies' dramatic strategy, as is that of Rowlands, who destroys the puppet theatre rather than see it desecrated by the philistines.

Tompkins' theory of postcolonial metatheatre may be aptly applied to the strategies Davies employs in *Fortune, My Foe*: "A play-within-a-play acts immediately as a device which *draws* attention: it mimics and reflects the original . . . but the meaning is refracted. When the actors on the stage watch the action, the audience's gaze is split, and paradoxically, multiplied, to further foreground the act of re-visioning. . . . [Such] plays demonstrate a specularity that is . . . the location of difference, ambivalence, and resistance" (45). Thus Rowlands' destruction of the puppet theatre and his ejection of the three ideologues, Simonds, Tapscott, and Philpott, invite a radical re-visioning in the outer play of Don Quixote as a representation of colonial resistance and self-assertion in the face of the United States and other superpowers. At this level, the analogy to Quixote's actions is no longer Nicholas' devotion to his patently shallow girlfriend's aspirations, but instead is re-conceived as his new commitment to stay and work in Canada, which commitment reflects and mimics the established intentions of Szabo. At the same time, at another level of metatheatricality, Davies uses the presentation of the Don Quixote scene to prove his commitment to the belief "that Realism in the theatre is a dead end" ("Jung" 146). *Fortune, My Foe* is the most realistic of Davies' plays, yet even here he uses realism only to undermine it: romance triumphs over realism not only in Quixote's story but in that of Nicholas Hayward. The play also demonstrates how absurdly unsuitable are small-mindedness and playing safe as strategies for survival in the new postmodern (and postcolonial) world: while Tapscott and Philpott will not look into the face of the enemy, Davies insists that his audience, like Nicholas Hayward, do so instead.

*Fortune, My Foe* was produced over a hundred times before 1967, its success during that time, as Stone-Blackburn notes, "no doubt due to its topicality" (70). Most other plays by Davies (*Overlaid* and *Eros at Breakfast* excepted) have been more ephemeral, precisely because they lack the element of realism that would make their topicality accessible. Excessively fanciful as most of the other plays are, they do, nevertheless, employ essentially the same counter-discursive strategies of metatheatrical, postcolonial resistance that are evident in *Fortune, My Foe*.

In *A Jig for a Gypsy* (1955), written for the professional Crest Theatre in 1954, the story of Benoni's reading of the politicians' tea leaves also serves to resist debased personal narratives: those of the politicians, both Liberal and Tory, who covet her assurances. The curious and sudden marriage of Benoni and Conjuror Jones at the end of the play is a dramatically awkward attempt to consolidate spiritual forces in the face of the material concerns of more worldly characters.

In *Hunting Stuart* (1955), Davies begins to use metatheatre more obviously as a vehicle for the psychological integration of the protagonist. A minor bureaucrat, Ben Stuart is told by visiting behavioural scientists, specialists in royal genealogy and traits, that he is the pretender to the British throne, by virtue of his apparent descent from Bonnie Prince Charlie. In view of this revelation, he is forced to find the means to resist not only the scientific excesses of Drs. Shrubsole and Sobieska, who wish to make him into a royal guinea pig, but also the half-baked psychological theories of his future son-in-law Fred (revealed through a magically induced trance to be descended from a charlatan of the old-fashioned kind). In addition, Ben Stuart must deal with the bourgeois dedication of his wife, Lilian, the daughter of an Arnprior postmaster, to using her own very tenuous genealogical connections to the nobility of the old country as a means of social climbing. A magical powder induces Stuart to become, for a while, his own lusty, uninhibited ancestor. His dramatic predicament, comparable with that of the Prime Minister in *Question Time*, is that he must decide whether or not to betray the Queen (both constitutional and psychic) and his wife alike by pursuing his claim to kingship–and, symbolically, to reclaim his right to be his own man. The result of Ben's new-found self-consciousness and psychic integration, gained through magical experiences of his other self, the pretender, is that he is seen at the end of the play, with telephone in hand, about to book his flight to Scotland.

In *Hunting Stuart,* instead of inserting a theatrical performance into the action as he does in *Fortune, My Foe*, Davies has progressed to using the device of magic–as he later would also do in *General Confession* (1962) and *Question Time*–to reveal hidden dimensions of consciousness. By this means, the protagonist may come to know his present limitations and recognise in himself the suppressed powers that will facilitate his transformation. In this play, the magic potion that can evoke ancestral powers in its consumer establishes clearly for the first time Davies' notion, most elaborately explored thirty years later in *What's Bred in the Bone* (1985), that, "for all the emphasis on environment in our modern social-psychological assessment of people, heredity is an undeniable, though perhaps concealed, factor in making us what we are" (Stone-Blackburn 126). Toward the end of the play, Fred states it explicitly: "Heredity is the old house we have over our heads; environment is the junk we put into it" (99). Davies thus uses this play to demonstrate once again–but in new terms–the difference between superficial material concerns, as well as faddish ideology, and the true source of the individual's potential: his own inherent qualities.

The metatheatricality of Davies' favourite (albeit unproduced) play, *General Confession* (1962), is differently structured from that of preceding plays. Here the playwright is less concerned with resistance to materialism and current ideology and more interested in the dramatisation of psychic wholeness itself. In this play, Davies consciously aims for a Jungian dramatisation of his hero Casanova's process of self-recognition. The framing play mirrors the inner action, which is much more prominent than that in earlier plays. The action begins as a seducer, his intended victim and a common-sense servant all intrude into Count Waldstein's library, of which Casanova was, at the end of his life, the custodian. Casanova is thus able to be a character in both inner and outer plays. Instead of presenting the originally planned seduction, the play metatheatrically enacts Casanova's encounters with his former selves, personified archetypally by three doubles, Voltaire, Cagliostro, and the Ideal Beloved. The dramatic strategy is to make the audience share the responses of on-stage spectators of Casanova's inner drama and, with them, as well as the protagonist himself, effect a transformation of their prejudgment of human nature. The aim of Casanova's trial, staged at the end of the play, is to establish that his guilt is no more than "universal guilt" itself (Stone-Blackburn 148).

Hornby defines the primary function of metatheatre as the manipulation of perception. In Davies' plays, as in so many others that use metatheatrical structures, the perceptual changes effected represent the transformation of self-consciousness. Davies' dramatisation of the self's dynamic complexities begins with the whimsy of *Eros at Breakfast* and raises itself to a more political form in *Fortune, My Foe*. It culminates in the last of Davies' plays, *Question Time*, and the unpublished "Pontiac and the Green Man," which deals with Major Robert Rogers as man of action, visionary, and dramatist. The more important of these two late plays is *Question Time*, because it represents an extraordinary shift in Davies' sense of theatricality. Given that it was commissioned for the St. Lawrence Centre's theatre program, the play's style and structure are partially the result of the availability of a large budget and superior technical resources. These factors, however, do not entirely account for the complexity of its conception, which is Davies' response to Canada's expanding sense of its own identity, so vastly changed since the writing of *Fortune, My Foe* and *At My Heart's Core*. In *Question Time*, the playwright deploys sound, light, video, elaborate costumes, and a split-level set to effect a complex interplay between a mythic realm (the Arctic) and political ritual (the question time of the title). No sign is single in this play: the Prime Minister argues with his own double, who is both the Leader of the Opposition and the Prime Minister's other self; the

Arctic shaman who leads the Prime Minister through his process of integration is also a physician with a degree from Edinburgh University; the national animal, the beaver, is at the same time a conventionally dressed man; the spirit of the land is a woman with the fairy-tale name La Sorcière des Montagnes de Glace, a title that contains its own doubleness, suggesting not only ice but also mirrors–thus symbolizing the reflections and refractions of the metatheatrical structure of the play. Isolated in the Arctic, the Prime Minister (his own double nature as both political leader of his country and a man evident in his name, Peter McAdam) is required to face his own private self and recognise the duality of his public/private life. The play's symbolic complexity and doubleness are intensified to force the audience to reconcile all the semiological differences with which it is presented and, through the hero's process, move toward a final sense of wholeness as the unity of the cultural, civic, and personal dimensions of existence.

Davies' metatheatricality is an alienation device that allows the audience to distinguish, in his words, the "inner life of the psyche" (usually the content of his play-within-a-play) from "the life of the daily papers" ("Jung" 151). In his theatre, as he himself has argued at length, the play of Jungian archetypes is equivalent to melodrama ("Jung" 151). This dramatic form, which has been the backbone of Western theatrical practice since the Renaissance, and is ubiquitous in the age of film, is based on the dynamic of the self enacted at one remove from the demands of society and the state–or, as Davies might prefer, "the life of the daily papers." Metadrama and melodrama, as they have been defined by contemporary theorists, are linked by their common rejection of the tragic conflict. Metadrama exists in the absence of the world, argues Lionel Abel: "[It] assumes there is no world except that created by human striving and imagination."[12] The same assumption also characterises melodrama, which promotes the regaining of wholeness after a battle of good and evil forces (whether in the protagonist's psyche or in a fictionalised environment) as a sufficient dramatic end.[13] Melodrama, in Davies' own words, is "a world of Myth . . . where Poetic Justice, however tardy, would manifest itself after many trials and vicissitudes. It was a world of romance" (*Mirror* 22).

Davies, then, as we have seen, devalues the capacity of realism to serve as an adequate mirror of nature (6). Instead, he argues that the melodrama of the Romantic and post-Romantic periods afforded a better mirror than more objective forms of social realism, by liberating the audience from its daily reality and offering it instead "Oblivion's balm, a forgetfulness of the world of everyday" (23). Melodrama allows the audience to see another dimension of existence, and this is what Abel, in his essay on metatheatre, refers to as "life already theatricalized" (60). (It is evident how closely related melodrama and metatheatre are if Davies' assessment of melodrama as "Oblivion's balm" is set beside Abel's definition of the metadramatic: "In this kind of a play fantasy is essential, it is what one finds at the heart of reality . . . in the metaplay life *must* be a dream and the world *must* be a stage" [79].) Paradoxical as it may seem, Davies' theatre of escapism, inspired by the nineteenth-century stage and evident in his own dramaturgy, is far from incompatible with the aims of contemporary theatre. Davies, as well as Abel, recognises in a self-referential theatre of dreams and fantasy the capacity to engage an audience in a degree of "metaphysical wonder" (85). It is often this kind of theatre that is favoured by postmodern dramatists, whose preoccupations differ radically from those of their predecessors of the 1960s and 1970s.

In contrast to the dramatists of the nationalist period, who aimed for a degree of social objectivity and primarily investigated communal identity, those of the 1980s and 1990s have tended to reject social realism–much as Davies did, and possibly for similar reasons. Chantal Hébert, assessing theatre in Québec since 1980, has examined this shift:

> The imagination of the collective project has . . . given way to the introspective questioning of the artist. If there were in fact one theme that took center stage . . . it was that of artistic creation. . . . The search for identity passes into the very act of writing, of recounting one's self . . . . This contemplation of self is no longer concerned with the question "Who am I?" . . . very much part of the great socio-political problematic . . . [of] the 1970s . . . [but] centers on "What am I doing?" The young . . . writers of today raise questions with respect to themselves and their function as artists in society.[14]

The turn toward representation of the "totally subjective," Hébert argues, indicates "a crisis of reality, or rather the death of reality in reality, as defined by traditional artistic codes" (41). This current preoccupation with the role of the artist has also been noted by Gilbert David, who argues that, as playwrights liberate themselves from the metanarratives of nationalism and Marxism, they still adhere to one metanarrative that survives in the postmodern era, albeit imbued with some scepticism: "l'émancipation du Sujet à travers l'art, à condition . . . de ne pas y chercher matière à consolation."[15] This quest for the self in art, argues David, is both a return to the modernist self-reflexivity of, for example, Pirandello, and, at the same time, the incorporation of heterogeneous elements (among them melodrama and parody), which serve to dispose of "des solutions de facilité (linéarité, psychologisme, naturalisme)" (156). If this latter project–the relativisation of modernist textual characteristics–can be set aside, together with the pessimistic turn of postmodernism, what remains of contemporary dramaturgy is evidently similar in its aim to Davies' project, as it is exemplified in *Overlaid, Fortune, My Foe, At My Heart's Core*, and, eventually, *Question Time*. In post-war Canada, which Kroetsch terms postmodern on account of its "invisibility" in "a high modern world with its privileged stories," Davies chose not to depict Canadian society in a realistic way, but rather to explore the very emancipation of the subject through art cited by David as the one remaining metanarrative in the postmodern era.

One need not look far in contemporary theatre to find metatheatre and melodrama employed to isolate the subject–often the subject as artist–from social reality. Some of the most prominent and powerful scripts of recent years have been the most self-reflexive and anti-realistic, especially, but not exclusively, in the theatre of Québec. In Michel Marc Bouchard's *Les Feluettes ou la Répétition d'un drame romantique* (1988), a priest, the director of a college production of D'Annunzio's "passion play" *The Martyrdom of St. Sebastian*, offers his intensely melodramatic view of the stage: "Au théâtre, on peut tout faire. . . . On peut être amoureux, jaloux, fou, tyran ou possédé . . . on peut mourir d'amour, de haine, de passion."[16] Within the doubly metatheatrical structure of Bouchard's play, the inner drama does indeed give rise to such passions–and a murder–among its cast. In a similar vein, in Normand Chaurette's *Provincetown Playhouse, juillet 1919, j'avais 19 ans* (1981), an institutionalised playwright infinitely re-enacts his own melodrama, "Le Théâtre de l'Immolation de la beauté," in which, years earlier, he had presented a real, in place of fictional, murder of a child.

In contrast to these two plays, both of which achieve their effect by confining the melodrama within outer frameworks and thus intensifying it, the theatrical scripts of Robert Lepage offer a very expansive, highly spatialised representation of the artist-subject; but here, too, the artifice of theatre is valorised over social reality. In *Vinci* (1987), Lepage transforms himself, through a series of ingenious illusions, from a Canadian visitor to Europe into Leonardo da Vinci. In *Plaques tectoniques/Tectonic Plates* (1987-89), he creates a complex nexus of relationships between contemporary North-American culture, pre-Christian Gaelic myth, and European Romanticism, to re-map the world of the Québec artist: the result is an intercontinental tapestry that, despite its postmodern decentredness, recalls Davies' own cultural mapping. A third work of Lepage, *Alanienouidet* (1992), dramatises the visit in 1826 of Edmund Kean to Québec, where he was invested as a chief by the Wyandot Indians of the area. Following his visit to the Wyandot community, Kean "according to his own later version of the story, went quite mad for a few days."[17] Kean's "madness" is dramatised here in a wilderness encounter with a shaman. Lepage's collaborator explains how the script arrived at its thematic core: "Madness . . . 'how to die' [became] the search for identity. In exploring Kean's state, we went through self destruction, to an identity crisis, to the wretched conditions of his birth in a whorehouse: civilisation *versus* purity" (Ackermann 34). Kean's spiritual death-and-resurrection among the Wyandot in the Canadian wilderness is strikingly similar to the Arctic self-confrontation of Prime Minister Peter McAdam in *Question Time*. Both plays present the destruction of the public persona for the purpose of psychic integration.

While these contemporary plays serve to provide some formal parallels to the explorations of the individual psyche and cultural position in Davies' plays, all of them lack Davies' characteristic comic stance. One contemporary script, Ann-Marie MacDonald's *Goodnight Desdemona (Good Morning Juliet)* (1990), stands out as strikingly close in spirit to Davies' Jungian "comedy company of the psyche." MacDonald's popular play concerns the attempt of a doctoral candidate, Constance Ledbelly, to prove from an arcane manuscript that Shakespeare intended *Othello* and *Romeo and Juliet* to be comedies: "Constance: 'The fact that [Othello and Romeo] do not save themselves, tends to characterise them as the unwitting victims of a practical joke–rather than the heroic instruments of an inexorable Fate.'"[18] She suspects that a "Wise Fool," erased from earlier plays, has created the "flimsy mistakes"–a lost hanky, a delayed wedding announcement–on which tragic fate depends for its workings (21). By magical means, Constance descends into her own unconscious (the world of the two plays) and redirects the outcome of each tragedy; she discovers that she herself is the Wise Fool, the author whom she sought by this process. The similarity to Davies' notion of drama becomes clear in MacDonald's Jungian framing of the play. The chorus' prologue is explicit: "What's alchemy? The hoax of charlatans?/Or mystic quest for stuff of life itself:/eternal search for the Philosopher's Stone,/where mingling and unmingling opposites,/ transforms base metal into precious gold./Hence, scientific metaphor of self:/divide the mind's opposing archetypes/–if you possess the courage for the task–/invite them from the shadows to the light;/unite these lurking shards of broken glass/into a mirror that reflects one soul" (13). In the epilogue, there are further echoes of the comic language of Davies' theatre of the unconscious: "The alchemy of ancient hieroglyphs/has permeated the unconscious mind/of Constance L. and manifested form,/where once there was subconscious dreamy thought./The best of friends and foes exist within,/where archetypal shadows come to light/and doff their monster masks when we say 'boo'" (87). MacDonald's script is primarily designed to turn the tragic action over to the heroines instead of the heroes, and in the process cause the audience to revise gender roles in Shakespeare; but in order to achieve this, as promised by the chorus, she creates a mischievous, alchemical play of archetypes, which resolves itself in a marriage of opposites. This play has achieved its popularity through a plot that is very similar in its playfulness to those of Davies (although admittedly his plays exhibit less formal flexibility than his novels). Davies' assessment of his plays as "old-fashioned" seems somewhat ironic in light of the success of MacDonald's Jungian comedy (Perkyns, vii). MacDonald, however, writes for an audience already jaundiced by realism, whereas Davies wrote his plays just as realism became a necessity for contemporary audiences, who were interested in art rather than in reflections of their society and culture, a novelty in Canada at the time.

Davies the playwright is like many postmodern playwrights in his dedication to staging (meta)theatrical games, in which the illusionistic confounding of two or more levels of reality brings about a transformation of self-perception and a final sense of having explored the totality of the subject. The wholeness depicted is pure fiction; it, too, is metatheatrical in that it refers to the integrity of the work, not that of the psyche. The postmodernists not only acknowledge but intensify the fiction, often pursuing, as David has pointed out, a vertiginous degree of relativisation and scepticism in their work (151). Where Davies is clearly not postmodern is in his complete faith in the notion of psychic wholeness, and in his insistence on a single interpretation of his plays. In a Davies play, as in a Davies novel, the authorial voice always eventually overrides the play of difference. It is never the illusionists–such as the puppeteer Szabo, Benoni the gypsy and her partner Conjuror Jones, Cagliostro, or the Sorcière des Montagnes de Glace–who have the last word. In Davies, it is always the moralist, not the magician, who prevails.

## NOTES

1. Susan Stone-Blackburn, *Robertson Davies, Playwright: A Search for the Self on the Canadian Stage* (Vancouver: University of British Columbia Press, 1985), 8.

2. Richard Perkyns, foreword to *Major Plays of the Canadian Theatre 1934-1984* (Toronto: Clarke, Irwin, 1984), vii.

3. For accounts of Davies' involvement with amateur theatre, see Stone-Blackburn and Lee. Davies himself said of the Dominion Drama Festival: "Though the DDF never succeeded in bringing a Canadian drama into being, it kept the whole country aware of what was being done in world theatre. . . . The time had to be right for audiences to accept the Canadian writer. Unfortunately they were not ready during the years of the DDF. It was nobody's fault really." In Betty Lee, *Love and Whiskey: The Story of the Dominion Drama Festival* (Toronto: McClelland & Stewart, 1973), xi, 298.

4. Robertson Davies, *At My Heart's Core* (Toronto: Clarke, Irwin, 1950); and *Overlaid* (Toronto: Clarke, Irwin, 1955), vii.

5. Robertson Davies, *A Masque of Mr. Punch* (Toronto: Oxford University Press, 1963), 39.

6. Robertson Davies, *Eros at Breakfast and Other Plays* (Toronto: Clarke, Irwin, 1949), 92.

7. Geraldine Anthony, ed., *Stage Voices: Twelve Canadian Playwrights Talk About Their Lives and Work* (Toronto: Doubleday Canada, 1978), 74; and Robertson Davies, "Jung and the Theatre," *One Half of Robertson Davies* (Harmondsworth: Penguin, 1978). Stephen Bonnycastle (1977) criticises Davies' tendency to combine moralizing with "showmanship" and spectacle in the Deptford novels. His critique of monologism as a means for a character to "[turn] his companions into an audience, and [hold] them because of . . . acknowledged superiority" has some validity with regard to Davies' own tendency to equate playwriting with monologism (39).

8. Patricia Monk, "'Quile Bookis': The Morality Plays of Robertson Davies," *Canadian Drama/L'Art dramatique canadien* 7 (1981): 82.

9. Richard Hornby, *Drama, Metadrama, and Perception* (Lewisburg: Bucknell University Press, 1986), 31.

10. Joanne Tompkins, "'Spectacular Resistance': Metatheatre in Post-Colonial Drama," *Modern Drama* 38 (1995): 42.

11. Robert Kroetsch, "Disunity as Unity: A Canadian Strategy," *The Lovely Treachery of Words: Essays Selected and New* (Toronto: Oxford University Press, 1989), 22.

12. Lionel Abel, *Metatheater: A New View of Dramatic Form* (New York: Hill and Wang, 1963), 113.

13. Robert Bechtold Heilman, *Tragedy and Melodrama: Versions of Experience* (Seattle: University of Washington Press, 1968), 79. Davies argues that the heroes of melodrama–he cites as examples Byron's Manfred and the Flying Dutchman–are archetypes "acting out their accustomed roles" ("Jung" 150). It is interesting to compare this view with that of Heilman: "In the structure of melodrama, man is essentially 'whole'; this word implies neither greatness nor moral perfection, but rather an absence of . . . basic inner conflict. . . . Melodrama accepts wholeness without question; for its purposes, man . . . is not troubled by motives that would distract him from the outer struggle in which he is engaged. He may be humanly incomplete; but his incompleteness is not the issue. It is in tragedy that man is divided; in melodrama, his troubles, though they may reflect some weakness or inadequacy, do not arise from the urgency of (un)reconciled impulses. In tragedy the conflict is within man; in melodrama, it is between men and things. Tragedy is concerned with the nature of man, melodrama with the habits of man. . . . A habit normally reflects a part of nature, and that part functions as if it were a whole. In melodrama we accept the part for the whole; it is a convention of form" (79). Though Davies permits his characters to undergo processes whereby they attain self-consciousness, they are, in the long run, restored to "wholeness" at a psychic level; the audience is left in no doubt that the apprehension of the self's integrity is a better goal than political risk, or any other form of sacrifice. Given Heilman's understanding of melodrama as an absence of conflict, it would seem that Davies' fondness for melodrama is related to the fondness for monologue that he demonstrates in his novels. Bonnycastle asks, "What if monologue is a sign of failure rather than triumph–a sign of isolation, of rightness, of estrangement from a changing world?" (171). If, like the Flying Dutchman, Davies' protagonists maintain their psychic wholeness at the expense of risking loss–including loss of control–then they do indeed operate in a partial manner, maintaining their integrity by the avoidance of conflict with the outer world.

14. Chantal Hébert, "The Theatre: Sounding Board for the Appeals and Dreams of the *Québécois* Collectivity," *Essays in Modern Quebec Theater*, ed. Joseph I. Donohue, Jr., and M. Weiss (Ann Arbor: University of Michigan Press, 1995), 41.

15. Gilbert David, "Dispositifs (post)modernes," *L'Annuaire théâtral* 21 (1997): 146.

16. Michel Marc Bouchard, *Les Feluettes ou la Répétition d'un drame romantique* (Montréal: Leméac, 1988), 130-31.

17. Marianne Ackermann, "'*Alanienouidet*': Simultaneous Space and Action," *Canadian Theatre Review* 70 (1997): 32.

18. Ann-Marie MacDonald, *Goodnight Desdemona (Good Morning Juliet)* (Toronto: Coach House, 1990), 15.

## WORKS CITED

Chaurette, Normand. *Provincetown Playhouse, juillet 1919, j'avais 19 ans*. Montréal: Éditions Leméac, 1981.

Davies, Robertson. *Eros at Breakfast and Other Plays*. Toronto: Clarke, Irwin, 1949.

–. *General Confession*. 1962. In *Hunting Stuart and Other Plays*. Toronto: New Press, 1972.

–. *Happy Alchemy: Writings on the Theatre and Other Lively Arts*. Ed. Jennifer Surridge and Brenda Davies. Toronto: McClelland & Stewart, 1997.

–. *Hope Deferred*. In *Eros at Breakfast and Other Plays*. Toronto: Clarke, Irwin, 1949.

–. *Hunting Stuart and Other Plays*. Toronto: New Press, 1972.

–. *A Jig for a Gypsy*. Toronto: Clarke, Irwin, 1955.

–. *King Phoenix*. 1947. In *Hunting Stuart and Other Plays*. Toronto: New Press, 1972.

–. *The King Who Could Not Dream*. 1945. Unpublished, unperformed.

–. Foreword to *Major Plays of the Canadian Theatre 1934-1984*. Ed. Richard Perkyns. Toronto: Clarke, Irwin, 1984.

–. *The Mirror of Nature*. Toronto: University of Toronto Press, 1983.

–. *Overlaid*. 1950. In *Eros at Breakfast and Other Plays*. With *At My Heart's Core*. Toronto: Simon and Pierre, 1991.

–. *Pontiac and the Green Man*. Unpublished. Performed at the Macmillan Theatre, University of Toronto, October 26, 1977.

–. *Question Time*. Toronto: Macmillan, 1975.

Donohue, Joseph I. Jr., and Jonathan M. Weiss, eds. *Essays in Modern Quebec Theater*. MSU Press Canadian Series 16. East Lansing, Ann Arbor: University of Michigan Press, 1995.

Lepage, Robert, with Marianne Ackermann. *Alanienouidet*. First performed at Théâtre 1774, Montréal, 1992, and National Arts Centre, Ottawa, February 4-29,

1992.

– and Théâtre Repère. *Plaques tectoniques/Tectonic Plates*. First performed Du Maurier World Festival, 1987, and Implanthéâtre, Québec, November 16 – December 9, 1989.

–. *Vinci*. First performed Théâtre de Quat'Sous, Montréal, 1986, and Dumaurier Quay Works, Toronto, January 20, 1988.

Moore, Mavor. *Four Canadian Playwrights*. Toronto: Holt, Rinehart and Winston, 1973.

# "Where There's a Will, There Are Always Two Ways": Doubling in *World of Wonders*

MARK SILVERBERG

In *World of Wonders* there are, as Magnus Eisengrim says, "double words for everything."[1] Like many of Davies' texts, *World of Wonders* is an intricate structure of dialogue and duality wherein Davies continually creates situations, images, and narrative structures that are doubled. Not only are they doubled, but this doubling is done in a duplicitous way. Like Eisengrim himself, who is named after that cunning animal the wolf, Doubles are often there to trick us. I intend to examine this doubling in two ways: in terms of narrative content and narrative structure. In the content phase, I will focus on the circus and theatre sections of the novel, examining images of doubling and considering the role of the uncanny and the grotesque as important preoccupations of the novel. In the narrative phase, I will briefly examine dialogism and double-voicing, as well as what I will call autobiographical duplicity. Finally, I will make some tentative suggestions about why doubling and the Double are key conceptual categories for understanding both *World of Wonders* and The Deptford Trilogy in general.

## The Circus Section

In the first stage of Magnus' story, we begin with what appears to be a series of radical inversions. His first step is from a life as the minister's son, memorizing Psalms, to a perverted life as a slave to Willard; a converted and inverted life as the inner workings of the "idol," Abdullah; and a life of subverted innocence as he sees himself as a Jonah-like figure "in the belly of hell" (111), a castaway from God and from the normal pleasures of childhood. With Paul we enter the subversive world of carnival–with its reversal of the sexes, of sacred and profane, of inner and outer.[2]

The interesting thing about this "second" home with Wanless World of Wonders is that it is not clearly the black flip side of a white past. Though there is a duality set up between these two worlds, there is also a surreptitious duplicity. Paul's first home in Deptford is full of equal, though certainly very different, terrors and humiliations. When we consider the religiously inspired beatings he receives from his father, the shame he feels for his mother, and the "pure malignance" of the neighbourhood children (24), Deptford makes the circus world look not half bad. The two homes, I would suggest, are not opposites but form a strange Double home: they inform each other and rely on each other. Lind remarks on the duplicity between these two worlds when he considers Paul's abduction into the circus: "The Bible obsession must somehow have supported the obsession with the conjuror. Not even a great revelation wipes out a childhood's indoctrination; the two must have come together in some way" (30). If Wanless is a "hell," as Magnus says, then I think we need to see it as a hell that ambiguously attracts as much as it repels. It is a hell that must be passed through to make the transition from Paul Dempster to Magnus Eisengrim.

Paul's entrance into the circus world seems to be a matter of both awful chance and directed compulsion. His encounter with Willard is one of uncanny fate that occurs at a powerful moment of intersecting vulnerability and desire. He says: "I ran off to the fair, and my heart was full of terrible joy. I was wicked, but O what a delicious release it was!" (25). This terrible joy describes the doubleness of Paul's reaction–there is something both wonderful and horrible about breaking taboos, about aligning himself with the devil, with shows that his father calls "utterly evil" (26). I would argue that the whole World of Wonders is permeated with this duplicity, and that readers are also implicated in Paul's ambiguous response. As with the power of real life Freak Shows, the World of Wonders compels attraction and repulsion from its viewers: we want to see, but we know we shouldn't want to. We therefore vicariously participate in Paul's satisfaction in breaking taboos. The more dreadful Paul's story gets, the more compulsively we want to read on. It is this double force of attraction and repulsion when faced with the grotesque or the bizarre that is at the centre of the novel's power. This is the same power that made Freak Shows of all stripes so popular, and that continues in different manifestations, for example, in our fascination with everything from car crashes (à la David Cronenberg) to Siamese twins. Our fascination here is partly with the Double, the other, in whom, with a little imagination, we can clearly see ourselves.

There are many different types of Doubles in the carnivalesque first section of the novel, as is obvious in a character like Andro the Hermaphrodite, who ritualistically neutralises the opposition of male and female in his act where he "wraps himself in his own arms" and we see "a beautiful woman in the arms of a half-naked muscular man, whirling rhythmically around the stage in a rapturous embrace" (99).

Another interesting Double is Rango, the Missing Link, who serves as Heinie's double or shadow, a primitive second self who can behave in ways even more uncivilised than his master. But Rango is more than just a buffoon; he is also Heinie's closest friend and a necessary adjunct to his identity, since without Rango, Heinie has no act and no livelihood. Rango later becomes Em Dark's double when Heinie dresses him in her best clothes and he parades down the hall. This leads to the tragicomic situation where Joe, who looks "like a man who has seen a ghost" (119)–which similitude parallels the description Macgregor later gives of someone who sees his Double in a dark alley–throws a knife, killing Rango. Rango proves to be not only Heinie's Double, but the Double of the circus itself, as his death brings the shadow of death to Sonny, Gus, and Abdullah.

Abdullah, the hideous papier-mâché automaton, is one of the most engaging Doubles of this first section. Abdullah can be seen as Paul's Double, or Paul as Abdullah's, as he describes himself as "the soul of Abdullah" and explains how Abdullah becomes "the face I presented to the world" (110). On the one hand, Abdullah is a sweaty, claustrophobic prison, permeated by "the strong whiff of hot dwarf" (54). Abdullah is the vessel in which Paul is kidnapped, and the dungeon in which he is kept for seven years. Abdullah, however, is much more than just "a very nasty coffin" (111): Magnus also describes it as "my kingdom," noting that within "I was possessed by an intensity of interest and ambition that was better than anything I had ever known in my life" (54). Abdullah offers a perhaps perverse but nonetheless meaningful and exciting occupation. It also offers, ironically enough, a means of escape from an equally stifling and confining life in Deptford. For Paul, this was a life of unmitigated shame as the son of a "hoor" who, in his mind, was also the cause of his mother's ruin. Thus to be anonymous, to be "Nobody" in "the smelly bowels of Abdullah" (61), came as a blessing. As Paul explains, "I very soon came to forget that it was I who was the prisoner: I was the one who saw clearly and saw the truth because I saw without being seen" (110). If Abdullah is a coffin, it is one that offers the possibility of being born again. Abdullah repeats one of the main paradoxes of the novel: to ascend one must descend, to become a master, one must first be a slave. The automaton belongs to a double world: he is responsible both for Paul's most dreadful imprisonment and for his most liberating step toward self-actualisation.

Abdullah is doubled not only from the inside, but also from the outside, as it were, in the reaction he provokes in onlookers. Abdullah is a great hit in the show because "there is something in humanity that is repelled and entranced by a machine that seems to have more than human powers" (60). The spectators' double reaction to Abdullah in the context of the circus, I would suggest, mirrors the readers' reaction to Abdullah in the context of the novel: like the carnival Rubes we are entranced and repelled, amazed and disgusted by this literary spectacle.

I began by talking about the double world of Paul's first and second homes. I would suggest that the two come together in a most uncanny way when Paul meets Willard. Paul's first description of Willard is very instructive in relation to Lind's comment on the double obsession of Bible and Magic. Paul sees Willard as a living embodiment of what is most powerful in the Bible: "For me the Book of Revelations came alive: here was an angel come down from heaven, having great power, and the earth was lightened with his glory; if only I could be like him, surely there would be no more sorrow, nor crying, nor any more pain" (29). The terrible duplicity and irony of these lines are not available to us on the first reading (since the rape scene is still to come)–and yet I think there is a strong sense of foreboding in this first description. Willard is, in a sense, an inverted angel who represents the majesty of everything that has been unrealised and excluded from Paul's first home and first self. Willard is Paul's second self, an uncanny figure who is the possessor of "breathtaking secrets" (27), but whose secrets are in fact strangely familiar, since they represent the most powerful and forbidden desires of the first self: "I longed with my whole soul to know what Willard knew. As the hart pants after the water brooks, even so my blasphemous soul panted after the Wizard" (28). For good and ill, Paul will become not only like Willard, he will become Willard's Double, and thus move a step further toward becoming himself.

The shifting relationship between Paul and Willard is extremely complicated, but let me make a few suggestions about their co-duplicity. To begin with, in a very real sense, neither can exist without the other. Paul is altogether completely reliant on Willard, with the complete dependence of a child, but Willard is also reliant on Paul. Significantly, it is Paul, now Cass Fletcher, who is the key to Willard's most important magic trick–Abdullah. And Abdullah is more than a trick; it is the central achievement and meaning of Willard's life, since being able to baffle and defeat the Rubes defines who Willard is, fundamentally constitutes his sense of identity. When Abdullah is burned, Willard mourns the loss of "the greatest thing in his life," which had served as an "an irreplaceable source of income" (126). But Abdullah is much more than a source of livelihood for Willard: it figures as much for his identity as it does for Paul's.

As Willard declines in illness, Cass rises in power, until Cass becomes his literal double, appearing on stage as Willard. And yet Willard's decline does not free Cass from his psychic bond. He says, "I had lived with him in dreadful servitude for almost half my life, and now I didn't know what I should do without him" (127). From here, and particularly from the time when they flee Canada, the master/slave relationship becomes inverted, though they still remain inseparable psychic doubles. Cass, now transformed into Jules Legrand, steps into Willard's old role: "This confused old wretch had been my master, my oppressor, the man who let me live hungry and dirty, who used my body shamefully and never let me lift my head above the shame. Now he was utterly mine: he was my thing" (131). Jules, the transformation of Willard into Wild Man, geek, and Shame of the Old South, is a neat mirror image inversion of Willard's transformation of Paul into Cass Fletcher. Yet one has the sense that more than just a spirit of revenge prompts Jules' actions; particularly in his refusal to help Willard die, one senses that the symbiotic double relationship is still in effect–and that Jules needs Willard as much as Willard needs Jules. Throughout, they remain preoccupied with, and essential to, each other's existence. Even after Willard's death, the Wizard remains a key feature in the makeup of Magnus' soul. Thus we hear the echo of Willard's "Mephistophelian laugh," which Magnus describes as having "a glorious command over lesser humanity" (29), in what Ramsay calls "Merlin's Laugh," which is also a laugh of power–the power to enchant and the power to destroy. And Magnus does so beguile and tear down in the next section in his encounter with Roland Ingestree.

## *The Theatre Section*

In the next long section Paul enters the theatre world, which seems at first to situate another inversion, in the form of a reversal of fortune. We soon discover, however, that this world, too, is in every way doubled, and we are duped if we think that Paul has evaded the duplicitous life. He escapes from the "shadow of Willard," as Cecelia Coulas notes, only to "emerge under the shadow of Irving"[3] where he is found juggling and is inducted into the theatre world where he becomes Sir John's Double in "Two, Two" of the double play, "Scaramouche" (162).

His role as Sir John's Double bears a striking resemblance to his acting as Willard's Double. Once again, neither can exist without the other. Sir John needs Paul, but this need is doubled: it contains both poles of opposition and affinity. On the one hand, as the company manager, Holyroyd, explains, Paul is repugnant to Sir John. As he notes, Sir John needs a Double:

> And when that Double comes—and such a Double that you can't
> deny him—he's a seedy little carnie, with the shifty eyes of a
> pickpocket and the breath of somebody that eats the cheapest food,
> and you wouldn't trust him with sixpenn'orth of copper, and every
> time you look at him you heave. He looks like everything inside
> yourself that you've choked off and shut out in order to be what you
> are now. (171)

In Jungian terms, Paul is Sir John's shadow. But though he is repulsive, he is also altogether absolutely necessary, for he makes available the one thing Sir John most desires: youth. Milady makes this clear when she is explaining his role as Double to Paul. "Sir John can and will do something extraordinary: he will make the public . . . believe he is doing those splendid, skilful things. He can make them want to believe he can do anything" (167). Of course, the great irony and duplicity is that Sir John needs Paul in order to achieve this height of his art.

Paul is likewise dependent on Sir John for his very existence. He cultivates the skill of being Nobody that he learned inside Abdullah and fills what Milady calls his "tabula rasa" with Sir John's very being (168). As Ingestree first suggests, and Magnus later confirms, Paul climbs into the body and soul of Sir John: "When I knew you," says Ingestree to Magnus, "you were inside Sir John, inside his body and inside his manner and voice and everything about him that a clever double could imitate" (227). Magnus at first doesn't very much like Ingestree's suggestion that he was trying to eat Sir John, but in the last section of the novel he admits his "wolfishness," his "hunger not just to be like him but to be him . . . to possess him, to make him mine" (307). These lines provide an eerie echo of what Magnus says about Willard as slave: "he was utterly mine: he was my thing" (131). And, of course, this relationship follows the same pattern; as Paul, now Mungo Fetch, ascends, Sir John descends, until in the final scene before Sir John's death, even his wife mistakes Fetch for John. Though in one sense the Double kills his twin, there remains a sneaky duplicity in the fact that both Willard and Sir John live on as significant factors in the soul of Magnus Eisengrim.

### Narrative Doubling

As I suggested earlier, doubling figures in the form as much as in the content of *World of Wonders*. Most obviously, Magnus' autobiographical text is doubled by Lind's film-like text. We learn from the beginning that the impetus for the telling of Magnus' story is that it will provide the subtext or, in a sense, the shadow text for Robert Houdin's life, a life that (so Ingestree believes) is full of "false modesty, exaggerated humility, greasy bourgeois assertions of respectability" (14). Certainly Magnus' story provides an ideal shadow text for Houdin's "gigantic whitewash job" (16). Magnus has no modesty or humility, and the world he takes us through no doubt inversely mirrors the "bland and cozy" respectability about which Ingestree complains. This doubling of the text might be compared to the way Ramsay's text doubles Lorne Packer's in *Fifth Business*. But film is an even more appropriate double, since the medium itself, like the photograph, has an uncanny aptitude for doubling life. Lind makes exactly this suggestion when he discusses the possibility of a filmed version of history (in this case the execution of Charles I) being more convincing than the real version.

We also see another way the text is doubled when we think of Ramsay's two productions of Magnus' life. *Phantasmata: The Life and Adventures of Magnus Eisengrim* is Ramsay's best-selling text book, which Magnus himself calls "a poetic autobiography, far more true to the man he has become than any merely factual account of his experience could be" (18). "Phantasmata" is doubled by "World of Wonders," which is the ostensible second record or "document" Ramsay makes of Magnus' life that he refers to at the beginning and end of the text. Together these documents comment on the doubleness and duplicity of "the truth" of autobiography and on the possibility of presenting a unified version of a life.

### Doubling the Record: Double Voices, Double Words

The overall structure of *World of Wonders* can be seen as complex, dialogical. What presents itself ostensibly as a monologue is broken up and dialogised by the inset passages where Lind, Ingestree, Kinghoven, Ramsay and Liesl debate, deride, question, and comment on the main story. In fact, three of these characters play even more important roles, as they act as narratological doubles for parts of the story, filling in essential details and giving us another, first-hand perspective on parts of Magnus' tale. Ramsay plays a part in the early stage of Magnus' life, and in both this text and *Fifth Business*, he doubles Magnus' story. Liesl points out that "you [Ramsay] precipitated, by a single action—and who could think you guilty just because you jumped out of the way of a snowball—everything that we have been hearing from Magnus during these nights past. Are you a precipitating figure in Magnus' story, or he in yours? Who could comb it all out?" (140). Next, Ingestree doubles Magnus' tale as they tell the story of the Tresize company "as a duet" (215), which performance by two also engenders an important debate in this section: between the Old and New Theatre, the nineteenth and twentieth century, the melodrama of feelings versus the contemporary theatre of ideas. Finally, Liesl doubles the last section of Magnus' tale, filling in her life as much as she does his. This double structure foregrounds and, in a sense, amends the usually suppressed duplicity of autobiography that, as Liesl says "can't be managed except by casting one person as the star of the drama, and arranging everybody else as supporting players" (136).

The dialogical nature of the text, its propensity for debate and discussion, is essential to understanding its double nature. The structure of the novel opposes different characters' discourses, as well as inviting and alluding to many other discourses outside the novel (we need only consider the huge number of intertexts—of film, magic, drama, and literature). Even when we are only hearing Magnus' voice, his language is what Bakhtin would call "double voiced": in other words, it is "directly, blatantly, oriented toward a future answer word. It provokes an answer, anticipates it and structures itself in the answer's direction."[4] This is most clear in the way Magnus' story shapes itself in response to the antagonistic presence of Ingestree. Here additional terms from Bakhtin are useful. Bakhtin talks about the "hidden polemic" and the "sideward glance" as aspects of double-voicing. "Here the author's discourse [I am thinking of Magnus' discourse] is directed towards its own referential object but at the same time a polemical blow is struck at the other's discourse. The speaker is anticipating an antagonistic response from the listener; he seems to cringe or take a sideward glance at another's hostile point of view."[5] In this way we begin to see how Magnus' discourse is doubled in that it shapes itself by looking not only inward (to the past), but also outward (to his audience). I would suggest that, if any of the other characters were not present, Magnus' story would necessarily be different. He speaks to and for Ramsay, Lind, Liesl, and Roly, and what he says has as much to do with who they are as who he is.

### Autobiographical Duplicity

Autobiography claims to present the facts of a life, but in it the present is always conflated with the past. There is always an unintentional duplicity in the act of autobiography. As Ingestree says, the "classic problem of autobiography is that it's inevitably life seen and understood backwards. However honest we try to be in our recollections we cannot help falsifying them in terms of later knowledge, and especially in terms of what we have become" (58). This embellishment of the past is often brought to the readers' attention through other characters' comments, not only on the content of Magnus' story, but also on his style and approach to telling it.

The irony and duplicity that build from the characters' comments on Magnus' narrative are starkly exemplified in Ingestree's comment on Magnus' story about the end of Willard:

> What I can't decide is how much of what we have heard we are to take as fact. It's the inescapable problem of the autobiography: how much is left out, how much has been genuinely forgotten, how much has been touched up to throw the subject into striking relief? That stuff about Revenge, for instance. Can he have been as horrible as he makes out? He doesn't seem a cruel man now. We must never forget that he's a conjuror by profession; his lifelong pose has been demonic. I think he'd like us to believe he played the demon in reality, as well. (135)

Roly points out the possible duplicity of Magnus' narrative, but it seems that

Davies is also having some fun in duping Roly, or the readers. For as we are about to discover in the proceeding narrative, Magnus will reveal a genuinely cruel streak in his "trampling" Roly; he there paints some of his less brilliant moments as "the genius" and the fool of the Tresize company (256). Here Davies dupes the character, who thinks he has caught on to the narrative's duplicity.

### Tentative Conclusions on the Meaning of Doubling in World of Wonders

My first suggestion is a reiteration of what I have said about a Bakhtinian reading of the novel. The doubling effect is essential to the novel's dialogical nature. Magnus tries to dominate us and the text with his monologue, but the other voices in the text provide resistance to such domination. *World of Wonders* is a novel of constant debate. Throughout the text, we experience ongoing debates between feeling and thinking, education and experience, reason and wonder, orality and textuality, simplicity and difficulty, the grotesque and the sublime, and God and the Devil. Finally, the novel engenders a debate between the communicative practices of monologue and dialogue.

Doubling also supports Davies' concept of the Magian World View as presented through Liesl. As Liesl explains that concept:

> It was the sense of the unfathomable wonder of the invisible world that existed side by side with a hard recognition of the roughness and cruelty and day-to-day demands of the tangible world. It was the readiness to see demons where nowadays we see neuroses, and to see the hand of a guardian angel in what we are apt to shrug off ungratefully as a stroke of luck. It was religion, but a religion with a thousand gods, none of them all-powerful and most of them ambiguous in their attitude toward man. (287)

The Magian World View is the view of a Double World, and Davies' acts of doubling bring this world to life. It is a world view that allows us to see events such as Paul's abduction into the circus as simultaneously marvellous and horrible, compelling and repelling. Liesl explains further: "We have educated ourselves into a world from which wonder, and the fear and dread and splendour and freedom of wonder have been banished. Of course wonder is costly. . . . Wonder is marvellous, but it is also cruel" (288). So although Paul's abduction is horrible, there is also something necessary and wonderful about it from the

Magian point of view, since it is this event that ultimately frees him to become a great magician, and to become himself.

The duplicity of the Magian World View highlights the substantial link between cruelty and creation. This pattern, of creation through destruction, runs through all three novels of the trilogy. Like the heroes of most Romances, Magnus must be degraded in order to be elevated; he must first be slave in order to become master. As Bakhtin notes, "Degradation digs a bodily grave for a new birth; it has not only a destructive, negative aspect, but also a regenerating one."[6] While Magnus suffers greatly, the suffering does not reduce, but enlarges him.

As I suggested, this pattern of creation through destruction seems to inform the entire trilogy, since it is Boy's two destructive acts–throwing the snowball with the stone, and "swallowing" the stone in his self-destructive suicide–that initiate all of the creative acts of the novels: Ramsay's, David's, and Magnus'. In a trilogy replete with characters "twice born," it is not surprising that the Double plays a number of crucial roles.

Another important purpose for Davies' doubling is that it supports the slippery philosophical musings about God and the Devil woven into the length of the texts. According to traditional Christian understanding, of course, the Devil represents God's opposite, and Evil the absence of Good. According to now established "psychological" understanding, the Devil images humanity's sense of its own evil, the gods its sense of its better self. Davies makes the Devil much more interesting and ambiguous than a simple projection of forbidden desires, since his Devil is very much God's Double. In *Fifth Business*, Father Blazon points out the power and insight of the Devil who "knows corners of us all of which Christ Himself is ignorant" (249). Like Liesl, who is certainly one of his spokespersons, or Willard the Wizard, the Devil is both attractive and repulsive in Davies' world. And like the Double, the Devil is also disconcertingly familiar. Meeting either the Double or the Devil means encountering essential parts of ourselves. The Double, in other words, is the Other finally recognised as the Self. Paul's encounters with Willard and Sir John are instances of self-meeting and figure as necessary stations on the road to self-actualisation.

Rather than trying to "untangle" the intricate relationship between God and the Devil (as Liesl laughs at Ramsay for trying to do at the end of the novel), I close with a quotation that maintains the duplicity of these two, often indistinguishable, voices:

> God wants to intervene in the world, and how is he to do it except
> though man? I think the Devil is in the same predicament. It would

be queer, wouldn't it, if the Devil had only made use of Magnus that one time? And God, too: yes, certainly God as well. It's the moment of decision–of will–when those Two nab us, and as they both speak so compellingly it's tricky work to know who's talking. Where there's a will, there are always two ways. (316)

## NOTES

1. Robertson Davies, *World of Wonders* (Harmondsworth: Penguin, 1977), 212.

2. For an extended account of the carnivalesque in Davies, see Barbara Godard, "*World of Wonders*: Robertson Davies' Carnival," *Essays on Canadian Writing* 30 (1985): 239-86.

3. Cecelia Coulas, "What is Known and Long Familiar: The Uncanny Effect in *World of Wonders*," *Studies in Canadian Literature* 15 (1990): 107.

4. David Lodge, *After Bakhtin* (London: Routledge, 1990), 21.

5. Phyllis Margaret Paryas, "Double-voicing/dialogism," *Encyclopedia of Contemporary Literary Theory: Approaches, Scholars, Terms*, ed. Irena R. Makaryk (Toronto: University of Toronto Press, 1993), 538.

6. Mikhail Bakhtin, *Rabelais and His World*, trans. Helene Iswolsky (Bloomington: Indiana University Press, 1984), 21.

# Authentic Forgeries: Hermeneutics, Artifice, and Authenticity in Robertson Davies' *What's Bred in the Bone*

DAVID HALLETT

W hen Simon Darcourt calls Francis Cornish a "true son of Hermes" early in *What's Bred in the Bone*, he provides a hermeneutic "skeleton key" both to meaning in the novel and to a comprehension of Davies' sense of self as moral fictionist.[1] The figure of Hermes organizes and gives meaning to the novel's many uses of artifice and invention, even as the hermeneutic notion of "horizon(s) of expectation" enables a recognition of the didactic component of Davies' fiction. Reference to devices such as retouched photos, player pianos, stories and lies that characters tell each other, and, especially, art restoration help to authenticate artifice as both an instrument for teaching and a record of genuine human emotion. Beginning with theories of the horizon of expectation, as developed by Hans Robert Jauss and Hans-Georg Gadamer, I will argue that all the artifices–imitations, copies, and genuine articles alike–and the novel that contains them represent efforts to shape and expand the *human* horizon of expectation. More importantly for Davies, the novel challenges specifically *Canadian* horizons of expectations, as held by Canadians of themselves and ostensibly as held by the rest of the world perceiving Canada. The novel, by engaging the real world of which it is a part, becomes an "authentic forgery." After making a very brief comparison of *What's Bred in the Bone* with William Gaddis' 1955 novel, *The Recognitions*, I will argue that in *What's Bred in the Bone* Davies creates a Sidney-esque "defence of fiction" by employing fiction both to define its own terms of authentification and to present a challenge to Canadians to find value in the self. Thus, though the novel displays many of the defining characteristics of what Stanley Fish calls the "self-consuming artifact," it is not self-consuming but self-authenticating.

Hermes figures significantly in *What's Bred in the Bone* as Mercury, "patron of crooks, the joker . . . the mischief-maker who upsets all calculations" (13). Hermes is also "the reconciler of opposites" (14). The potential of artifice to convey truth rests in this reconciliation of opposites, which proposition immediately suggests the aptness of reading of *What's Bred in the Bone* with the hermeneutic circle in mind: "a part of something is always understood in terms of the whole and vice versa."[2] For example: the words of a sentence may only be understood in relation to the sentence as a whole, and a sentence may only be understood by analysis of its component words. Gadamer proposes that we understand, not in spite of our historical and cultural prejudices but because of them. Paul Ricoeur adds one further refinement to the hermeneutic process: "the self . . . cannot be understood by . . . direct scrutiny, but only by way of a detour through cultural works, particularly works of art" (Kerby 92). Thus, if our historical and cultural prejudices can be actively changed, so can our understanding; *through* art, we can come to understand something of ourselves.

Hermeneutics stresses "the crucial importance of interpretation to most if not all aspects of human endeavour and culture" (Kerby 90). *What's Bred in the Bone* repeatedly emphasizes the importance of interpretation, from Aunt Mary-Ben's certainty that her skullcaps are "the head-dress of servitude" (45), through Dr. Joseph Ambrosius Jerome (itself a "loaded" name full of hermeneutic possibilities) and his reading of the world as "a huge disease" of which humans "are all part" (196), to the narrator's comment that the role of "the experts" is "to sink their learned teeth into [a work] and worry it to some sort of satisfactory interpretation" (392). The "crucial importance of interpretation" is always in the foreground of the novel,[3] and the horizon of expectation is vital to any act of interpretation.

Gadamer considers the horizon as "an essential part of every interpretive situation":[4] it provides a vantage point "that limits the possibility of vision, resulting from our necessary situatedness in the world" (Holub 553). Most important to analysis of Davies' novel is that this horizon is not fixed, but a "continuously evolving vantage point . . . intimately linked to the prejudices we bring to any situation, since they represent a 'horizon' over which we cannot see" (553). The "historical" bent of *What's Bred in the Bone*, its assertion that knowledge of what *was* "bred in the bone" of a given individual is essential to a comprehension of whatever that individual eventually becomes (18-19, 59,

379, 435), seems to encourage a hermeneutic analysis. For my purposes, the horizon of expectation is a useful label for one of Davies' obsessions: the challenge to Canada and Canadians to revise views of Canada.

Davies regularly proselytised about a more self-aware and self-authenticating Canada. References both in his fiction and in interviews to changing, maturing, and evolving perceptions of Canada, and a need for greater recognition of Canada's worth, are certainly not difficult to find. From criticizing provincial platitudes in the Canadian approach to art in 1968,[5] to challenging "the stereotyped notion of Canada as a dreadfully dull place where nothing interesting could happen" nearly twenty years later,[6] Davies encouraged Canadians to realize the "astonishing" nature of "what crops up in our national life,"[7] to believe that Canada "is just as full of extraordinary potentiality . . . as anywhere else in the world."[8] He criticised the frequency with which any achievement by a Canadian in any field is received as "the Canadian somebody else" (Penman 150), instead of being recognised in its own right, without need for some sort of external comparison.

These challenges inform *What's Bred in the Bone*. At school, Francis, who knows "about pictures," is "beset" with queries from other boys about his attitude to the Group of Seven. The queries are frequently negative, labelling the Group's work as "outrageously modern" or "like what the Swedish cook used to paint on her day off" (161-62). "Can you see Georgian Bay in it?" asks one lad (162), voicing the widely held perception that the only true measure of quality in a work of art is its precise mimicry of external features. Saraceni, an "outsider," criticizes Canada by telling Francis that his options include returning to his "frozen country, with its frozen art" (331). A commonplace of Canadian definition, both at home and abroad, is ridiculed when Aylwin Ross, lambasted by the public for his efforts to purchase Old Masters for the National Gallery of Canada, has his sin defined in "the more extreme papers" as "blasphem[ing] against hockey" (421).

By far, Davies' most direct challenge to Canada's sense of itself is voiced by his character Ruth Nibsmith: "Canada is an introverted country straining like hell to behave like an extrovert. Wake up! Be yourself, not a bad copy of something else!" (312). Here, Davies asserts his belief that Canada, in order to grow into full recognition of its own merits on its own terms, must interrogate its old belief that it has "no reality except in relation to some other standard."[9] When Francis Cornish returns to Canada after his lengthy European career, the narrator observes that "the land of his birth had not stood still since

Francis had left it" (411). The reader anticipates a positive comment. However, alluding directly to Ruth Nibsmith's charge earlier in the novel, the narrator continues:

> The little country with the big body, which had always been introverted in its psychology . . . was striving now to assume the extroversion of [its] mighty neighbour. Because Canada could not really understand the American extroversion, it imitated the obvious elements of it, and the effect was often tawdry. Canada had lost its way, had suffered what the anthropologists call Loss of Soul. (411)

The extreme pessimism of this description of the country is only offset, if at all, by the actions of the framing characters in the last pages of the novel, when the younger Arthur Cornish decides to allow his uncle's official life to be written despite the possibility of resultant scandal (435).

All these calls for a more confident Canada, with a broader horizon of expectation situated in a more perceptive, less dismissive world, grow from Davies' sense of himself as a moralist. The role of the artist in conveying a moral vision is another regular concern in the novel. *What's Bred in the Bone*, I would contend, is a didactic novel. "I am a moralist," Davies overtly claims in his lecture "Painting, Fiction, and Faking" (75). He is frequently concerned with the Jungian-influenced concept of individuation. The significance of myth, and of its language and symbolic systems, is also a common subject. Another regular moral issue in Davies' fiction is the importance so often placed on maintaining a perceived respectability in social/moral ordering. Davies also regularly insists on the validity of the psychological notion that human life is inevitably a mixture of the sublime and the disgusting. Together with changing Canadian self-image and the role of art, *What's Bred in the Bone* addresses these moral concerns.

Davies is concerned with what Patricia Monk calls "the smaller infinity,"[10] with how the growth of the individual self is crucial to the growth of humanity. As Monk cautions, Davies sees his work as a "map" of inner reality but "not the territory" (184); it is the individual's responsibility to explore one's own territory. And every map needs a symbolic language. For Davies, it is "the language of faith and mythology," one that might safely have been assumed at one time as common knowledge in an audience, but now "almost a dead language."[11] In *What's Bred in the Bone*, that language, together with a lament for the decay in the ability of ordinary readers to recognize it, is foundational, from character naming, through direct advice given by characters ("Can't understand the present if you don't know the past" [171]), to plot points in a historical "process" (for example, the almost total ignorance of the Cornishes about Arthurian legend [177-8]).

Maintaining the appearance of respectability is a major concern in the Blairlogie of Francis' childhood, and remains significant throughout his life. This concern seems basic to the Davies ordering of Canadian living. In 1981, Davies said that "Canadians are still a people who don't want to admit that they are frequently torn by passion and driven by feelings that they frequently can't control" (Hay, in *Conversations* 215). In *What's Bred in the Bone*, the Daimon Maimas and the Recording Angel, the Lesser Zadkiel–our hermeneutic commentators throughout[12]–stress the need to "understand what respectability meant to these people," that respectability means far more than "What will the neighbours think?"; it may affect the entire course of one's life (44). Concern for respectable appearance is also a form of "emotion, disguising itself as reason" (44). Throughout the text, the value of apparent respectability is undermined by the frequency with which such respectability is revealed as a false front.

Most significant for all the novel's discourses of respectability is the figure of the Looner, Francis Cornish the first, the child almost but not quite destroyed in the womb by his grandmother's efforts to induce an abortion in her unwed daughter (38,147-48), the child effectively buried, as it were, before he was dead (68, 131). With the Looner, discourses of respectability merge with Davies' stated "unrepentant" belief in the mixture of opposites in the human psyche, "the ineffable, the elegant, and the praiseworthy ... inextricably mingled with the grubby, the commonplace, and the reputedly inadmissible" ("Painting" 83). The novel reiterates that belief through Francis' internal monologue: "what was he to make of this terrible house where the pious refinement of Aunt was under the same roof as the animal lust of the Looner" (137). The virtually rhetorical question is answered by our hermeneutic guides, who tell us that "the Looner was a lifelong reminder of the inadmissible primitive in the most cultivated life" (207).

There remains among Davies' regular didactic concerns the role of art, which returns us to the beginning of the discussion. "All art," Davies argues, "is created in the hope that it will say something to interested people" (68). The crucial question is not "What is this object . . . and how does it conform to the aesthetic principles I have made my own?" but–and in this Davies concurs with Gadamer's theories of the horizon of expectation–"What does this *say* to me?" (68). This premise is found in *What's Bred in the Bone* as Francis tries to explain his emerging comprehension of art to Jack Copplestone. Explaining that he understands the modern view that "a picture shouldn't really be *about* anything," Francis finds himself unable to accept that modern painters such as Picasso are producing "just form and colour on a flat surface" (183). The works of the Old Masters, Francis insists, "are statements" (184) and any contemporary critical discourses that would deny the presence of meaning in art, classic or contemporary, "won't work" (184). Francis then discusses Bronzino's *Allegory of Love*[13] and concludes that "it's saying something. . . . Nobody is going to tell me it's just an arrangement of form and colour" (185).

Francis understands as he reaches the end of his apprenticeship that a great painting (here we may read "a great work of art") "must have its foundation in a sustaining myth" (358). As Francis considers the subject for the painting that Saraceni has challenged him to make, he reaches "the only possible, the inescapable answer. He would paint the myth of Francis Cornish" (359). Francis' epiphany is significant in two respects. First, it points toward the contemporary methodology of art, which has largely supplanted creation enabled by a "universal grammar" with creation founded on individual myth and symbol. Second, it keeps us focused on the parallels between the character and his author, who is, of course, engaged throughout the novel in "painting" the myth of Francis Cornish.

What modern art has to say, argues Davies, "is expressed by the painter as it arises from his unconscious, creative centre" (81). The language of modern painting is thus "a secret language" and, therefore, "a special and subtle temptation assails the modern painter . . . : the temptation to fake the secret language and to paint mysteriously where there is no real mystery" (81).[14] Francis Cornish confronts this idea directly, and Saraceni offers him the following advice:

> Nothing is so easy to fake as the inner vision. . . . The moderns . . . find something in the inner vision that is so personal that to most people it looks like chaos. . . . Not very pretty and not very communicative, but they have to find their way through that to something that is communicative. . . . Don't try to fake the modern manner if it isn't right for you. Find your legend. Find your personal myth. (227)

Once again, the advice offered in the fictional context is also, in part, autobiographical. As Judith Skelton Grant observes, part of Davies' motivation in writing *What's Bred in the Bone* lay in his "annoyance with the critics who accused him of being old-fashioned." This annoyance "led him to create an artist whose genius is to paint in the manner and with the technique and materials of the sixteenth century" (*Man of Myth* 571). Here, Davies has found and is expressing his own "personal myth."

The deliberate borrowing of detail from Davies' past for Francis' character reminds us that *What's Bred in the Bone* is, of course, a partly autobiographical novel. A comparing of *What's Bred in the Bone* with William Gaddis' novel *The Recognitions* (1955) that does not take into account such autobiographical elements as there are in Davies' novel might plausibly conclude that Davies had simply rewritten the older work with a Canadian context. In many respects, *What's Bred in the Bone* is a Canadian *Recognitions*–which assertion uneasily sits with his assertion in conversation with Margaret Penman to the effect that he has been critical of the usage "the Canadian 'X'" "since childhood" (150; see also Marshall 70). To those who would say it is "nothing more," however, it is also "nothing less." If we apply a precept of convicted forger, suspected poisoner, former art critic and eventual portrait painter in Australia, Thomas Griffiths Wainwright (quoted approvingly by Davies in his essay "Painting, Fiction, and Faking"), *What's Bred in the Bone* authenticates itself on its own terms. Wainwright said that "I hold that no work of art can be tried otherwise than by laws deduced from itself: whether or not it be consistent with itself is the question" (76). Thus if the remarkable similarities of Davies' novel to the earlier Gaddis novel mean anything, it is solely that two men with similar concerns as moral fictionists have, after considering alchemy, art and forgery, medieval and Renaissance symbolism and faith, and the peculiar role of the artist, independently arrived at similar plot structures because of similarity in their conceptual, philosophical, moral, and spiritual frameworks.[15]

There is, as *What's Bred in the Bone* phrases it, "a division between art and deviousness and . . . crime" that is "sometimes as thin as cigarette paper" (405). It is with that division and its subtle distinctions that Francis Cornish struggles. To understand the importance of this division, we must examine what it is about the "fake" that so disturbs us.

In Davies' view, the fake scares us because it makes "the experts look foolish, which is unendurable, because experts of all kinds are our modern priests and we want to think them infallible" ("Painting" 86). He alludes to the case of Henricus van Meegeren (in part a model for Letztpfennig in *What's Bred in the Bone*) and to the question van Meegeren posed at his trial for forgery:

"Yesterday, this picture was worth millions of guilders, and experts and art lovers would come from all over the world and pay money to see it. Today, it is worth nothing, and nobody would cross the street to see it free. But the picture has not changed. What has?" (quoted in "Painting" 87). Davies says that the only "honest" reply he has heard to this question from any art critic is, "simply, 'The magic has gone out of it'" (87). Finally, consider the question raised by Davies in 1986: "If you sign a famous name . . . to a portrait, you're trying to sell something which is wicked. But the picture itself, if you didn't sign it–isn't it fit to hang with [the Master it imitates]?" (*Conversations* 264).

*What's Bred in the Bone* directly engages these questions. The novel details a world rich in people, attitudes, and objects of occasionally dubious authenticity. Amongst these elements of uncertain virtue, sometimes called art, sometimes forgery, are the retouching of photographs (88-89), the use of chalk and ink by Zadok Hoyle to lighten or darken his clothing (91), and Aunt Mary-Ben's "Phonoliszt" player-piano, on which she always performs *before* admitting the trick to guests (105-106). Zadok's cosmetician work at the funeral home is also an "art": he makes corpses "look as they'd have looked on their wedding day, maybe better," despite the fact that they "never clean their nails from Easter to Easter" because "all the rough part" of a funeral "is no business of the public's" (116, 116-17, 111). Perhaps the only act of legal forgery in the novel, outside the art world, occurs when Ismay copies Francis' signature on a cheque (245-247). These sundry examples of "fakery," apart from the last (and even that is defended by its perpetrator), are represented in the novel as helpful fiction in the business of getting through life.

But it is in the world of painterly art, of course, that the most important examination of the paper-thin division between artifice and forgery occurs. *What's Bred in the Bone* posits the idea that restoration might be considered "re-creation" (258). Francis insists that he wants "to be a painter, not a craftsman who tarts up paintings that have been allowed to decay" (280); but Francis is bound to his mentor for a period of servitude during which the distinction between art restoration and art forgery grows almost impossible to make with any real assurance. Saraceni insists that the "true work of restoration" demands choosing the materials and techniques employed by the Old Masters, which choice he puts forward as "the honesty" of the craft, simultaneously noting that such materials are "undetectable" (292). When Francis asks whether Saraceni's restoration is not going "a bit farther than is necessary," the mentor responds: "speak what is on your mind. The word you want to use is faking, isn't it?"

(295). Francis then takes on the task that I argue is analogous to Davies' task in writing the novel: to create a work that is all his own but that would not look out of place among the earlier works it resembles. Francis accepts the challenge, eventually thinking of himself as "The Happy Faker" as he begins to enjoy the work (303). The painting he creates is so good that Prince Max, who is heading the project to bamboozle the Nazis with their own preference for art from the Reich, insists on including Cornish's painting with the others that he is "returning" to Germany by first smuggling them out of Germany. The painting may be a fake "in the substance," Max concedes, but is "certainly not [a fake] in the spirit" (318). The distinction is a fine one, with profound implications for the soul of Francis Cornish.

In Davies' novel, time is tentatively suggested as the one element that authenticates "the magic" alluded to above (346-47). "Experts" cannot validate true art, and, in fact, come off rather poorly in the course of the fiction. When they are "shown the obvious" during the Letztpfennig Van Eyck "trial," the experts "[make] haste to declare that it was indeed obvious" (352). They are described soon after as "those who profess to rank artists as if they were schoolboys" (353), and it is suggested that the reaction of experts is frequently dictated not by what they are seeing, but by what they think they are supposed to see. Their inability to recognize what is in front of their noses is a recurring motif in the text: they can fill "a whole day" with "an orgy of happy haggling, of high-powered knowing-best" (389). And though Aylwin Ross defends the critic as the only person who can make "a considered and sometimes a final judgment" (407), he dies a disgraced suicide. Compare Ross' fate with that of Saraceni, who largely gets whatever he wants in life and who performs his most dubious act of "restoration," as Dave Little observes (*Conversations* 86), in an effort to exploit the Nazis. Saraceni also echoes Davies' subtle distinction between the fake for commercial exploitation and a work in the mode, method, and manner of the Old Master that is unsigned: "faking"–from which, of course, he shrinks "in holy terror"–"is contemptible" and is clearly distinguished from "the ability to work truly in the technique and also in the spirit of the past" (325, 356).

An attending to Wainwright's dictum makes understandable the major reason for the artistic success of *What's Bred in the Bone*: "whether or not it be consistent with itself is the question" ("Painting" 76). *What's Bred in the Bone* is undeniably consistent with itself: its very composition argues that it is possible to make "a picture that is all your own" and that does not "look out of place" among earlier pictures in an earlier mode (296). In producing a didactic, moral work of art in a modernist manner in the midst of the postmodern era, Davies achieves just that: the 1985 novel does not look out of place set beside its 1955 predecessor, nor is it merely a "copy." *What's Bred in the Bone* authenticates itself.

That self-authentication I assert as a contradiction to the idea of the self-consuming artifact as argued by Stanley Fish and applied to texts of the seventeenth century. I employ it deliberately in application to a twentieth-century text because that text makes overt, conscious use of the idea of a contemporary artist working effectively in the mode of an earlier era. *What's Bred in the Bone* refutes the idea of "self-consumption." Rather than consuming its own usefulness by challenging its readers to seek answers that cannot be contained within the text, the novel affirms such a challenge to its readers as the *raison d'être* of art.

*What's Bred in the Bone* meets many of the criteria for the self-consuming artifact that Fish proposes. It is a "dialectical presentation" that does require of its readers "a searching and rigorous scrutiny of everything they believe in and live by."[16] It is "didactic in a special sense; it . . . asks that its readers discover the truth for themselves" (1). Fish evokes the image of The Good Physician, who "tells his patients what they *don't* want to hear in the hope that by forcing them to see themselves clearly, they may be moved to change the selves they see" (3). Davies' overt challenge to Canadians to improve their self-image, and to individual readers to find their own personal myth as the only authenticator of the self's own "art" (in whatever literal or metaphorical sense we may understand that to be), seems to square with Fish's definition of the dialectical text as "practised" by a Good Physician. Fish characterizes the dialectical way as one that moves its reader toward "an all-embracing unity"–once more perfectly in harmony with both the commentary of the hermeneutic guides cited above and with the figure of Hermes/Mercury, "the reconciler of opposites" (14).

It is Fish's third premise with which I disagree. "It follows then," writes Fish, "that a dialectical presentation succeeds at its own expense" (3), becoming a self-consuming artifact by conveying its reader to a point at which the reader no longer needs the "medicine" offered by the text. "A self-consuming artifact signifies most successfully when it fails, when it points *away* from itself to something its forms cannot capture" (4)–what might be understood as a text reaching the limits of its own horizons. My contradicting argument here is twofold. First, my view of humanity suggests that we may need to confront a dialectical challenge more than once before truly reaching the point at which we can no longer be made "better persons" (Fish 4) through our reading. Secondly, while I would agree that *What's Bred in the Bone* points away from itself to something its forms cannot capture—namely each individual reader's personal myth and path toward individuation—I would also suggest that it *does* capture a model of how that eternally external to itself "something" might be pursued by the actively engaged reader. Here, the hermeneutic circle returns: the novel needs the reader, *and* the reader needs the novel. It is on those grounds that I argue that *What's Bred in the Bone* is not self-consuming but self-authenticating. Further, what it is for its principal character and for its reader, it is for its author: self-authentication is exactly what Davies has been encouraging for Canadian art and for Canadian life throughout his career.

Thus arises the idea of a Sidney-esque "defence of fiction."[17] As Saraceni tells Francis, "art is a way of telling the truth" (327). Davies' novel argues, without specifically stating, a point explicitly affirmed by a character in Anthony Powell's *Hearing Secret Harmonies*: "Because a novel's invented, it is true."[18] "Nobody ever knows the whole of anything," the narrator asserts near the close of *What's Bred in the Bone* (431). My unwillingness to accept Fish's argument that a reader might reach the point at which the medicinal value of the dialectical text is only truly felt in the consumption of the medicine accords with that premise. Being human is a chronic condition; the prescription of challenging art always needs renewal.


## NOTES

1. Robertson Davies, *What's Bred in the Bone* (Toronto: Macmillan, 1985), 15.

2. Anthony Kerby, "Hermeneutics," *Encyclopedia of Contemporary Literary Theory: Approaches, Scholars, Terms*, ed. Irena R. Makaryk (Toronto: University of Toronto Press, 1993), 90.

3. Other sites in the novel at which the importance of interpretation can be seen include the Doctor's pretense at being greedy as he scoops up "the remains of the cake tray" for "children in the Polish section" (*WBB* 50); "the spite of that Tory rag" in reporting the Cornish wedding without overtly naming its Protestant aspect (51); Blairlogie's hierarchical structure for the determining of the respect due various servants according to their positions (89); the pictures displayed at St. Kilda for the tacit edification of Fathers Devlin and Beaudry (104-105); Zadok Hoyle's affirmation of the Harry Furniss

principle that "most people don't see what's in front of their nose" coupled with his encouragement to young Francis to "encourage people to see what they think they ought to see" (112); Francis' treatment of Eastwood, his "superior" at school (155); the revelation of Francis' true feelings for Ismay as read by Charlie Fremantle in Francis' drawings of her (235); Saraceni's lengthy discourse on Bronzino's *Allegory of Love* (261); the advice Francis receives during the Blitz to dress so that he can be properly identified should he be killed (369-70); the presumption of many that Francis and Aylwin Ross are homosexual lovers (387); and the last dig at the obnoxious Urquhart McVarish (who features prominently in *The Rebel Angels*) through his reception of a literary insult as a compliment (429)–to draw up a not exhaustive list of such textual sites.

4. Robert Holub, "Horizon of Expectation," *Encyclopedia of Contemporary Literary Theory: Approaches, Scholars, Terms*, ed. Irena R. Makaryk (Toronto: University of Toronto Press, 1993), 553.

5. Gordon Roper, "Conversations with Gordon Roper," *Conversations with Robertson Davies*, ed. J. Madison Davis (Jackson: University Press of Mississippi, 1989), 40-41.

6. J. Madison Davis, ed. *Conversations with Robertson Davies*, 254.

7. Peter Gzowski, "Morningside," *Conversations with Robertson Davies*, 245.

8. Margaret Penman, "Sunday Supplement," *Conversations with Robertson Davies*, 147.

9. As quoted in Douglas Marshall's "The Merlin of Massey College,"*Conversations with Robertson Davies*, 70.

10. Patricia Monk, *The Smaller Infinity: The Jungian Self in the Novels of Robertson Davies* (Toronto: University of Toronto Press, 1982), 4.

11. Robertson Davies, "Painting, Fiction, and Faking," *The Merry Heart: Selections 1980-1995* (Toronto: McClelland & Stewart, 1996), 68.

12. The Daimon Maimas, personally responsible for the direction of Francis Cornish's life, and the Lesser Zadkiel, Recording Angel, make their first appearance in *What's Bred in the Bone* directly following Simon Darcourt's lamentation that he lacks the hermeneutic key to understanding what Francis became. Attracted "by the sound of their own names" (18) from their position in the First Order to the Second Order discourse of the mere mortals, they accompany the reader on a tour through all that Simon Darcourt cannot know (at least at this stage in his researches). The two become

hermeneutic keys to the reader's interpretation of Davies' novel, interrupting at crucial points to explain the significance of actions and ideas in Francis' development and summarizing at the end of most chapters the significance of the proverbial story-so-far, their interventions growing increasingly spaced as the novel progresses, then more frequent once again as the narrative draws to a close (cf. 18-9, 23, 43-4, 58-9, 72-3, 83, 93, 103, 113, 123-25, 147-48, 175-76, 206-07, 283-84, 322-23, 355, 398-99, 426-27, 434-35).

13. Also an important subject of Davies' lecture "Painting, Fiction, and Faking."

14. While it is not the main purpose of this paper to argue that Davies' thoughts on painting are directly transferable to the art of writing fiction, I will point out that he continues his speech with the words "I know that this happens in literature . . ." ("Painting" 81).

15. There is no evidence in either Judith Skelton Grant's biography of Davies, *Robertson Davies: Man of Myth*, nor in her collection of his reviews and critical essays, *The Enthusiasms of Robertson Davies*, that Davies was at all familiar with the Gaddis novel. Grant does, however, cite an instance of Davies being concerned with "the subtle relationships between art, deception and truth" at least "as early as 1955" (555)–the year in which Gaddis published *The Recognitions*. The book that prompts Davies' written consideration of these issues in 1955, however, is Thomas Mann's *Confessions of Felix Krull, Confidence Man*. If there is influence, it is less, if at all, that of one fictional text upon another, and more, if not exclusively, the product of the prevalence of such discourses in the intellectual climate in which both authors were working.

    The concern with fakery and authenticity is shared philosophical ground for the two texts. Many other overlapping elements exist. Each protagonist is an art restorer who works with techniques and materials of an earlier age, and grows as an individual within a world that seems to be static or, perhaps, "devolving"; growth is achieved through facing a serious crisis in self-confidence, with the assistance of a mentor figure from whom each becomes ultimately independent. Each mentor is a suspicious figure, whose integrity in matters of recognizing authentic works of art is significant but whose moral character is dubious; each mentor is also associated with hermetic mysteries, dark powers, suspected but never confirmed. Each is faced with the temptation to use his restorative skills in acts of forgery. Each must go to Europe in order to discover something about his North-American self, an epiphany that is facilitated for each by a lengthy period of living in isolation from the world at large while working on art restoration projects. Each is brought up in a family both divided on certain religious issues and with household members who are adherents of various minority faiths or sects. Each learns significant lessons from his grandfather. Each has a failed marriage, and each has one "relationship," more satisfying than not, arbitrarily cut short after he begins to assimilate the practical effects of his epiphany.

The only similarity that is not easily classified as a fairly regular feature of the North-American version of the *Künstlerroman* is the fact that both are art restorers. But there are similarities at more minuscule sites. Alchemy plays a major role in each novel, with certain alchemical texts and definitions cited in each. Even zoos play a role in each novel, foregrounding ideas about medieval and Renaissance iconography and the various symbolic roles filled by animals in paintings. Both Francis and Wyatt are involved in forgery questions involving Van Eyck—Hubertus Van Eyck and not his far better known brother Jan. Both deal with paintings of "The Harrowing of Hell." Both are influenced by Hieronymus Bosch. Each uses as a model a young woman for whom he has some sexual feeling but with whom further development of a sexual impulse is temporarily impeded. Francis struggles in his relationship with Ismay; Wyatt faces similar difficulties with Esme.

16. Stanley Fish, *Self-Consuming Artifacts* (Berkeley: University of California Press, 1972), 1.

17. This is a deliberate echo of Sidney's *Defense of Poesie*, not least because of Davies' own comments on the importance of Sidney to his own comprehension of self as artist (cf. "A Canadian Author" 185).

18. Anthony Powell, *Hearing Secret Harmonies* (London: Heinemann, 1975), 80.

## WORKS CITED

Davies, Robertson. *The Rebel Angels*. Markham, Ont.: Penguin, 1983.

Davis, J. Madison, ed. *Conversations with Robertson Davies*. Jackson: University Press of Mississippi, 1989.

Gaddis, William. *The Recognitions*. New York: Harcourt, Brace & World, 1955.

Grant, Judith Skelton. *The Enthusiasms of Robertson Davies*. New York: Viking, 1990.

–. *Robertson Davies: Man of Myth*. Toronto: Viking, 1994.

Makaryk, Irena R., ed. *Encyclopedia of Contemporary Literary Theory: Approaches, Scholars, Terms*. Toronto: University of Toronto Press, 1993.

# The Myth and Magic of a Textual and/or a Metaphorical Reading of The Deptford Trilogy

## TATJANA TAKSEVA CHORNEY

In an interview with Michael Hulse in 1986, Robertson Davies responded at length to a question concerning the structure and themes of his novels and concluded by saying:

> You have to think about readers. This is where I get in trouble with some of my academic critics. I am interested in having as many readers as possible, reaching as wide an audience as possible. . . . My books are not novels in the sense of being artistic constructs formed on something which reaches back to a French origin, or Henry James, or something. They're romances. I just write romances, and when you write romances you have to be Scheherezade and bear in mind that if you do not hold the Caliph's attention he will cut your head off in the morning.[1]

This is a fine Davies-like observation: symptomatically uncomplicated and rich in allusion as only the uncomplicated can be. It echoes a number of his comments that relate to the act of reading and to the actual reader. Condensed, all of them in one way or another convey what Davies succinctly noted in *A Voice from the Attic*: "The reader can only interpret, giving the author a fair chance to make his impression . . . the reader allows the writer to act upon him."[2] Since I am a reader, and since this is helplessly and from its conception an interpretive inquiry into The Deptford Trilogy, treated here as the body of one text, I feel at liberty to begin unravelling some of the interpretive possibilities.

My hope is that in the course of this unravelling I preserve at least a shaving of the spirit of Davies' text, one of buoyant earnestness. It is often made clear in numerous literary texts that any interpretation, as an informative principle, is both at best and at worst only an opinion. In emphatic agreement, the only thing I would state unequivocally is that I approach The Deptford Trilogy with "sympathy and respect" arising from a kind of reading that Davies called "opening oneself to a text" (Davis 238).

Davies' recommendation to the reader to keep his mind open while reading and the clearly stated generic classification of his works as romances, reveal a desire for an accessibility of writing that contrasts with the hermeticism of many modernist texts. Although I am unwilling to suggest that (with the reference to Scheherezade) his comment consciously alludes to the paradigm of the high modernist narrator who, exhausted and threatened by death, is still inventing, I call upon it with interest because it points by implication toward the narrator's own identity with which the storytelling magic begins. "The good writer is first of all an enchanter," writes Davies in *Reading and Writing*. He further explains that "the longer I live, the more I become convinced that the only thing that matters in literature is the (more or less irrationally) *shamanstvo* of a book" and defines *shamanstvo* as the "real quality of the enchanter, the weaver of spells who may, through his spells, reveal unexpected and marvellous things about life, and thus about ourselves" (*A Voice from the Attic* 56-57). The writer who conceives of his art in these terms, just like the magician/enchanter, is in continual intercommunication with his audience/readers. He needs their participation (partially, of course) to sanction his performance; he makes them participate but in the sense that they are expected to open themselves to enchantment and, to absorb the magic of his performance, his text.

The reader of the Davies-like text is thus urged to share in the magic of the text, not as its co-creator, but as one who accepts its gift appreciatively and with an undeniable freedom to interpret it. This sort of reader-participation is affiliated with an often neglected atavism (at times described in terms of naïveté) in the way we understand works of literature, allowing them to act upon us in their immense versatility of form and content and all the shades of and in between the two. This ebb-like aspect of reading is usually the one responsible for the immediate, often silent responses created in us that form the steps of the ritualistic dance in which we engage with works of literature, a dance performed concurrently with the organised, progressive pursuit of ideas shaped into visible thoughts that call for understanding; this is a subtle and an uneven dance around issues that concern smaller or larger bits of (our) humanity in a very (close) fundamental yet a (distant) universal sense.[3] The romances to which Davies refers in the Hulse interview have their fair share in the eventfulness of this miscellany of responses called reading. As a genre, they are widely consumed by the general reading public with an appetite that apparently never abates; they are often rebuked and at least as often applauded on account of the genre's wide appeal. It is a genre that at best, and at its most traditional, carries eternally familiar resonances of patterns that we (as readers) are naturally disposed to recognise.[4] Such a statement, with all that it implies of indiscriminate conventionalisation, brings me closer to my subject.

After all, I have begun this paper with Davies' reference to the *Arabian Nights*. A brief digressive rehearsing of the facts of the story is in order: the Caliph, spellbound, listened to Scheherezade's spinning the web of a thousand and one stories. Why? We are told why *she* did it: to save her life. We have even made her the paradigm of the high modernist narrator, who creates under the threat of death. But the Caliph, although very cruel and unreasonably vengeful (as we are told), deserves some attention too, if for no other reason than for the singularly unwavering interest he took in those stories. It is true, we are told, that Scheherezade's beauty very much appealed to his wicked appetites and that this is why he agreed to the unusual proposition she made: he began to listen to her stories. But a thousand and one? The inextinguishable relish of the Caliph in listening holds the power to intrigue. What was it about those stories that made him wait for more and more and, in the end, that made him spare her life, turning him into her loving spouse mended from his intractable ways? It was love, of course, but a love born of a particular kind of "literary" appreciation, a wonderful example of love for something other than the narrator herself. If Scheherezade is the paradigm of the narrator, the skillful storytelling enchantress, the Caliph is the paradigm of the "ideal" recipient of the storytelling/literary magic: he is a paradigm of the reader.

All this is only to rephrase the questions: Why do we read? Why do we enjoy it? What is the textual truth (we assume that any text conveys a certain cohesion of problems referred to as truth) of a work embedded in romance? And *how* do we read the truth of such a work? More particularly, why do we read and enjoy Davies' Deptford Trilogy, and how do we read and enjoy it?

This is where I will unabashedly declare the subject of this meditation: magic. How does one, in good faith, begin? Perhaps the best way, under these literary circumstances, is precisely by way of a meditative inquiry. Choosing magic as the answer to all the questions I have posed is an attempt at a seriously fanciful investigation of the ways in which the characters of The Deptford Trilogy reach out from the page toward the reader. That the reader of any text enters into an active relationship with that text, interpreting its gaps, completing, or misreading the meaning of that text, I take to be true without much questioning, as I believe Davies did too. All the references to the truth of a text, or a textual truth, in this context, will necessarily deal with the *shamanstvo* of the text; and it is because of–and despite–this that I chose to consider this very unfashionable and infamously inconclusive topic: the magic of the text–and specifically, the text of The Deptford Trilogy–and its effects upon the reader.

I will begin by suggesting that the act of reading the Trilogy is chronologically related to the way one reads myth as *mythos*: a story told in time and spatially related to the experience of the action of metaphor, fashionably understood as a verb. I will attempt an account of this as I go along, but it is vital to note that the Spatial and the Chronological, as dimensions in human perception, just like myth and metaphor, are often interwoven and that sometimes the only way to speak of or attempt to understand one is to speak of and attempt to understand the other. All four of these categories belong to the field of understanding; but while the Spatial and the Chronological, on the one hand, yield more or less "palpable,"describable cognizance, myth and metaphor, on the other hand, abiding as they do within the sphere of art, mystery, and the human spirit, bear truths substantially linked to visions that ultimately lead to discoveries. These are discoveries of the kind that here concern this reader, discoveries of the kind that are most aptly approached by way of evocation and suggestion rather than by close definition and argument.

Since I am writing about the experience of reading the Trilogy, and since I take reading also to be a process during which a medley of irregular and unaccountable responses takes place, the issue I would like to consider is one that may be referred to as "identification." By identification here I mean not only the irregular and unaccountable association a reader forms with a text, the power of the text to exert an associative pattern, but also the taxonomy involved in reading (intuitive or knowing), the classifying, cataloguing, and naming that accompanies reading in its linear progression. Much of the pleasure of reading and the reason for it depends on the (un)willing indulgence in the surrender to the magic of the text speaking "through" one of its textual faces–the indulgence in the experience of a (discerning) identification, or a desire for it, which is inevitable, and which is, in part, responsible for the opinion one forms of that text. This sort of identification, despite its invincible vulnerability and uncertainty, has a beginning and an end. This is so because the identification in the reading of fiction, in fact, poses or passes for a (sub)liminal awareness of the elusive and often receding dividing line between the mimetic and the magical, understood as the mythical, the metaphoric, the unlikely.

Thus, how does the reader attempt to identify with Liselotte Vitzlipützli, for example, who, in the Trilogy, acts as the *phantasia,* an embodied wealth of mental imagery? Or Magnus Eisengrim, who embodies the magical itself? What is the space that they occupy, both in the text and in the spatio-temporal extension of their text-character, lodged in the reader's mind? Where lies their textual truth, true but never conclusive?

My venture here is to suggest that their truth is "like" the truth of metaphor. It is effected through imagination, chiefly that of the reader. As a response to a spatial reading of text and character, the phenomenon of metaphor (even in the Ricoeurian sense) is capable of expanding our vision of the boundaries of what is real and is charged with a tensional but logical "incongruence." It is an action of thought rather than a figure of speech, and, as such, it works at the juncture of finite denotation and infinite connotation. The consequence of this action is always a reward in understanding, a discovery that pushes the limits of a structurally defined thought; it is that action that occasions the magic of metaphor. Metaphor is the figurative and sprightly child of symbol.[5] The potential for symbolism is rooted in a function common to all words, which are inherently mediations: they obscure while they seek to reveal, but they also reveal by obscuring. In this light, (and this is not news) metaphor conveys two contradictory messages: it suggests "a state of things in which there is no sharp or consistent distinction between subject and object," in the sense in which Northrop Frye defined it.[6] Yet, at the same time, it suggests a state of things, or, rather, a state of perception where dis/similarity as a mode of distinction between "proper" and "novel" is continually sensed. The "literal" and the "novel" meanings of metaphor (the operating tension of which informs the action of equipoise required to stand, for a moment, at the "blind point" of metaphoric, surprised delight) correspond to the "literal" (mimetic) and the "novel," supra-narrative (magical, if you will) grip that Davies' text possesses. Metaphorically and perceptually speaking, then, the "blind spot" created by this sort of narrative, emerging from the almost-caught glimpse of the place where the "truthfulness" of successful literary creations such as Magnus or Liesl begins; it represents the point where the reader's identification with them may begin, but, at the same time, is also the point where that identification ends. It is a point where magical thought, as presented and sustained in the Trilogy, most notably via Liesl, begins to effect an (un)recognised "realness" of those creations as separate beings, separate (that is, from the reader) as creations of a word-as-image truthfulness, in a fundamental pictorial sense, and whose relation to the reader can be expressed, disappointingly perhaps but adequately, only in degrees of (dis)pleasing affective responses. They are and they are not. The way in which Davies' literary creations of the Trilogy reach out from their textual space intruding into the spatial dimension of the reader resembles the metaphoric action of reaching out in perpetual tension for an equilibrium between two dis/similar concepts, or images, in order to furnish thought with a better understanding of itself.[7] Understood in this way, the stereoscopic effect exerted by the magical narrative of the Trilogy implies a magic-as-truth-as-symbol reading, both comfortably and surprisingly placed as a magical counterpart to a "novelistic/realist" narration, without disturbing the requirements of a compelling plot.

I return to Liesl. The power she wields upon her co-characters and the reader is based on the fact that she becomes, metaphorically, the textual embodiment of *phantasia,* understood both as fantasy and a wealth of mental imagery. Tzvetan Todorov's definition of the "fantastic" serves to illustrate a part of her dimension: "the fantastic . . . is characterized by a brutal intrusion of mystery into the context of real life. . . . [It] implies an integration of the reader into the world of the characters; that world is defined by the reader's own ambiguous perception of the events narrated."[8] Although Todorov refers to no actual reader (except the reader implicit in the text), the point here concerns precisely the actual reader who is faced with Liesl: the brutal intrusion of mystery into the context of real life in this case turns into the real mystery of self-discovery, and the context of real life becomes the unexplored self as a context for what it, the self, has learned or decided to call real life. Throughout the Trilogy Liesl propounds new laws (which brings her closer to Todorov's definition of the marvellous), laws that in the Trilogy call for a fruitful if tensional balance (armistice) between thought and feeling, logos and eros, all on the uncertain battleground of the yet unreconciled self: the self of Ramsay and David Staunton primarily.[9] In the Trilogy, Liesl acts as the metaphor for this fruitful association that pushes the limits of both thought and feeling. And like the marvellous and the metaphoric, Liesl is intriguing, immediate, and an authority unto herself.

Our heroes, by and large, have no objection to this. They would not have been those Davies meant them to be, or to become, had they not eventually gathered around and under Liesl's mesmerizing hegemony. Liesl's sentences, and the phrases she employs, are the verbal equivalents of potent visual images that imprint themselves on the listener's/viewer's/reader's mind and that, quite simply, oblige consideration. And the force of it all is unsurprisingly distressing. To the unsuspecting, ordered Ramsay, Liesl says:

> You despise almost everybody except Paul's mother. No wonder she seems like a saint to you; you have made her carry the affection you should have spread among fifty people. Do not look at me with that tragic face. You should thank me. At fifty years old you should be glad to know something of yourself. That horrid village and your hateful Scots family made you a moral monster. Well, it is not too late for you to enjoy a few years of almost normal humanity.[10]

Ramsay bears the cross of his Deptford past dutifully and with a sense of obsessive devotion. He also seems to be better prepared for his encounter with the miraculous, being by nature inclined to look for truth beyond the one of the phenomenal world. But Ramsay's difficulty, as Liesl points out, is the constraining influence of his Presbyterian upbringing, which is partly responsible for his rigid religious rationalism. Ramsay must tear down the wall of intellectual fascination with the miraculous and magical in order to allow some of that fascination to be converted into emotion, into his living flesh, reconciling with it and reclaiming the part of himself responsible for turning him into Fifth Business. Like the High Priestess of the Tarot deck, Liesl unrelentingly and harshly opens doors, points to obvious but unconsidered signs and is, in turn, seen herself. In *The Manticore* she furnishes Jo von Haller's contribution to David Staunton's re-acquaintance with himself with the immediacy and insolence of emotional severity—the very element, apparently, lacking in his formal analysis:

> So? It isn't everybody who is triumphantly the hero of his own romance, and when we meet one he is likely to be a fascinating monster, like my dear Eisengrim. But just because you are not a roaring egotist, you needn't fall for the fashionable twaddle of the anti-hero and the mini-soul. That is what we might call the Shadow of democracy; it makes it so laudable, so cosy and right and easy to be a spiritual runt and lean on all the other runts for support and

applause in a splendid apotheosis of runtdom. Thinking runts, of course—oh, yes, thinking away as hard as a runt can without getting into danger. But, there are heroes, still. The modern hero is the man who conquers in the inner struggle. How do you know you aren't that kind of hero?[11]

Through this particular kind of instruction, Liesl is more than aggravating. She forcefully offers what Ramsay and David Staunton want (in both usual senses of the word). She obliges them to open to a world informed by the knowing magic of personal feeling, integrated into the self's various realities. She drives them to grant entrance to the cognitive possibilities that hover just beyond the realm of the orderly logos. She also has an emblematic role in the universe of the text: through her body she acts as a metaphor, transforming experience into ambiguous ritual actions. Her body "transmutes sensations and beliefs into the physical art" of life and self, and the magic of daily life.[12] She offers an insight that, in its embryonic phase at least, belongs to the nonverbal form of cognition.

For the greenhorn recipient this means a blend of silent thought and silent feeling, just below the threshold of articulation. Ultimately, it is the individual psychic baggage of Ramsay and David Staunton that eventually determines the singular but unified sensibility and that represents their silent reaction to Liesl's instructive (verbal) imagery. This is why Liesl expresses herself essentially through monologues: being the *phantasia*, and the marvellous, she is awesome. She verbalises silent, still unarticulated representations of the self (that of Ramsay and David Staunton) drawn primarily from the store of sense experience. And this is why those around her appear to be silent, or silenced. But all this is not news. In the mythology of The Deptford Trilogy, Liesl is the goddess and the high power: she is both the eternal womb and the power of male energy. As far as the reader is concerned, positioned at the blind spot of this active space that Liesl inhabits, he reacts effectively to the brazen but undeniable force of *phantasia*: he is either annoyed or he smiles with degrees of recognition. (Indifference is admittedly an option, but I would think a very rare one, and one that would imply a set of entirely different considerations.) The recognition is qualified and conditional (as is the annoyance) because of the essential ambivalence with which we respond to the phenomenon of metaphor. Something of Liesl at once pleases, surprises, and annoys us; however, we do not identify *with* metaphor, we experience it. At best, the experience of metaphor is one of surprised recognition. We recognise the tensional space that Liesl as a character inhabits as a space of metaphoric (im)possibility. Like a metaphor, she remains throughout the Trilogy the supreme priestess of the rituals that concern the rebirth of the knowing self: she vanishes for a time and then appears again to state that nothing is ultimate except the cycle, the ritual of the self. In the role that she performs in the Trilogy, Liesl embodies originality and illusion; she "represents wisdom and serene knowledge; intuition and penetrating understanding . . . [who] is a delicate contradiction: obscured clarity, earthy empress, and a guardian of secrets who, inevitably, illuminates what exists only in the shadows . . . where mystery becomes discovery and discovery remains mysterious" (Highwater 69). Like the metaphor and myth of the High Priestess in the Tarot deck, Liesl exists as a contradiction without the need for resolution or mediation. And this is how the reader "reads" her–on the edge.

Since this essay is only covertly Jungian, I will refer to Magnus simply as one of Liesl's kind. But, while Liesl's truth *corresponds* to the truth of metaphor, Magnus, unconditionally, *is* the un-self-conscious metaphor. Even Liesl, in her enlightened glory, acknowledges him as a teacher whose power lies precisely in his faults. It is tempting to see Magnus, also within the figures of the Tarot deck, as "The Magician" who holds a rod in his left hand that points to the heavens and who points downward with his right hand toward earth (Highwater 53). Metaphorically, then, he occupies a space somewhere between heaven and earth, representing free will, unfettered creativity and imagination, deception and trickery. Existing between heaven and earth he is amoral, pure, and unqualified, neither good nor evil. He *is* the raw, unprocessed marvel founded on instinct and fed on intuition unmitigated by logos, a marvel that in its inexplicability and might verges on (but never veers into) self-sufficient brutality. "Wonder is marvellous but it is also cruel, cruel, cruel. It is undemocratic, discriminatory, and pitiless," says Liesl (*World of Wonders* 324); and the perilous implications of this statement are confirmed when Magnus himself, in *Fifth Business*, says "One always learns one's mystery at the price of one's innocence" (259). The mystery, for Magnus, is the hard-earned recognition and welcoming of his instincts (at once both feeling and thought–unified, and thus un-self-conscious), which never fail him. As the self-conscious, embodied balance between the logos and eros principle, Liesl can explain Magnus' strengths in terms of the Magian World View. It was:

> A sense of the unfathomable wonder of the invisible world that existed side by side with a hard recognition of the roughness and cruelty and day-to-day demands of the tangible world. . . . It was poetry and wonder which might reveal themselves in the dunghill,

> and it was an understanding of the dunghill which lurks in poetry
> and wonder. It was a sense of living in what Spengler called a
> quavering cavern-light which is always in danger of being
> swallowed up in the surrounding, impenetrable darkness. . . . I knew
> about the Magian World View and recognized in my teacher. He
> knew nothing of it . . . it was so much in the grain of the life he had
> lived, so much a part of him, that he didn't understand that
> everybody else didn't think–no, didn't feel–as he did. I would not
> for the world have attempted to explain it to him, because that
> would have endangered it." (*WW* 325)

Being an un-self-conscious metaphor for feeling and intuition, Magnus
*is* the feeling and intuition, and is brutal as they are in their unmitigated forms.
And we can most certainly recognise them and sense their intensity. He is also
the "naked magician,"[13] whose power derives from these two pure properties,
and on account of which he has established himself successfully in the fictional
world of the Trilogy. It is because of these two properties that Magnus has
metabolised into his sanguine fluid that he reconciles the tensions between what
is real and what is unreal, in more than one sense. He is "really" Paul Dempster,
but, at the same time, in *Fifth Business*, he tells Boy Staunton: "My real name
is Magnus Eisengrim. That is who I am and that is how the world knows me"
(258); and in *The Manticore*, upon meeting David Staunton and inquiring
whether he had read the story of his, Magnus', life written by Ramsay, he says:
"*Phantasmata* says what it is quite frankly what it is in its title: it is an illusion,
a vision. Which is what I am . . . . [But] it is truer to the essence of my life than
the dowdy facts could ever be. Do you understand? I am what I have made
myself. . . . Do the facts suggest or explain what I am? No. But Ramsay's book
does. I am truly Magnus Eisengrim. The illusion, the lie, is a Canadian called
Paul Dempster" (260). Illusion as fact, and magic as a principle of truth:
unlikely–but in the un/real figure of Magnus they are there, reconciled. The
reconciliation forged within the fiction of Magnus' textual world does not
diminish the tension established between Magnus and the reader, who balances
within *himself* while reading the sense of Magnus' "unreality" and magic, his
(im)possibility, with the degrees of recognition and discovery, as forms of
identification.

Therefore, even in the spatio-temporal extension of Magnus'
character/figure, he (just like the whole of The Deptford Trilogy) acts as a
liminal being: he is not "supernatural" (which would compel the reader to think

in terms of belief/disbelief, or even in terms of the hesitation that characterises the fantastic as defined by Todorov), but he stands at the threshold between the Infinite, universal, and the Finite, temporal and personal. In that sense Magnus is also a mythological protagonist engaged in an archetypal story of which characters and readers alike know the pattern: "What is the mythical element in his story? Simply the very old tale of a man who is in search of his soul, and who must struggle with the monster to secure it. All myth and Christianity–which has never been able to avoid the mythical pull of human experience–are full of similar instances, and people all around us are living out this basic human pattern every day" (*WW* 155). Without daring to go into any further commentary on the similarities between religion and myth, I would note that it is this pattern that makes it unlikely that the young reader (who is very often the one who reads and enjoys the Trilogy) upon reading *World of Wonders*, for example, would be tempted to pack his bags and join an inferior troop of travelling showmen to lead a life of ambiguous ethical merit.

Reading texts that in their entirety are attuned to the familiar resonance that every myth(os) carries does not prompt one to action. The identification that involves the ambivalent, surprised recognition is more likely to create something akin to "an aesthetic arrest," similar to the arrest effected by the action of metaphor, which holds in balancing tension two concepts (without prompting one to action). This is the point where metaphor and myth in the reading of character in the Trilogy converge upon the issue of recognition and identification. Magnus' (sometimes seen as) "dubious" claim to the role of the hero stops being dubious if understood in terms of the Magian World View, which is in its essence mythical, and which finds a direct parallel in the nature of the romance form of the fairytale, itself a form of the hero-myth, where "devils and evil spirits threaten man, angels and fairies protect him" and where the "division of the spirits into good and bad . . . is a part of that dualism which, ever the same under its thousand forms, fills the Magian world" including "polarities in the most primary sensations which mingle with those of the refined critical understanding" (Monk 168). While this suggests the kind of adventure of individuation that Magnus undergoes, it also suggests the way the reader perceives the text that deals with it. Reading Magnus as the mythical hero who undertakes a metaphorical journey implies an acceptance of a textual truth that cancels issues of credibility of character. One does not "believe in" metaphor. Neither does one "believe in" myth. One *conceives of* their (im)possibility, absorbing them, but with the edge of doubleness and ambivalence that define them.[14] It is true that the references to this inescapable ambivalence carry Jungian overtones, in that the magical is allowed to encompass an expression of a universal truth. Brought forth through the shared mythical background, the "collective unconscious," this (textual) truth, the element of recognition and familiarity, is as instantaneous and immediate as is the perceptual (spatial and temporal) distance that such a text carries with it:

> Whoever speaks in primordial images speaks with a thousand voices; he enthrals and overpowers while at the same time he lifts the idea he is seeking to express out of the occasional and the transitory into the realm of the ever-enduring. He transmutes our personal destiny into the destiny of mankind, and evokes in us all those beneficent forces that ever and anon have enabled humanity to find a refuge from every peril and to outlive the longest night.[15]

Magnus and Liesl speak in primordial images: this is how they act upon the reader. As far as the "actions" of Ramsay and David Staunton are concerned, their accepting and loving Liesl, as well as understanding Magnus, implies a concept of self-perfectibility. In its optimism this concept is realised as a reciprocal, double dialectic independent of the external—the establishment of a balance between the dynamism intrinsic to the process of individuation and the passive receptivity of the higher forces of fate, or divinity, as predicated in Jung's theory of the universal archetypes. The mystery of self-discovery, in this (Romanticist) sense, becomes the parallel of a golden reality.

The way this relates to the chronological reading of the Trilogy as a *mythos*, a story told in time, becomes evident through a similar action of recognition and identification that takes place both within the textual universe and within its inhabitants who exist at the border of their and the reader's universe. Frye locates the centre of gravity of myth as the narrative of all literature. Joseph Campbell argues that the material of myth is the material of our life, our body and the material of our environment. The Deptford Trilogy, as a literary artifact that, as has been noted, aims at representing the necessity for a complete (re)integration of the fragmented self (into) the material of our life, body and environment, is perhaps best comprehended if we assume that its text is a formation of style and the essence of art and life, all "suspended in the gap between imagination and reality," blurring the borderlines of subjective and subject-independent truth. This ambivalence and doubt are also inherent in the term "myth(os)" in its chronological dimension: "A myth," writes Frye, " . . . is a narrative that suggests two inconsistent responses: first, it says, 'this is what is said to have happened,' and second, 'this almost certainly is not what happened, at least, in precisely the way described'" (4). What metaphor does to space, myth does to time, Frye asserts. Myth condenses time: it freezes it in the present moment, which in itself becomes ambivalent, since it is the present that (paraphrasing T.S. Eliot) is comprised of the past and the future at once. The presence of the present time, thus frozen through myth, implies a core, a centre.

The centre around which the individual myths of the Trilogy circle is Deptford (as the birthplace of Ramsay, Magnus/Paul Dempster, Boy Staunton; as the genealogical root of David Staunton; and also the centre that obscures the death of Boy Staunton). The core is at once that which is known and that which is unknown, and, therefore, mysterious. The Deptford core binds them all together; but again, like every core, it is an elusive centre that separates them. It is the source, the shared, originating past of the central figures in the Trilogy, acting as a kind of "collective unconscious" to Ramsay, Eisengrim, and the Stauntons, haunting them all in different ways. Each of the figures linked to it has to reclaim and reread it in a wholly personal way. It is the history that binds them; but, then, history is just as unlikely as myth and magic. History needs to be confronted, used and overcome, or integrated. Deptford is the mythical core; all three narrators weave their *mythoi* against the (historical) shadow of Deptford. At the core of every *mythos* is a historical event, but because of its ambivalence, myth is, in part, an imaginative construct, and being a story (*histoire*) told in time, it implies the presence of the storyteller/narrator, inescapably burdened by subjectivity. Ramsay's narrative (most notably in *Fifth Business*, but also in all the instances in *The Manticore* and *World of Wonders*) exemplifies such a subjectivity. He is a historian and a hagiographer; he is also the storyteller "before" Davies and behind *Fifth Business*; he makes–and I emphasise the logocentricity, the implied personal (self-conscious) presence in this verb–records of the past, of the event of Paul Dempster's birth, the "facts" of Boy Staunton's and his own life, the number of Staunton's marriages, the names of his two children, the places of their education, his own war service, the accident, and the women in his life.

But the texture of his narrative, of his textual space, is coloured by the (interpretive) personal, the "magical." (I am aware of the immeasurable freedom of use that this term allows; I take this to be the synchronous cause for its immense appeal and for the analytical discontent it may provoke.) Just as metaphor is counter-logical rather than illogical, and just as myth is counter-historical, the magical is counter-realistic. The reader is aware of this historical interplay in Ramsay's narration (remembering the close and controversial ties between "history" and "story"), not only in the sense that his character possesses an archetypal flavouring, being the sort of life-wonder- teaching history teacher, fallible and fascinating, that many of us have had, or wished to have had, but also in the way that he searchingly adumbrates that which resists articulation: "I clung to my notion, ill defined though it was, that a serious study of any important body of human knowledge, or theory, or belief, if undertaken with a critical but not a cruel mind, would in the end yield some secret, some valuable permanent insight, into the nature of life and the true end of man" (*Fifth Business* 169). The reader's impressions of Ramsay, and of his narrative, are equally stereoscopic when he, Ramsay, hidden in a corner of the Byzantine basilica in Guadeloupe, watches the endless crowd of men and women as they shuffle on their knees to get as close as possible to the miraculous picture of the Virgin, "whose faces had the beauty virtually every face reveals in the presence of the goddess of mercy. . . . Very different, these, from the squinnying, lip-biting, calculating faces of the art lovers one sees looking at Madonnas in galleries. These petitioners had no conception of art. To them a picture was a symbol of something else, and very readily the symbol became the reality" (*FB* 199). The created background of the basilica against which Ramsay gains an awed and profound understanding of what he calls a "psychological truth" is as magical as the "real" thing. The awed recognition of the psychological realism of something as magical as faith is perhaps as old-fashioned as Ramsay himself, but it could also be a meaningful metafictional commentary on the way we are to read the story, or history, not only of *Fifth Business*, but of the Trilogy as a whole.

In the course of his confessional narrative, Ramsay has accordingly to recognise and befriend his personal Devil. The reader has to recognise and learn to deal accordingly with the truth of a text that is inspired by myth, magic, and romance, interlocked elements all related "to the shaping of the universe of the human mind" (Monk 14). Ramsay's is an account of factual events shaped to adhere to his intuitive vision of what "true" reality is, interwoven with his propensity for mythologising and shaped to adhere to his sense of a reality learned. Synecdochically, this is true for the whole of the Trilogy: the entangled and intertwined *mythoi* of Ramsay, Magnus, David and Boy Staunton, and Liesl, are to be regarded as both typical/mimetic and highly unusual/magical; tales that for better comprehension must be embraced both actually and symbolically.

The symbol, in its mimetic and fictional sense (at once Ramsay's only senses), is and is not reality. Metaphor is not to be taken literally (and it would be very difficult to do so when metaphor is understood as a verb) for the fruits of its truth. These are effected only through imagination, and there is no other faculty more magical and unlikely in its power than imagination. Liesl and Magnus know this all along; Ramsay senses it and has to relate it, apply it to his "self," which he does; David Staunton wants and needs this insight in order to continue his life in a fulfilling way, learning from his father's mistakes retrospectively, most notably from Boy Staunton's continual gliding upon the surface of his personal myth, that of the handsome and capable tycoon, without recognizing the need to probe beneath the surface for other meanings. Boy Staunton, the man who "couldn't keep anything to himself," uses Ramsay as the "keeper of his conscience," and, in the end (his end as told in *Fifth Business*), dismisses even the indirect but insightful advice this keeper gives him: "You created a God in Your own image, and when you found out he was no good you abolished him. It's a quite common form of psychological suicide" (241). As the core event around which the tales eccentrically revolve, his death leaves a lot of ambiguities. Is it the symbol became reality? Very likely. The facts, as we know them, are not really important.

In *World of Wonders*, Magnus builds his narrative around the recognizably same events (recognizable, sequentially, after *Fifth Business*), but he encircles them with the colours of his experience. He is also a tricky narrator, conscious of the relativity of (historical) truth and conscious that because of that relativity there are many ways in which his audience—as viewers or listeners—can be reoriented and, indeed, manipulated. At the beginning of *World of Wonders* he decides to tell his audience at Sorgenfrei "a few things" about his magic and his life, which events are naturally interchangeable. The reader may or may not be on guard, depending on his inner disposition, but he remembers the virtuosity Magnus displays on the stage, satisfying his audiences' desire for magic. So, what Magnus tells is his own *mythos*—a story that says, "this is what (is said) to have happened" and at the same time "this almost certainly is not what happened, at least in precisely the way described." Being the magician, one who invents reality, Magnus toys even with the sources of his own identity, remaking himself, like his own story, to conform to what his experience has made of him and to conform to his most prominent traits, as powers: feeling and intuition. The beneficial consequence of this is the question of his identity, which is finally "resolved" in ambivalence.

David Staunton learns that understanding and experience are not interchangeable, and Liesl is the one who makes a promise to show him the need for their happy union. In the course of his analysis, he recognises the doubt of reality itself while contextualizing himself within his own universe: "[recognizing] the objectivity of the world, while knowing also that because of who I am and what I am, I both perceive the world in terms of who and what I am and project onto the world a great deal of who and what I am. If I know this, I ought to escape the stupider kinds of illusion" (*The Manticore* 244). Staunton's (hi)story is formally framed as a Jungian analysis that validates (the "realness" of) his self-exploration even as that self-exploration proceeds from submission to learning from another. That is why he is modestly and less imposingly ready to acknowledge the weakness, and, possibly, the erroneousness of his perspective. The magical grip of the text in *The Manticore* is subtler; it comes through dreams and recalls the affinity between myth, and literature, and dream. The interpretation of the dream-myth is "gradual and it comes from an exploration, by the head, of [one's] own wisdom" (95). This is what David does: his narrative is an exploration *of* his self and *to* himself. While Ramsay's narrative stance was at least a striving (even if knowingly futile) toward a dispassionate account of events, David's is from the very outset private; the purpose of his narrative is to explain himself to himself, and he is not concerned with the consistency of his perspective, either spatially or chronologically: time shifts are frequent, and the time given to events in the different sections varies.

All this, however, reveals the congruity of message delivered by the whole of the Trilogy, which is the concern with meaning–as the subjective, un/real and infinite product of interpretation, rather than as truth ("Without being a verbatim report, this is the essence of what passed between us," says David of his sessions with Dr. Jo von Haller [*TM* 67]). Thus the nature of un/reality and the secrets of (his) human identity are taught to David, or unveiled to him with the help of Jo von Haller and, magnificently, with the help of Liesl. As the mythical hero who must undergo the standard path of individuation, David Staunton must pass (in a symbolic form presented as) "a pseudo-death, or a death-analogue, which in mythical narratives serves as a catalyst for the achievement of the desired goal, the symbolic re-birth" (Monk 140). In *The Manticore*, and for David Staunton, this death-analogue, which carries within it the seed of new life, is the moment in the bear cave, which affords a memorable representation of magical thought. In other words, this scene is the culmination of a kind of psychological realism, itself ambivalent in its paradoxical emphasis on a magic that is exposed simultaneously as truth and illusion. David Staunton, in the midst of it all, shows promise to emerge all the better for it, and the reader, still between two books, begins to hear echoes of "all things are *as if* they were. . . . *Real* things are *effects* of something unknown. . . . We have no idea of absolute reality, because 'reality' is always something 'observed'" (Monk 146).

One of the subtly distressing effects of reading an atypical romance, which in its essence is mythical and metaphoric but which is neither myth nor metaphor, is the fact that the skilled reader might feel manipulated through the text's insistence on ambivalence, revealed in and through every narrative perspective, especially when this ambivalence touches upon some vital ontological and epistemological issues. To fight this or to define it is simply a matter of choice, even if the reader does not allow the magic of the text to work in its mysterious way. In fact, this sort of narrative presents the reader with multiple perspectives converging (sometimes slightly off-centre) on one (un/real) event. It also presents him with a curiously lifelike layering in perception, and it involves him in a quasi-historical process of reconstruction: the search for a credible fictional meaning, somewhere around the elusive narrative core. The ambivalent nature of this search further confirms the uncertain (and already platitudinous) boundaries between truth and fiction/reality and magic. Only the process of reading itself is, in fact, more magical and ambivalent than anything else, since it is always a magical, quasi-historical quest for a totality of understanding that always remains out of epistemological and ontological reach. This is not to say that the prospect for marvels and wonder is forsaken; on the contrary, it remains the quintessential condition for the interplay between literature and being. But the details of this interaction are always the matter of autobiography.

Liesl, Ramsay, Eisengrim, Boy and David Staunton, as well as the characters of which I have not spoken, particularly Padre Blason and Father Knopwood, are condensed figurations of character; they are, so to speak, essences of character. In the tensional continuum between reader and text, they act as magical, polyvalent pointers in the (textual) maze of the self's metaphorical journey toward itself. Their significant vigour rests upon their ability, or, rather, Davies' ability to evoke pictorial images related to familiar systems of ideas, both in the reader's fancy and imagination, resulting in what might be called an "infinite text." They act upon the reading mind in the way primary colours act upon the seeing eye. Through their symbolic and/or textual lives, which carry implications of mythic images translated into discourse, they are the fictional, textual practice of what Joseph Campbell called the Perennial Philosophy–they are universal pictorial images translated into textual faces. This approach to the reading of The Deptford Trilogy invites a "split" thought: one that encompasses both magic presented as fact (albeit a psychological one) and a "rational" contemplation of the literal, the mimetic aspect of fiction, a thought that operates through the continual "pulling together"of the two perspectives that touch on an edge of recognition and perception, the simultaneity of which the reader is aware of as a prolonged action that stirs him. The continuities we recognise in myth prompt or initiate responses based as much on affective, intuitive impulses as on articulated, acquired systems of thought. This is one of the reasons why the "moral" dimension of the Trilogy is "magical" in more than one way: it is one that concerns itself with the individual, who is still and despite all "the greatest hope of mankind," and the "mysticism of happiness," which is another way of describing the up-swelling of wonder, the sense of well-being, the coming together, the expanding, the unfolding, the kind of "marvellous sense of the glory, splendour, gorgeousness of life" (Davis 61); it is a message that invites a glance at and a reach beyond the limits of the knowable–"You have to be on reasonable terms with yourself; you've got to forgive yourself for being an awful lot of things which you just are" (Davis 138)–and a message that if it ever "promotes" anything, it is "a moral concern . . . not as an advocacy of a particular kind of morality, but a deep concern with certain basic things" (Davis 234).

The message is wonderfully clear and bright, if not shockingly new. Being new, in this case, is thoroughly beside the point. It is in its clarity and brightness that it reaches its wide audiences, and it is in these magical qualities that its main strength resides. ("A good piece of magic is a work of art and should be respected as such; it is a flower, not an alarm clock, and if you pull it to pieces to find out what makes it work, you have destroyed it, and your own pleasure.")[16]

After I have written all this, chasing after the mood of the Trilogy, staying in between sentences and at the beginning of thoughts, some of the many questions that logically arise (when one belongs to a scientifically and analytically oriented era) go like this: does all this talk of magic and the truth of a text produce a distancing effect, distancing, that is, in all the imaginable ways a distance can be sensed? Or, simply, what is (if any) the effect it produces? These are perfectly valid, somewhat self-conscious questions, which I acknowledge, but leave unanswered. Attempting answers would collapse the arching outlines of this essay (and the topic itself). The notion that there is much magic in what Davies called "psychological realism" and that even an atypical romance such as The Deptford Trilogy may strike a responsive chord in the reader only implies a rejection of (interpretive) absolutisms. The idea of a causal (even interpretive) universe and a social (even critical) order built on seemingly universal (moral) laws is always qualified by an ultimate principle of uncertainty: the only thing there is to know is our own knowing. This is at once the metaphor and the myth(os) of our existence.

In the way of a(n) (im)possible finalisation, I believe it is only appropriate to let Davies impart, at some length, a few of his own ideas on the topic of the magic and text. *The Merry Heart,* a posthumous collection of his essays, contains a transcription of a 1989 lecture "The Novelist and Magic," delivered in the Medical Building at University of Toronto:

> I have already said that the novel is wholly personal in its appeal; one reader, with one book, encounters the mind of one author. Not all the science in the world can explain or chart the different ways in which the book reaches its reader.... When I first began writing novels I was often criticised for elements in the plots which seemed to the critics to be inadmissible in any serious work of fiction.... What most annoyed them, however, was my way of introducing things into my novels which hinted at what they called the supernatural–at a life existing at the same time as ours, and influencing ours in a variety of great and small ways.... But I did not mean these things to be supernatural because that is a stupid term.... No, my novels were simply psychological.... I was not interested in realism in the ordinary acceptance of the word; my realism was psychological realism, and the way in which it manifested itself in my stories could not be accommodated to a narrower conception of reality.... I was not a photographer, catching in black and white what the lens of the camera could see; I was a painter in oils, including what I, as an author could see.
>
> Why? It is here that I have to tell you one or two things which I have not spoken of in public, because I thought they would be misunderstood. But I have now come to a time in life when I really don't care very much whether people understand me, because I have spent my life trying with my best efforts to understand myself. I am one of those creatures–by no means uncommon–who were called by Bernard Shaw ... Galtonic Visualizers. It is not a

very good term, but it strives for scientific accuracy and therefore I offer it to this scientific audience. Things of importance come to me not in philosophical reflections, but in flashes, in sudden perceptions of the unseen, indeed I suppose I must say in visions. It is not, I assure you, because I have a screw loose, but because my arrangement of screws is wholly personal.

... Has that anything to do with the novel, which you pick up, put down at will, use to beguile an idle hour, and perhaps think of as a modest contribution to the ever changing culture of the time?

Well, yes, it has, if you will permit me to be shameless in asserting the essence of the art of which I am a humble but careful practitioner..For the novelist, indirectly perhaps, but persuasively, he hopes, is pointing you in the direction of the new discovery. ... That is, if you want to call it by an ambiguous name, his magic, his enchanter quality. (138-43)

## NOTES

1. J. Madison Davis, ed. *Conversations with Robertson Davies* (Jackson: University Press of Mississippi, 1989), 267.

2. Robertson Davies, *A Voice From the Attic* (Toronto: McClelland & Stewart, 1960), 18-19.

3. This article is clearly an interpretive meditation on a direct experience of a work of literature; a meditation that in its sweep is archetypal and inclined toward synthesis (alluding both to Jung and Romanticism) and, also, one comfortable with "logical" ambiguities. I believe this to be in agreement with Davies' perspective on his own work and in agreement with his outlook on his art and life, of which he spoke and wrote in his lectures and books of essays.

4. In the essay entitled "A Rake at Reading," in *The Merry Heart* (Toronto: McClelland & Stewart, 1996), Davies writes about John Cowper Powys as the author through whose work he encountered the world of romance:

In 1933 I discovered an author, by no means widely popular yet, though I think him one of the giants of our century. ... It was in that year that *A Glastonbury Romance* appeared; it was just what I wanted and I read its 1,174 pages with wonderment, sometimes with bafflement, but eventually with breathtaking illumination. ... Very often he described his best fictions

... as romances, which is a better name for them than novels, for they break every rule that the high priests of the novel have devised. . . . He attempted, with variable success . . . to extend the boundaries of what language can do in evoking rare and unusual modes of feeling. His books are romances in the old Celtic sense, for in them the point of view changes whenever he pleases, the prevailing mood varies and bypaths are pursued with what is sometimes maddening caprice. But they enlarge the reader's concept of what may be comprised within a single consciousness. . . . Yet, he was not describable as a romantic; sometimes he is a realist, sometimes a cynic. He is, to put it as simply as possible, a very great man of a Blake-like breadth of perception. (14)

What is clearly perceived is the hesitation on Davies' part to refer to Powys as either a romantic or a realist. These adjectives are, at any rate, very imprecise, but they are capable of intimations with regard to the style of a work of fiction. The Deptford Trilogy itself stands in between these two connoting fields. It is in this "in-between" sense that the Trilogy harmonises with Franz Roh's definition of the term "magic realism" in the context of the visual arts, where magic suggests neither a return to the spiritual in an ethnological sense, nor to a demonic irrationalism, nor naive vitalism, but understood as "the magic of Being" it refers to an "authentic rationalism" (quoted in Irene Guenther's "Magic Realism in the Weimar Republic" in *Magic Realism: Theory, History, Community* [Durham: Duke University Press, 1995], 35).

5. In her insightful and sensitive discussion of ancient Greek lyric poetry, in *Eros the Bittersweet: An Essay* (Princeton: Princeton University Press, 1986), Anne Carson traces the etymology of symbol to the ancient world, to *symbolon*, describing it as "one half of a knucklebone carried as a token of identity to someone who has the other half. Together the two halves compose one meaning" (75).

6. Northrop Frye, *Myth and Metaphor: Selected Essays, 1974-1988*, ed. Robert D. Denham (Charlottesville: University of Virginia Press, 1990), 7.

7. Stereoscopically, then, one sees the "sameness" and, at the same time, one sees the difference between the two wor(l)ds. Somewhere in between, in this essentially atavistic, violent and stereoscopic space, stands a possibility of grasping a truer meaning (not a truth).

8. Tzvetan Todorov, *The Fantastic: A Structural Approach to a Literary Genre*, trans. Richard Howard (Ithaca, N.Y.: Cornell University Press, 1973), 28-30.

9. It is very fitting that Liesl, in her marvellous dimension, is apparently displeasing at first sight. The reaction of all three–Ramsay, Eisengrim, and David Staunton–upon first

seeing her is unpleasant surprise.

10. Robertson Davies, *Fifth Business* (Toronto: Macmillan, 1970), 255.

11. Robertson Davies, *The Manticore* (Toronto: Macmillan, 1972), 267.

12. Jamake Highwater, *The Language of Vision: Meditations on Myth and Metaphor* (New York: Grove, 1994), 33.

13. Patricia Monk, *The Smaller Infinity: The Jungian Self in the Novels of Robertson Davies* (Toronto: University of Toronto Press, 1982), 147.

14. This is why myth, and narratives with mythical overtones, cannot be accused of advocating a particular ideology. Even though they cannot be dissociated from their social milieu, they do not promote a systematised set of beliefs, because, as Frye notes in *Myth and Metaphor*, they have the quality of fine ambivalence, existing on the edge between the individual/personal and social/universal (7).

15. Carl Gustav Jung, "On the Relation of Analytical Psychology to Poetry," *The Spirit of Man, Art, and Literature*, in *The Collected Works of C.G. Jung*, ed. Sir Herbert Read et al., trans. R.F.C. Hull (Princeton, N.J.: Princeton University Press, 1953), 82.

16. Robertson Davies, "World of Wonders," *The Merry Heart: Selections 1980-1995* (Toronto: McClelland & Stewart, 1996), 283. This essay is a transcription of a lecture delivered in 1992 at the Avon Theatre during the Stratford Festival Celebrated Writers Series, when his novel *World of Wonders* was adapted for the stage. In a letter to a friend, written in the same year, he commented with pleasure on the warm reception with which the play was met by the audiences, especially the part when the actor who played Eisengrim showed some of his illusions: "Perhaps the most popular [illusion] was . . . when Eisengrim . . . took the notes that had been made by the man who wanted to make a television show of his life, and threw them out into the audience, where they flew up into the roof of the theatre and disappeared! A very good ending for a play about magic–the magic of the stage, and the magic of life" (264).

# "Converting the Clerisy": Quest/ioning, Contradictions, and Ethics in The Cornish Triptych

ANDREA C. COLE

In *The Lyre of Orpheus*, academic Penny Raven (a professor of Comparative Literature) comments on the significance of a piece of literature for an understanding of the project that the Cornish Foundation has undertaken:

> You see, there's a very great poem by Lewis Carroll about the Hunting of the Snark; a lot of crazy creatures set off, they know not whither, in search of they know not what. . . . It's just about a crazy voyage that somehow, in an unfathomable way, makes a kind of eerie sense.[1]

Canadians can be great seekers, or questers, for identity. The quest for identity is not one that can be achieved by the individual, for persons always evolve, and a conclusion to a quest must necessarily indicate some form of closure, just as we expect our stories to have a beginning, a middle, and an end. It is in this context that I see Robertson Davies' work. We set off, a company of crazy creatures (because readers can be crazy creatures with their social and historical expectations, and their critical methodologies in hand) in search of we know not what. Sometimes we have an idea whither, if we are searching toward or within a specific idea or context. Davies says: "As for my own books, I hope that readers will have to use their heads and be collaborators . . . in creating the work of art that is the book. It's just a script."[2] In this, he echoes Northrop Frye, who avers that "eventually it dawns on us that it is the reader who achieves the Quest."[3] Davies likes to remind us, in a very specific way, that it is we as readers who "achieve" the quest, although I have no doubt that the context of the word is very different for Davies than it is for Frye.

I am particularly interested in the sorts of narrative oppositions that Davies sets up in his novels, especially where they seem to interfere with the linear progression of a chronological narrative. They are often thematic, but more often they are technical; for example, the voices of the living world set against the voices of a "dead" or afterworld, which "voicing" has interesting implications for both theme and technique. This trait is apparent in *The Lyre of Orpheus*, and it is a technique that developed in the Cornish triptych, which peaks in the penultimate novel, *Murther and Walking Spirits*.

Narrative voices or lines that oppose or question each other are certainly not new techniques, if we think of the intrusive authorial voices, however omniscient, of Thomas Hardy in *The Dynasts*; having more than one character tell a story is certainly not unique either. That is simply a matter of point of view. But it is interesting that in response to Davies' work, no less than a small critical furor has been raging over the last decade or so in just these areas. Barbara Godard, for instance, believes that Davies' writing evinces a clear example of the multi-voiced Bakhtinian dialogue, that he works within her interpretation of the carnivalesque.[4] In contrast, there are those who argue, as does Stephen Bonnycastle (also within Bakhtinian constraints), that Davies writes monologue, the insistent drone of one voice–in this case, his authorial own.[5] Jamie Dopp supports this point with what he admits is theoretically shady psychoanalysing, "that perhaps the tendency to monologue has become a problem [for Davies] (self-defeatingly dogmatic? Too old fashioned?)."[6] W.J. Keith, on the other hand, extols Davies' position "in the van-guard of post-modernism . . . ; [he] is as capable as any post-modernist of deconstructing the conventional theories of fictive decorum."[7] But Davies has seldom, if ever, voiced his views on the politics of the postmodern.

Davies is eminently aware of the importance of his position in Canadian letters and has often voiced his opinions on the sorts of readers he wants to cultivate, what he calls his "clerisy," an audience that is educated and sophisticated in literary taste. Clearly for Davies, educating the reader is of primary concern, and that impulse to educate is inscribed in a narrative in which the tension between character and point of view is foregrounded. As readers, we are conditioned to expect certain things of our stories. Structuralist critics argue that we are also conditioned to accept only certain types of plot constructions as well; in an academic dogfight in *The Lyre of Orpheus*, even Davies slyly allows one character to posit the supposed fact that there are only nine plots in all story-telling. But for Davies, the elegance of his paired and repeated plots, his inter-textuality, is played out in an arena where technique is foregrounded, where the obviousness of the narrative takes precedence over the story; in other words, the real story is how the story is told, not how it proceeds. For Davies, the process of writing, like the process of the quest for identity, is paramount. In fact, the processes of the two are so intricately intertwined that it would be hard to untangle them. It is thus easier to see Davies' writing as the quest for identity, a quest in which the reader has an intimate and necessary part. As he says, the "excitement of art is in the doing, the becoming."[8] It is not just a matter of individual psychology, but one of social necessity, an intrinsic way of positioning a culture (problematic though that word is) within its own space.

If we accept the dictionary definition of the word "boundary" as something that indicates limits, a line that encloses something, we see something of the attitude that Davies likes to parody. The tendency among his unsympathetic characters is to label and define, and often those labels and definitions are shown as too harsh or ignorant. His characters often cannot see beyond the limits of their background or upbringing. Even Geraint Powell, the character in *The Lyre of Orpheus* who most embodies the lust for living, cannot escape what's bred in the bone–in his case, the strict religious doctrine of his upbringing. This is a thematic metaphor that reappears time and again in Davies' work, so much so that an entire novel is dedicated to the concept, which then informs the work that comes after it. It is, however, an important focus of repetition, and one that the alert reader should interpret as a message about the art of the writer and the job of the reader. Neither can wholly escape the limits, or boundaries, of what is bred in the bone–that is, the expectations with which we work and read.

Davies has been faulted, as has Frye, for the repetitions in his work. A.C. Hamilton, in defending Frye, points out that in many other art forms, repetition is an important means of renewing or re-creating an idea. Context is important; it gives us a new view, makes us think differently about the pre-sentation of the whole.[9] Davies uses repetitions and retellings to blur readers' expectations and distinctions. The foregrounding of readerly expectation helps us see not only the boundaries of those expectations, but also the space between them. It is within this space, this "gap" between antithetical elements in the narrative, where Davies operates best.

It is, of course, a Janus-faced distinction. In *The Lyre of Orpheus*, the gap within which Davies operates is a type of narrative tension, a border space that encompasses thematic and technical contrasts. Inherent in these contrasts is the embedded narrative of ETAH, a "dead" character, outside of the boundaries of the more conventional narrative in terms of space and chronology. Davies has used a similar structure in *What's Bred in the Bone*, with a corresponding emphasis generative of problems for his readers.

ETAH, as he is known by the characters of the living world of the text, is E.T.A. Hoffmann, composer, writer, and lawyer. Problematically, he was once also a real person in our own world and thus has a great deal of baggage attached to him. He, too, is a "storyteller" in more than one artistic medium, so it is easy for even the most alert reader to become prey to the seduction of the text's tangential enticements. But if we ignore Hoffmann's thematic purposes for a moment, we will see that the character, as a narrator, has important technical significance.

Like the narrative "structure" of the Angel and the Daimon in *What's Bred in the Bone*, the narrative voice of ETAH is separated from the text by its italicisation. That separation draws attention to itself as a narrative structure, which also forces the reader to recognise it as a break in the other narrative, a not-so-subtle way of signalling a certain level of self-reflexivity. Unlike the Angel and the Daimon, those other-worldly beings watching a sort of videotape of Francis Cornish's life, Hoffmann observes and comments on the present world of the text. In *What's Bred in the Bone*, the "present" world of the Angel and Daimon comments on the past world of Francis' life, a structure somehow more congruent with readerly expectation. Readers, as critics and clerisy, are more conditioned to accept a clearly linear temporal narrative than an intersection of competing chronological frames. In *The Lyre of Orpheus*, Hoffmann sounds like the voice of the past, commenting upon the present action. The character is part of the gap, emphasising how much influence the past has over the creation of the present.

As a narrator, Hoffmann seems omniscient: that is, a narrator who sees from behind.[10] But for Davies, as we have seen previously in *What's Bred in the Bone*, omniscience is a category in question. The authority of its position in narrative theory rests on its objectivity, to some extent, and on the limitlessness of its view and interpretation of events. We have already seen that omniscience is very flawed and limited in *What's Bred in the Bone*. The Angel and Daimon admit their inadequacy as omniscient narrators. In *The Lyre of Orpheus*, the same trouble, which is compounded by character construction, resurfaces.

Hoffmann, recounting his memories and impressions, speaks in the first person. In addition, he comments on the impact that the "present" story has on him. His omniscience is vouchsafed by the fact that he is dead, and therefore, by readerly expectation, able to see all that the characters who are still alive cannot. He is also able to see the motivations from which they operate:

> What an amusing drama life is when one is not obliged to be one of the characters! . . . The remoteness, the removal, of my afterlife is vastly agreeable. I see all the people who are preparing my opera; I comprehend their feelings without needing to share them painfully; I applaud their ambitions and I pity their follies. But as I am wholly unable to do anything about them, I am not torn by guilt or responsibility. It is thus, I suppose, that the gods view humankind. . . . Of course, the gods could intervene and frequently did so, but not always happily from a human standpoint. (368)

This quotation highlights two technical problems. First, in true omniscient categorisation, Hoffmann displays his ability, from his "privileged Position," to see all without needing to share the lived experience. Also, he recognises his impotence to influence the action. But herein lies the stickiness of the boundary of contradiction: in relating events in the story that are not known to those in the story, and in commenting upon the motivations and events of those in the past, now long dead, Hoffmann, as narrator, does influence the action in the sense that he is an integral part of its construction and creation for the reader. We have the double irony of knowing that Hoffmann is as much a character (for the purposes of this work of fiction) as any of the others. His omniscience is as non-authoritative as that of the Angel and Daimon, who also defer to a higher authority (in their case, a metaphorical "they"). So here we have a narrative subtly highlighting its own importance in the text, set apart as it is in structure and form, yet abdicating its responsibility for the events it comments upon.

Not only is the narrative "bent" by ETAH's interpretation of his supposedly omniscient position, but it is also subject to the boundaries of another category of narrative, that of the first person. By definition, this is a narrator who is a participant in situations and events that he recounts, both past and present. Hoffmann is only "omniscient" by reason of the story's event–that is, by authority of his death or "absence" from the story. Davies defies chronology by reaching into an inaccessible realm where time and space, as readers might quotidianly understand those concepts, have no order. As a first-person narrator, Hoffmann cannot be trusted to have a completely objective view; no matter what he perceives or comments upon, we know that his "future" or freedom from Limbo depends entirely upon the success of events in the real time of the story. Since he is powerless to influence the events of the story, there is in this level of the narrative a degree of anxiety created almost entirely by the tension between the contrasting distinctions of the categories of narrator. It is, in fact, a type of suspense.

Suspense is a function of plot, and it is on this level that thematic tension is created between past and present. The suspense here centres on the notion of ETAH's pending freedom from Limbo to whatever his future holds. That future is predicated completely on the creation, or rather the re-creation, of his opera, "Arthur, the Magnanimous Cuckold." It is not the success of the opera that matters in this instance; it is its completion, its resolution or closure, that will create an unseen future, a progression for ETAH's character to some new level.

This notion of creation and re-creation is foregrounded thematically. We have been presented with what are essentially two "presents," the present of the story, in which the conventional action occurs, and the present of ETAH in his static or dead world. For readers, the distinction between past and present is a blurry one. We accept, on some level, that what is dead is necessarily past, and we discount its active influence on the present. But we cannot simplify to this extent in *The Lyre of Orpheus*: ETAH's notion of his time happens parallel to the time of the story, even though he is not visibly present in the same dimension as the other characters. He functions as a literal bridge over the gap between past and future, since he constantly comments and questions how the re-creation of his opera is possible. There are two stories of re-creation at stake: ETAH and his opera, and the story or myth of King Arthur in its various incarnations.

The story of Hoffmann's life, at least insofar as it concerns his opera, seems very much to be a matter of record. Penelope Raven and even Hulda Schnakenburg can guess, albeit learnedly, at Hoffmann's life and motivations. As readers, we are privileged (as Hoffmann says) to have more access to his first-person point of view. We can hear the dead man talking. So we have knowledge, at least in matters of personal life, from an incontrovertible source that the academics can never have access to, the kind of knowledge that Darcourt desperately wants for his biography of Francis Cornish.

In this way, Davies comments subtly on the non-resolution that all biographers face: a fundamental inability to portray their subject's identity in its truest form. We cannot live the past, or even present, experience of another person, or, in this case, character. We cannot appropriate that space in order to know an evanescent identity. So, as Darcourt masterfully manipulates the framing device of Francis Cornish's biography into place (the Marriage at Cana triptych), we are well aware of the fictional liberties he is taking, and of the lack of reference libraries in Limbo. Even if there were such, the libraries would not suffice. The type of knowledge it takes to reach the kind of closure we are taught to expect, says Davies, says the narrative, is simply not accessible.

This is a thematic point that is repeated in the main plot. There is no attempt to hide the Arthurian myth's retelling. We are told point blank, in both narrative lines, exactly what that plot is there for. Hoffmann tells us: "I can see however, that their fate is different and who may hope to escape his fate? They are living out, in a comic mimesis, the fate of Arthur and Guenevere, but to be ruled by a comic fate is not to feel oneself as a figure of comedy" (370-71).

Thus emerges a comic mimesis perhaps because the story does not have the tragic dimensions of Mallory's story, or, for that matter, of any of the other retellings of the Arthurian legend. But then, Arthur, Guenevere, and Lancelot, as characters in those past tellings, did not know what was expected of them. They were not privileged to know the conclusion of their story. It seems that, armed with the knowledge of expectation that comes from knowing the story, Arthur, Maria, and Geraint, the parallel Arthurian characters in *The Lyre of Orpheus*, are not doomed to repeat written history. They are keenly aware of their mythical entrapment, even if they fight the notion that it is happening.

Arthur does not want to read the myth the way it has played out in his life, since it simply does not meet his expectations. He did not live and die, as the legendary Arthur did, to uphold the great ideal of civilisation. I think that the suggestion signed by such a resistance is that this particular re-creation is significant primarily because it departs from tradition, mocks it and flies in the face of readerly expectation. Arthur, who is one "reader" (albeit within the narrative) can face neither the departure from tradition nor the parody of it. That departure displaces his notions of the centre's traditions too forcefully. This is a very common strategy in works where a culture is searching for identity apart from a motherland; such works are concerned with place and displacement, for example, and how the crisis of identity erodes the notion of a valid and creative sense of self. This sense of discomfort and dislocation triggers a quest for identity, or the questioning of identity, especially since "place, displacement and a pervasive concern with myths of identity and authenticity are a feature common to all post-colonial literatures in english."[11]

There is also usually a heavy reliance on contrasts, which we see frequently in the technical and thematic oppositions in Davies' works, and in his intentional blurring of distinctions. There is, of course, his reliance on the retellings of the Arthurian myth. It *is* myth, however overtly psychological it may seem compared to the older Roman and Greek myths. I would suggest that myths today must have this psychological facet to appeal to our more sceptical minds, but what is important in this retelling is that it is parody. It seeks to invert itself, shows us its rough underbelly. From the Canadian margin, Davies' re-creation pokes at us, as readers, to accept that our landscape, our psychomachia, can be mythologised. He shows the reader how to tap into an unprecedented source of creative energy.

It is clear that Davies is working to subvert the reader's expectations on many levels, both technical and thematic. W.H. New suggests that "Canada and New Zealand's literary relationship to Britain is subversive rather than filialistic, counter-discursive rather than a continuing expression of the original imperial discourse."[12] While Davies may not subscribe to the politics of the postcolonial position in its entirety, his parody of the Arthurian myth is clearly not a loyal filialistic representation of the imperial discourse. His parody is counter-discursive in its challenge to tradition, to expectation. What is important is that Davies has gone beyond the limits, the boundaries of the geographical and political and even beyond the boundaries of literary socialisation. By focusing on the dynamic between past and present, in the gap that allows a new type of creativity, he invites his readers to achieve the quest for themselves by learning how to question. It is no accident that "quest" is the dominant construction in the word "question." Davies highlights the questions inherent in the quest, from how we know what we think we know to how we set those facts down on paper. They are necessary touchstones for the intellectual education of his clerisy. By leaving the reader no comfortable stance, no encompassing point of view, he creates in his narrative a metaphor for questioning the boundaries of what we only think are contradictions. Davies' creation of the novel reasserts that "one of the functions of the artist is the questing inside himself; it is toward self-discovery. But then he is not doing this just for self-satisfaction, but eventually to be able to get over the gulf to other people" (Roper 47). However, the reader is not meant to accept any position unquestioningly; a true clerical, or ethical, reading must remain open. This conjunction of writer and reader is necessary. The collision of epistemology and hermeneutics is, in Davies' work, an epiphany.

## NOTES

1. Robertson Davies, *The Lyre of Orpheus* (Markham, Ont.: Penguin, 1989), 211-212.

2. Robertson Davies, interview by Robert Fulford, "The Grand Old Man of CanLit," TVOntario, 1988.

3. Northrop Frye, *Anatomy of Criticism* (Princeton, N.J.: Princeton University Press, 1957), 323-24.

4. Barbara Godard, "Robertson Davies' Dialogic Imagination," *Essays on Canadian Writing* 34 (1987): 64-80.

5. Stephen Bonnycastle, "Robertson Davies and the Ethics of Monologue," *Journal of Canadian Studies* 12 (1977): 20-40.

6. Jamie Dopp, "Metanarrative as Inoculation in *What's Bred in the Bone*," *English Studies in Canada* (1995): 91.

7. W.J. Keith, "Robertson Davies and the Cornish Trilogy," *Journal of Canadian Studies* 24 (1989): 145.

8. Robertson Davies, "Interview with Gordon Roper (1968)," *Conversations with Robertson Davies*, ed. J. Madison Davis (Jackson: University Press of Mississippi, 1989), 55.

9. A.C. Hamilton, *Northrop Frye: Anatomy of His Criticism* (Toronto: University of Toronto Press, 1990), 188.

10. Gerald Prince, *A Dictionary of Narratology* (Lincoln: University of Nebraska Press, 1987).

11. Bill Ashcroft et al., *The Empire Writes Back: Theory and Practice in Post-Colonial Literatures* (London: Routledge, 1989), 9.

12. W.H. New, *Dreams of Speech and Violence: The Art of the Short Story in Canada and New Zealand* (Toronto: University of Toronto Press, 1987), 200.

# "Medical Consultation" for *Murther and Walking Spirits* and *The Cunning Man*

RICK DAVIS, M.D., and PETER BRIGG

This is not an academic paper but a story with academic interest. It is the story of a book collector who particularly collected the books of Robertson Davies and who contacted him to ask if he would sign some books. From this grew an acquaintance of eight years and from that acquaintance came a correspondence in which that highly encyclopaedic among modern writers began to ask the book collector, who happened to be a physician–my physician, in fact–if he could provide answers to some unusual medical questions.

In what follows, Dr. Rick Davis shall read from his own letter to Robertson Davies and I, Peter Brigg, shall read Davies' letters to Dr. Davis and the related segments of Davies' texts.

Robertson Davies' letters are reprinted here with the kind permission of the Davies Estate; quotations from *Murther and Walking Spirits* and *The Cunning Man* are from the McClelland & Stewart first hardback editions.

\*     \*     \*     \*     \*     \*

*The background of the medical research for* The Cunning Man *was some medical research for* Murther and Walking Spirits. *On December 27, 1989, after thanking Dr. Davis for Christmas books, Robertson Davies wrote:*

**Brigg:** "Your choice of *Recollections of Death* must have been intuitive, for at the moment I am embarking on a new novel, to which that book is strongly relevant. Medical friends of mine have talked to me from time to time about such phenomena, and I have long been acquainted with C.G. Jung's description of his apparent leaving of the body during a heart attack (he didn't want to return, and was annoyed when he was resuscitated) but this is the latest word on the subject. And because I am, as I have said, starting a new book, your kindness emboldens me to ask you some technical questions which only a medical man can answer. It would help me greatly if you could drop me a line about these things:

(1) Could a man who was struck from in front, on the head, with a weighted cudgel, be killed instantly? Where on the head would it be necessary to strike him?

(2) Is it always necessary to have an inquest in a case of murder? How long after the murder does it take place? Do the police release the body for burial before the inquest, or must they keep it until afterward?

I want to be sure to get my details right, for readers are quick to notice any mistake. I am not writing a murder mystery, but my book begins with a murder, and I don't want to say anything stupid.

Again, thanks for your kindness, and I wish you and yours a very happy and prosperous New Year.

Robertson Davies"

*Dr. Davis answered these questions, and here is part of those answers.*

**Davis:** (in a letter dated January 4,1990)

"I am very pleased that you are finding *Recollections of Death* useful and I am honoured that you would ask my medical opinion on some matters. My own field is that of family medicine, with special interest in Obstetrics, Hypnosis and Psychotherapy. The questions you ask fall mainly in the realm of Forensic Medicine, so I took the liberty of consulting with Dr. Ross C. Bennett–Chief Coroner of Ontario–to provide you with, hopefully, some accurate information.
1. Can a man be killed instantly when struck with a blunt object, from in front, on the head?

Yes. Basically he can die from massive brain damage from a blow anywhere on top of the head. This may be sufficient to cause a fracture with direct damage to the brain tissue. A person may also be killed by a major disruption of blood vessels, such as a direct blow to either temple, which can cause severing of a major arterial supply to the brain.

When you ask "instant death," do you mean *instantaneous death*, i.e. death at the second of impact? Death, I suppose, could occur relatively quickly but it does take some time for the heart to stop beating, although I don't know how long. What I am saying is that loss of consciousness may be immediate but it may take some time (perhaps a minute?) for all bodily functions to cease. Furthermore, a blow to the temple may cause immediate loss of consciousness, but *some* period of time may have to pass, while haemorrhaging, before actual *death ensues*. I don't know if it is pertinent to your novel that the victim appears to die instantly, or that it is necessary for him or her to have some indeterminate amount of time pass before all bodily functions cease. I think, in general, it is basically accepted that a blow to the skull sufficient to cause major brain damage could be said to have caused instant death. (Note: the first part of this answer: "Yes," is Dr. Bennett's. The rest is mine.)"

*This, of course, turned into the opening of the novel* Murther *and* Walking Spirits:

**Brigg:** "I was never so amazed in my life as when the Sniffer drew his concealed weapon from its case and struck me to the ground, stone dead.

How did I know that I was dead? As it seemed to me, I recovered consciousness in an instant after the blow, and heard the Sniffer saying, in a quavering voice: 'He's dead! My God, I've killed him!' My wife was kneeling by my side, feeling my pulse, her ear to my heart; she said, with what I thought was remarkable self-possession in the circumstances. 'Yes, you've killed him.'(2)

Where was I? I was surveying the scene at close range but I was not in the body that lay on the floor." (3)

*On December 27, 1992, Dr. Davis received another letter that began a correspondence about medical matters:*

**Brigg:** "I am beginning a new novel, as I think Moira has told you, and if I may

160

I should like to turn to you for some expert advice. Would you like a note at the beginning saying: 'I am indebted to Dr. Richard Davis for medical advice?' I will tell you what my problem is: I want to make use of a poison which is virtually instantaneous in its effect, and so far I have not been able to run one down. The situation is this: an old priest–over 80–is celebrating Communion in his Anglican Church. As usual, he breaks the wafer and eats it, is overcome, and falls dead–or so near death that in the confusion nobody does the right thing, if indeed there is a right thing, and he dies. The wafer has been poisoned, but again in the confusion nobody finds it out. Now–what was the poison? It has to be something that the murderer–not an expert person–could get hold of pretty easily. My best solution so far is that the wafer has been poisoned with a strong extract of yew-twigs; they poison cattle, and if the extract was (sic) strong enough, they might also poison an old man. (But apparently it takes half an hour: in a man of 80 would it work more speedily?) But fast enough? I can't tell, but perhaps you have an opinion, or some suggestion. Could we get together for lunch later in January, and talk about it? Meanwhile, keep it under your hat, or under the seal of your Aesculapian Oath, or whatever, as I don't want somebody else to pinch my plot.

We are in the country, and it is very beautiful. I sometimes wonder if Canada is not the most beautiful country in the world, when you get outside the towns. Friends who have visited us from all over are always astonished at how lovely it is, at all seasons except Spring, which is decidedly not our best.

Every good wish to you and your family for 1993,
Robertson Davies"

*Dr. Davis proposed the following answer, dated January 18, 1993:*

**Davis:** "Your questions relating to the poisoning of the elderly priest entailed some interesting problems, but I think now I have some usable and credible solutions for you. I solicited the help of a number of Toxicological experts, and I would like to mention them: Ronald Brecher, Ph.D. of Globotox International Consultants, Guelph; James G. Young, M.D., Chief Coroner of Ontario; and Joel Mayer, M.D., Head of Toxicology at the Centre for Forensic Sciences, Toronto.

Apparently, poisoning is not much in vogue now. I must say that even over the telephone I sensed some raised eyebrows when the specifications you gave me were so precise, and I must also admit that I did feel a little funny asking around–again (!)–about how to commit a quick, clean murder, in view of the research I did three years ago for *Murther*. It *was* a lot of fun.

However . . .

There are really only two poisons which would be appropriate. One is cyanide, which is fairly accessible (e.g. chemistry labs) and quick but it is hard to know how much could be put on a single wafer, and there is no guarantee that it would be immediate. Also, it would cause convulsions (and therefore even more drama before death), and it has the taste of burnt almonds. A discerning member of the congregation might see the priest screw up his face, thus providing an important forensic clue. Furthermore, it is treatable, if medical help is available.

Probably the best is RICIN, a very potent poison from the plant *Ricinis communis*. It is extremely toxic, and is sold as a powder or oil. It is easily ordered through the Sigma Chemical Company in St. Louis, Missouri. The seeds of the plant also contain the active ingredient, and apparently as few as two to twenty can kill a man. A person may collapse immediately. There are no convulsions. There is no antidote. Cardiopulmonary resuscitation would not save a victim. One of its byproducts is cyanide. It has been used effectively by the KGB in assassinations. Evidently it has a wide use in Industry, from the treatment of wool fibre and printing inks to use in paints and varnishes. My understanding, also, is that it is odourless and tasteless and Dr. Mayer felt it was credible to simply sprinkle (sic) it on a wafer and that a very quick death from ingestion would result. Sounds pretty devastating!

I hope this information is useful to you and that you incorporate it into your new novel. I will look forward to meeting with you next week to talk about this a little more.

Sincerely,
Rick"

*It was this information that was transmuted into the following:*

**Brigg:** ". . . But all I said was: 'How?'

'The wafer. . . . The old man always ate the whole wafer himself. . . . If he'd given any of it to the rest of us at the altar it would have been a mass murder. . . . But I knew he wouldn't. . . . Never did.'

'You did something to the wafer?'

'Jon . . . you're being stupid . . . I poisoned it.'

'Don't be absurd! He died instantly–well within ten seconds.'

'Yes. . . . That's the kind of poison it was.'

'What kind?'

'Jon . . . feel dreadful can't really talk anymore. . . . Could I have a drink?'

'No, Charlie, you damn well can't have a drink. It could kill you. Here's a nitroglycerine tablet. Put it under your tongue. Now tell me what was the poison?'

'It's called ricinus communis . . . comes from castor oil . . . a dryer . . . no taste, no smell, and damn near instantaneous.'

Could I be unjust in thinking that Charlie was looking the least bit pleased with himself? Life is not wholly a dull fabric of commonplaces and likelihoods. He *was* pleased with himself.

'Where did you get it?'

'Russell.'

'The printer? The Church warden? How did he get it?'

'He makes his own inks. . . . Point of pride. . . . He gets it from a company in St. Louis, Missouri. . . . The KGB used it a lot.'

'And Russell gave it to you?'

'Stole it. . . . He printed the service orders for the church. . . . When he was out of the room I pinched a small quantity. A few drops on the wafer . . . no smell, no taste . . . and that's it.'" (*The Cunning Man* 443-44)

*But this was not the end of matters. In fact, it was quite close to the beginning. After a few months that must have been seminal in the creation of the text, news came that more questions were in the wind. After thanking Dr. Davis for a birthday book, Robertson Davies added, in a letter dated August 31, 1993:*

**Brigg:** "I hope to send you a few more medical questions before too long but I am being intentionally vague in what I write as the book does not hang entirely on its medical interest and I don't want to get into any arguments with the medical profession.

With all good wishes,

Yours sincerely,

Robertson Davies"

*What followed, on November 7, 1993, was in the order of a barrage, and to clarify these exchanges, we are going to follow one query at a time through the remaining correspondence and into the text.*

**Brigg:** "I would not trouble you with professional questions, were it not that Moira has told me that you said you might find them a welcome distraction. I am winding up the novel, and there are a few things on which I would be glad to have your advice. So here goes:

(1) A character dies of breast cancer. It has been ignored and therefore neglected. When she has to have the operation might it be necessary to remove the shoulder and arm as well? Moira says she knows of such a case. And if that were so, and all of the cancer were still not removed, how long might it take her to die? Much pain? Depression? Heavy sedation? What about mental attitude? If she just gave up all hope–knowing that death was inevitable–would the death come quickly?

(2) Another character dies, really of despair, but he is a heavy drinker–very heavy. Osler talks of something called alcoholic's pneumonia which brings quick death. Is it still recognized? What would carry off an alcoholic who was almost starved (refuses food) but who kept on drinking? I would like him, if possible, to be clear in his mind before death. A very intelligent man, dying of despair.

When the book is published I should like to acknowledge your help in a brief note at the beginning. Something like: 'I am greatly obliged to Dr. Richard Davis for advice about some of the medical matters that appear in this book. Any errors, or simple stupidities, however, are my own.' Would that be all right? Or would your colleagues be scornful of your association with low fellows like novelists?

Again, with our warmest good wishes. . . .

Rob Davies

[Sorry! one more question overleaf]


ADDITIONAL QUESTION: the chief character in the book, a doctor, suffers a freak accident during World War 2; he is in a hotel in London, having a bath,

164

when a bomb strikes nearby and wrecks several buildings including his hotel; he is trapped in the bathtub for about ninety hours before he is rescued. The water grows very cold, is full of plaster and debris, and of course as time goes on, urine. He hates having to drink it, but must–though as little as he can. What would his symptoms be–a man in his twenties in good health and very intelligent? Would he have spells of unconsciousness? The weather is spring, so though it is chilly it is not freezing. What would be his condition when he was rescued? Shock? How long would it take him to recover? What, in fact, would starvation and dehydration do to him and how would he be restored to health?

Don't exert yourself unduly about these questions: I cannot use a full clinical description in a novel–just chief symptoms and anything the ordinary reader would not think of.

R.D."

*Dr. Davis answered on November 16, 1993, but let us first follow his answer to–*

## QUERY I: THE CANCER CASE

**Davis:** "The lady with breast cancer–is it possible to get some idea of the year, or even decade, in which she presents to the physician? Treatments vary markedly in time, and this could help me a great deal. When asking how she might die, is it possible to get some idea of her "pre-morbid personality," i.e., what she was like before her illness? She is obviously in great denial, and I don't know if you want to highlight that; certainly mental attitude could play a role here."

*This produced a fax from Robertson Davies on Nov 19, 1993:*

**Brigg:** "The Breast Cancer Woman–suffering from serious depression, as she feels her career has been a failure. Has been sent home from hospital as no more can be done for her after left breast and shoulder have been removed (this was her working hand as a sculptor). Could she die within a month? Gradual decline? Would she be ill-tempered and snappish to her devoted friend?"

*Dr. Davis' final and full medical description came on November 28, 1993:*

**Davis:** "I spoke to a retired surgeon (Dr. Phil LeBlanc) who had a case very similar to this–a rich lady who was a gifted pianist who married below her station and was considered a failure by her family. She was presented with neglected breast cancer which, after radical surgery, left her without the use of her dominant arm. She died denying her disease to the very end.

Patients like this can indeed be short and snappish with close friends, because they don't want them to be solicitous, as it may remind them that they are ill.

I believe that the patient presents in the 1970's. The treatment at that time usually involved a radical mastectomy and often an axillary node dissection. (Radical mastectomy means the removal of the entire breast plus underlying chest wall muscle down to bone. Axillary node dissection means removal of all the lymph drainage in the armpit [hence swelling of the arm].) This was usually followed by a course of radiation, but not chemotherapy. Often doctors, who would know at presentation she was doomed, would not discuss the diagnosis with the patient–'she mightn't be able to handle the information.' Indeed, the patient might not want to know. Chest x-rays and/or bone scans would probably reveal metastatic disease to the lungs or bone. Amputation of the arm or shoulder was not done; however, after a course of radiation therapy, it is quite reasonable to expect that the afflicted side would show gross swelling of the arm (lymphedema)–double the size or more, so as to impair totally all artistic use of the arm.

The patient may wish to hide the effects of the surgery (she would be able to go home). She might wear loose fitting, long-sleeved gowns with or without a glove. The skin would be thick and tawny or somewhat bronzed–certainly unnatural.

The life expectancy in such a case is usually four to six months, but could easily be less, especially if she gave up. She would likely suffer a "pulmonary death" (sic) i.e. death due to spread of the disease to her lungs. She might represent to the physician with wheeziness, shortness of breath, cough, weight loss, fever from pneumonia, and weakness. She may have severe bone pain from spread to these areas, especially the ribs, which could make her breathing even more painful and difficult. At this terminal stage, she would probably have oxygen by mask or be in a tent and eventually would lapse into unconsciousness with death ensuing in seven to ten days, or even less. She would probably be too unwell to eat. Death may be welcomed."

*When we come to* The Cunning Man *we find this material subsumed into art in various places*:

**Brigg:** ". . . and that very day she was taken to hospital and the following morning underwent a radical mastectomy and axillary node dissection. I knew very well that this might not be the complete solution of her trouble, and I arranged matters so that I happened, quite casually, to meet both Dumoulin and the surgeon later in the day, for they both lunched at my Club.

'I expect you'll get her onto radiation as soon as possible,' said the surgeon, who was practising his art on a pair of lamb chops.

'Oh certainly. Not an instant's delay,' said Dumoulin, who was busy with some gravy soup; 'goes without saying.'

'But what precisely are you going to say to her?' I said. I was having oysters before my chops.

'That it's the very best course to pursue,' said Dumoulin. 'We'd be very remiss if we neglected it.'

'But you won't tell her it will put her back at work, I suppose?' said I.

'That would be premature,' said Dumoulin.

'Look, George,' said I, 'you don't have to pull your punches with me.'

'Well, you are a friend of the patient, after all.'

'But a physician, like yourself. It's all up, isn't it?'

'I never say that,' said the surgeon, who was a large, fleshy, powerful man who looked as if he never said anything disagreeable under any circumstances. 'I've seen the most extraordinary recoveries in cases where you could never have predicted them.'

'But more often you've seen metastases that proliferated and made short work of things, haven't you?' said I.

'That's always a possibility, of course,' said Dumoulin, 'but we must wait for the X-rays. Never does to be in a hurry.'

'What are you going to tell her?' said I.

'Least said, soonest mended, is what I always find. A cheerful attitude, you know. No long faces.'

'A merry heart doeth good like a medicine,' said I.

'Bible, isn't it? Never been put better,' said the surgeon.

'But a broken spirit drieth the bones,' said I, concluding the quotation.

'I think I want a cognac, to top off,' said the surgeon. 'It'll be my last drop for twenty-four hours. A very full schedule tomorrow. Will you fellows join me? Steward!'

They were not callous, or devious. Merely experienced in the profession which was ruled, when all the cards were down, by Fate, against which there is no armour.'

\* \* \* \* \* \*

'I gave what comfort I could, but to my eye Emily looked like a dying woman. She wore loose-fitting tunics, to conceal the damage of her operation, Chips said, as if Emily's little breasts were so prominent that anyone would notice that one had vanished. What could not be concealed was that her right arm was swelling with lymphadenosis, and she wore a glove to conceal the bronzing of the skin on her hand.'

\* \* \* \* \* \*

'Surely they can do something?'

But 'they' could do nothing. Nor could they do a great deal to ease the pain which was growing in her chest. She wheezed now, coughed, suffered shortness of breath, and even Chips could not pretend that she was not losing weight; though she had always been a small, delicately formed woman, she was now a wraith." (*The Cunning Man* 426-28 and 437)

## *QUERY II: THE ALCOHOLIC*

*Dr. Davis "treated" the problem of the dying alcoholic in stages.*

**Davis:** "November 16, 1993:

I have some ideas about the alcoholic which will meet your needs–i.e., the starving, despaired man with clear mentation. However, do you want him to die quickly (i.e. less than one or two hours), or slowly–over days? I can give him a heart condition for a broken heart (?)"

*Robertson Davies responded in his fax on November 19, 1993:*

**Brigg:** "The Alcoholic priest–in bad physical shape as he has not been eating, and drinking heavily. I would like him to die over a period of two or three weeks. Suffers keen disappointment and self-reproach; feels he has sinned inexcusably and is beyond God's mercy. Your suggestion that he die of a broken heart is just what I want; please, what is the clinical description of a broken heart?"

*With the author's more precise desires to hand, Dr. Davis submitted what was to become the skeletal outline of Charlie's fate.*

**Davis:** "December 6, 1993

Regarding the alcoholic priest, there are a number of ways he could die. Certainly the most common ones could be by cirrhosis of the liver, with jaundice, a large, protruding abdomen, swelling of the extremities as well as a general decline in mental function. However, this man is quite depressed, and you wish him to retain his mental faculties, and to die gradually over two to three weeks. You might consider this: he could die of a 'broken heart' with his death caused by an alcoholic cardiomyopathy. In this condition, caused by excessive alcohol intake and complicated by poor nutrition, he would suffer a 'pump failure.' He would become lethargic and easily fatigued. He would develop shortness of breath as his lungs filled with fluid. His ankles would probably swell. He might need to prop his head up with more and more pillows (three to four). He would probably have difficulty dressing and later walking and eventually even speaking because of fatigue and breathlessness. He may only have enough energy to get himself another drink (perhaps aftershave or communion wine).

Very little effort would lead to drenching and exhaustion. His tolerance to the effects of alcohol would disappear. Generally an otherwise 'healthy' alcoholic has to take in large quantities of alcohol to feel the effects. In advanced alcoholic cardiomyopathy, he may require only one or possibly two drinks to become intoxicated. He would most likely experience palpitations or flutterings of the heart, which may remind him of his own mortality. Through all of this his thinking could be clear. The death of this man would come through fatal arrhythmia (lethal abnormality in heart rate and rhythm) which would carry him off almost immediately, or surely in less than one hour. His musings and self-reproaches during all this time I leave to your creative hand."

*In* The Cunning Man, *Charlie Iredale's "self-reproaches" about the poisoning are one of the high dramatic points of the text, but Charlie certainly declines closely to the medical script (although, it must be added, without the assistance of aftershave).*

**Brigg:** "He slept for many hours, and could not endure much company.

    I visited him twice a day; a morning call before I saw patients; a visit after dinner, when we chatted for a while. Even a slight measure of alcohol was out of the question; his condition was advanced alcoholic cardiomyopathy–very weak heart, in lay terms. He had spells of fluttering heartbeat, and palpitations, and these alarmed him greatly, for although he knew he was dying, he had a very human dread of doing so. But in all of this his mind was clear, and he spent his waking hours in unhappy reflection. One of our later conversations was typical.

    'Made a mess of things.'

    'You could have done worse. Don't scold yourself.'" (439)

## QUERY III: THE MAN IN THE TUB

*This is last of the medical matters dealt with in any depth in the correspondence, although Dr. Davis had conversations with Robertson Davies about the sinus operation, read that section of the manuscript and commented on it in a medical light, and provided a number of juicy small bits about medical training, including his own experience of beheading in the dissection laboratory:*

**Brigg:** "The strain on memory in Anatomy, the cynicism that seemed to underlie Pharmacology, the toughness demanded by dissecting–it took a strong constitution and it changed your outlook on the world. I remember once meeting a fellow I knew in my year, and asking him what he had been doing. 'Nothing special,' he said, 'took off a woman's head this morning, then I had lunch, and now I've really got to get down to the anatomy of the hand.' That kind of thing. I met him again recently, nearly forty years later. He's made a big name as a surgeon and his divorced wife owns an almost-Picasso. But whether he's rounded or not I really couldn't say." (*The Cunning Man* 151-52)

*The challenge of the man in the tub took Dr. Davis' fancy from the start.*

**Davis:** "November 16, 1993

    Fascinating! I think I can help you with this as well. You might look up a little arcane book I gave you three years ago called *Tips By Tarsus*–a little handbook of mnemonics used by medical students. ·Your character may spend some of his time trying to recall them. Also, a new word: 'adipocere,' a waxy film which covers the skin when immersed in soil or water for prolonged periods of time. More about this later."

*Robertson Davies' fax of November 19, 1993, presented a problem.*

**Brigg:** "The man who is Trapped In the Bathtub: thanks for the suggestion about adipocere (addy-po-seer) which I shall thankfully use. BUT–I have been unable to find the copy you gave me of *Tips By Tarsus* and your suggestion is an excellent one. May I borrow your copy for a week or two? Return in good condition guaranteed."

*The problem of the mnemonics got bigger.*

**Davis:** "November 28, 1993
   Unfortunately, the copy of *Tips By Tarsus* that I had given to you was my only one. I have tried the Medical Arts Library (Toronto) and the Osler Library (McGill) with no luck, but I'm sure it will turn up. In any case, I think I can supply a few good mnemonics if you can use them."

*In this same letter of November 28, 1993, however, Dr. Davis offered the full scenario for the man trapped in the tub.*

**Davis:** "The scenario of the man trapped in the tub is not at all unlikely. In order for him to survive for 90 hours when it is chilly does require some setup.
   Firstly, although he may be pinned, his chest must be free enough to let him breathe. It would be good if he could move his limbs to some extent, albeit not enough to extricate himself. The ambient temperature should really not fall below 10 °C (50 °F), or else true hypothermia may set in, and he really could die."

**Brigg:** "If the temperature in the English spring dropped much below 50 degrees Fahrenheit I would be in serious danger. I could breathe freely, move my legs and arms to some extent so that clotting of blood could be avoided. . . ." (*The Cunning Man* 218)

*Dr. Davis continued:*

**Davis:** "In this situation, an otherwise healthy twentyish man (plus hopefully a strong character) would likely experience starvation, weight loss of six to ten pounds, progressive weakness and periods of lassitude, especially as time wore on. As a physician he would know the importance of moving his limbs–both for warmth and to prevent clotting of blood in his legs due to immobility (deep vein thrombosis). He could survive on the water vitiated by urine. It would not be necessary (but would be effective) for him to defecate into the bath water. He would shiver a great deal–to maintain body heat. As time passed, he would probably swell in the hands and lower legs, and feet . . ."

**Brigg:** "Late in the second day I could no longer repress a bowel movement, and my water became a cold faecal soup, of which I could not force myself to drink . . . because as time wore on I suffered from lassitude and progressive weakness. I shivered a great deal, this helped to maintain my bodily heat. Hunger was a torment, and I could not long keep my mind off food. After the second day my hands, my lower legs and feet began to swell." (*The Cunning Man* 218)

**Davis:** " . . . and develop 'pitting oedema'–the type of swelling that will leave impressions of fingers on it after the skin is compressed (may be good if the rescuers lift him from the tub and leave their finger impressions on his shins). This resolves in time. He would probably have pressure sores, which may or may not be open; again, if he can move somewhat he may be able to minimize them. He may have small vesicles (blisters) on his extremities and trunk. His skin would become macerated if pinned against a beam. He would be able to sleep, but probably not for long, and would likely be awakened by shivering. Unfortunately, it does not look as if adipocere would develop."

**Brigg:** "I knew perfectly well that I was not developing the waxy skin coating that I had so often seen in my days as a police physician on the bodies of drowned men and women, but nevertheless I feared it, and felt my body for it, and wondered if I were not indeed experiencing a novel form of drowning, while fully conscious." *(The Cunning Man* 218-19)

**(Brigg's comment:** How breathtakingly delicious this manipulation is as

Robertson Davies makes a great peril out of a problem Hullah is not having!)

**Brigg:** "Of course I was almost ten pounds lighter, I was dehydrated, I had some pitting oedema, the localized dropsy to be expected, and a few pressure sores." (*The Cunning Man* 221)

**Davis:** "How he spent his time would be important. Does he see any daylight? Are there rats? Does he hear a rescue team trying to get to him? If so–for how long? (a time of great hope). He might have periods of despair."

**Brigg:** " . . . with enough of the rubbish above me open to the air.

(219) . . . Once or twice I heard scramblings that I supposed must be rats, and all that I had ever read about prisoners plagued by filthy rodents began to torment me . . .

(218) . . . I could hear the workers . . ." (*The Cunning Man*)

**Davis:** "As mentioned, he could review some colourful medical mnemonics (I'll try to get you some), count plaster chips, recall symphonic music (if musical), yell for help, tap out code, etc. He would weaken as time passed.

When found he would be swollen, stiff and cold, exhausted, unshaven, conscious, probably happy, but again probably slightly incoherent. The rescue team may give him their coats, warm blankets, and offer a cup of tea. He would be transported to hospital (if it still stood; ironic if he went to the one he worked in) and would be rehydrated with intravenous fluids. His recovery time would be two to three days."

*The delightful part of comparing this last paragraph of Dr. Davis' letter to the text is that it shows creative selection at work. Except for the mnemonic and the yelling for help, the latter a pretty obvious activity, none of these suggestions were put into play. For one thing, there is no real rescue scene in the text, and, secondly, Hullah has other things to think about that lead up to the vital self-discovery that is the mental action of the whole section.*

*In fact, all that the text says of the rescue is:*

"At last I was fished out of my tank and carried off to a hospital."

\*     \*     \*     \*     \*     \*

*CONCLUSION*

There are several footnotes to this correspondence.

First, *Tips By Tarsus* never turned up to provide the required medical mnemonics, but its place was taken by *Irving's Anatomical Mnemonics*, which Dr. Davis found and provided for the author. In addition, Dr. Davis himself provided in a letter the gleefully erotic *Guide to the Cranial Nerves of the Brain Stem*, which appears in the bathtub scene.

Second, on January 3, 1994, Davies wrote to Dr. Davis one last time about the medical advice.

**Brigg**: "I have been pegging away at the book, and am now in the home stretch. Little by little I am killing off all those who have to be killed, with your expert help. What you will think of the book when it is finished, I cannot say; many of my doctor friends, I think, will be annoyed by it, because it stresses the doctrine of Paracelsus that there are diseases, certainly, but that far more important are patients, and to treat the disease and forget the human creature is bad medicine, for every presentation of a disease is individual. But enough. . . . I have been most grateful to you during the past few weeks, for your guidance and help, and I shall say so in the printed book. Or is that likely to expose you to the scorn of your colleagues? . . . .
Again good wishes to you and your wife and children for 1994.
Robertson Davies"

Third, I suppose you may be wondering what moved us to report on this correspondence. Dr. Davis might want to speak for himself of the immense pleasure of his acquaintance with the Mage of Caledon East and to mention that he has gone on to advise several other writers since his work with Robertson Davies.

Both Dr. Davis and I want to dedicate this presentation to the memory of Moira Whalen, Robertson Davies' personal secretary for forty years, who

174

died in March 1998.

But I, too, have my reasons for assisting Rick. Robertson Davies was the director of my two graduate theses nearly thirty years ago at the University of Toronto, and I owe him an immeasurable debt for steering me through the sharp shoals of Graduate School with common sense, insistence on the Plain Style, and immense forbearance. And I think he fixed it so that I got a comfortable billet in Massey College.

We are constantly amazed and moved by the lightness of touch with which he turned experience, knowledge, wisdom, and the fruits of his extraordinary curiosity into art of the highest order–art that can contain at one and the same time a texture of common living and the roots of the great trees of myth and pattern. Dr. Davis and I think that knowing what he worked from in some sections of *The Cunning Man* enhances our appreciation of his art, and we hope that it has done so for you as well.

# CONTRIBUTORS

Faith Balisch

Department of English
Memorial University

Peter Brigg

Department of English
University of Guelph

Tatjana Takseva Chorney

Independent Scholar

Andrea Cole

Department of English
Queen's University

David Creelman

Department of Humanities & Languages
University of New Brunswick

Rick Davis

Medical Doctor

David Hallett

Department of English
Memorial University

Camille R. La Bossière

Department of English
University of Ottawa

Michael Peterman

Department of English
Trent University

Todd Pettigrew

Department of Languages & Letters
University of Cape Breton

Lois Sherlow

Department of English
Memorial University

Mark Silverberg

Department of English
Dalhousie University

K.P. Stich

Department of English
University of Ottawa

# REAPPRAISALS: CANADIAN WRITERS

Reappraisals: Canadian Writers was begun in 1973 in response to a need for single volumes of essays on Canadian authors who had not received the critical attention they deserved or who warranted extensive and intensive reconsideration. It is the longest running series dedicated to the study of Canadian literary subjects. The annual symposium hosted by the Department of English at the University of Ottawa began in 1972 and the following year University of Ottawa Press published the first title in the series, *The Grove Symposium*. Since then our editorial policy has remained straightforward: each year to make permanently available in a single volume the best of the criticism and evaluation presented at our symposia on Canadian literature, thereby creating a body of work on, and a critical base for the study of, Canadian writers and literary subjects.

Gerald Lynch
General Editor

**Titles in the series:**

THE GROVE SYMPOSIUM, edited and with an introduction by John Nause

THE A. M. KLEIN SYMPOSIUM, edited and with an introduction by Seymour Mayne

THE LAMPMAN SYMPOSIUM, edited and with an introduction by Lorraine McMullen

THE E. J. PRATT SYMPOSIUM, edited and with an introduction by Glenn Clever

THE ISABELLA VALANCY CRAWFORD SYMPOSIUM, edited and with an introduction by Frank M. Tierney

THE DUNCAN CAMPBELL SCOTT SYMPOSIUM, edited and with an introduction by K. P. Stich

THE CALLAGHAN SYMPOSIUM, edited and with an introduction by David Staines

THE ETHEL WILSON SYMPOSIUM, edited and with an introduction by Lorraine McMullen

TRANSLATION IN CANADIAN LITERATURE, edited and with an introduction by Camille R. La Bossière

THE SIR CHARLES G. D. ROBERTS SYMPOSIUM, edited and with an introduction by Glenn Clever

THE THOMAS CHANDLER HALIBURTON SYMPOSIUM, edited and with an introduction by Frank M. Tierney

STEPHEN LEACOCK: A REAPPRAISAL, edited and with an introduction by David Staines

FUTURE INDICATIVE: LITERARY THEORY AND CANADIAN LITERATURE, edited and with an introduction by John Moss

REFLECTIONS: AUTOBIOGRAPHY AND CANADIAN LITERATURE, edited and with an introduction by K. P. Stich

RE(DIS)COVERING OUR FOREMOTHERS: NINETEENTH-CENTURY CANADIAN WOMEN WRITERS, edited and with an introduction by Lorraine McMullen

BLISS CARMAN: A REAPPRAISAL, edited and with an introduction by Gerald Lynch

FROM THE HEART OF THE HEARTLAND: THE FICTION OF SINCLAIR ROSS, edited by John Moss

CONTEXT NORTH AMERICA: CANADIAN/U.S. LITERARY RELATIONS, edited by Camille R. La Bossière

HUGH MACLENNAN, edited by Frank M. Tierney

ECHOING SILENCE: ESSAYS ON ARCTIC NARRATIVE, edited and with a preface by John Moss

BOLDER FLIGHTS: ESSAYS ON THE CANADIAN LONG POEM, edited and with a preface by Frank M. Tierney and Angela Robbeson

DOMINANT IMPRESSIONS: ESSAYS ON THE CANADIAN SHORT STORY, edited by Gerald Lynch and Angela Arnold Robbeson

MARGARET LAURENCE: CRITICAL REFLECTIONS, edited and with an introduction by David Staines

ROBERTSON DAVIES: A MINGLING OF CONTRARIETIES, edited by Camille R. La Bossière and Linda M. Morra